OXFORD WORLD'S CLASSICS

DIALOGUES AND ESSAYS

Lucius Annaeus Seneca (*c.*1 BC–AD 65) was born in Corduba, Spain, and educated in Rome. Plagued all his life by ill health, he embarked on a political career after a stay in Egypt. In 41 he was exiled by the emperor Claudius and only returned to Rome in 49, when he became tutor to the young Nero. Together with the prefect of the Praetorian Guard Sextus Afranius Burrus, he acted as a senior adviser to Nero until 62, withdrew to private life, and was forced to commit suicide in 65. He had taken up writing as a young man. His earliest extant treatises date from the period before his exile. He continued to write throughout his life and was particularly productive in his final years. His treatises are recognized as the most important body of work on Stoicism in Latin. He also wrote the *Letters to Lucilius* and several tragedies, the earliest extant specimens of the genre in Latin.

John Davie was Head of Classics at St Paul's School, London until 1999. He is the author of a number of articles on classical subjects and has recently translated the complete surviving plays of Euripides for Penguin Classics (four volumes). A member of the Hellenic Society's and Roman Society's Visiting Panel of Lecturers, he divides his time between London and Oxford, where he teaches Classics to undergraduates at Balliol and other colleges.

Tobias Reinhardt is Fellow and Tutor in Latin and Greek at Somerville College, Oxford. He has published books on Aristotle, Cicero, and (jointly with Michael Winterbottom) on Quintilian.

OXFORD WORLD'S CLASSICS

For over 100 years Oxford World's Classics have brought readers closer to the world's great literature. Now with over 700 titles—from the 4,000-year-old myths of Mesopotamia to the twentieth century's greatest novels—the series makes available lesser-known as well as celebrated writing.

The pocket-sized hardbacks of the early years contained introductions by Virginia Woolf, T. S. Eliot, Graham Greene, and other literary figures which enriched the experience of reading. Today the series is recognized for its fine scholarship and reliability in texts that span world literature, drama and poetry, religion, philosophy and politics. Each edition includes perceptive commentary and essential background information to meet the changing needs of readers.

OXFORD WORLD'S CLASSICS

SENECA

Dialogues and Essays

Translated by
JOHN DAVIE

With an Introduction and Notes by
TOBIAS REINHARDT

OXFORD
UNIVERSITY PRESS

OXFORD

UNIVERSITY PRESS

Great Clarendon Street, Oxford OX2 6DP

Oxford University Press is a department of the University of Oxford.
It furthers the University's objective of excellence in research, scholarship,
and education by publishing worldwide in

Oxford New York

Auckland Cape Town Dar es Salaam Hong Kong Karachi
Kuala Lumpur Madrid Melbourne Mexico City Nairobi
New Delhi Shanghai Taipei Toronto

With offices in

Argentina Austria Brazil Chile Czech Republic France Greece
Guatemala Hungary Italy Japan Poland Portugal Singapore
South Korea Switzerland Thailand Turkey Ukraine Vietnam

Oxford is a registered trade mark of Oxford University Press
in the UK and in certain other countries

Published in the United States
by Oxford University Press Inc., New York

British Library Cataloguing in Publication Data

Data available

Library of Congress Cataloging-in-Publication Data

Seneca, Lucius Annaeus, ca. 4 B.C.–65 A.D.
[Selections. English. 2007]
Dialogues and essays / Seneca; translated by John Davie; with an
introduction and notes by Tobias Reinhardt.
p. cm.—(Oxford World's classics)
Includes bibliographical references.
ISBN-13: 978–0–19–280714–4 (alk. paper) 1. Seneca, Lucius Annaeus,
ca. 4 B.C.–65 A.D.—Translations into English. 2. Conduct of
life—Early works to 1800. 3. Ethics—Early works to 1800. I. Davie,
John N. II. Reinhardt, Tobias. III. Title.
PA6661.A7S46 2007
878'.0109—dc22   2007016351

ISBN 978–0–19–955240–5

9

Typeset by Cepha Imaging Private Ltd., Bangalore, India
Printed in Great Britain
on acid-free paper by
Clays Ltd, St Ives plc

CONTENTS

INTRODUCTION

Seneca's Life and Career

Lucius Annaeus Seneca was born around 1 BC as the second of three sons into a wealthy family of the equestrian class in what is today Cordoba in southern Spain. His father, likewise born in Spain but of Italian descent, is known as Seneca the rhetor; he had a keen interest in rhetorical education and wrote, late in his life, probably between AD 37 and 41, summary accounts of performances which he had witnessed in the rhetorical schools as a young man.[1] The elder Seneca mainly pursued the family's business interests, as was not unusual for someone of his social order, and apparently did not appear as an advocate. In his son's writings he is presented as an educated, old-fashioned, and down-to-earth Roman, whose attitude to philosophy was a reserved one, although it appears that practical moral philosophy had some appeal for him too. Seneca's mother, Helvia, was probably of Spanish descent; she is the addressee of one of the consolations included in this volume. Seneca's older brother, Annaeus Novatus, later changed his name due to adoption to Junius Gallio, had a distinguished political career, and became a proconsul of Achaia, where he met the apostle Paul (Acts 18: 12).[2] His younger brother, Annaeus Mela, on whom apparently the elder Seneca's hopes had rested more than on his brothers (*Controv.* 2 pref. 3–4), withdrew from public life as a young man; Mela's son was the poet Lucan, whose epic on the civil war is extant.

Seneca, along with his brothers, was soon sent to Rome, where he started the conventional course of education pursued by wealthy young Romans who were to embark on a career as an advocate or politician; their father accompanied them in order to oversee their education. In due course this academic training involved substantial reading of

---

[1] These are partially extant, and known as the *Controversiae* and *Suasoriae*; see the Loeb edition with translation by Michael Winterbottom (Cambridge, Mass., 1974), and below, p. xxiv. Such exercises would also represent the standard form of advanced rhetorical education for the young Seneca.

[2] See p. xxvi on the spurious correspondence between Seneca and St Paul, which circulated in the Middle Ages.

literary and historical texts and rhetorical practice, notably in declamation. In addition, Seneca had a series of teachers in philosophy whom he later credited with having a formative influence on him;[3] notably, they exposed him not just to Stoic moral doctrine, but to a wide range of other intellectual influences, and this breadth of outlook is reflected in Seneca's works. Two of his teachers, Papirius Fabianus and the Greek Sotion from Alexandria, had been pupils of Q. Sextius, who had founded Rome's only native philosophical school, which fused elements of traditional Stoicism with Pythagoreanism.[4] Fabianus had started out as a declaimer (Seneca the elder, *Controv.* 2 pref. 1), and his speaking retained its rhetorical power when he turned to philosophy; he had an interest in science and inquiry into natural phenomena, which might help to explain Seneca's interest in these matters. That one's everyday habits and customs need to be seen in a broad context was suggested by the teachings of Sotion, who, like Pythagoras, abstained from the consumption of meat because of his belief in the transmigration of souls (*Letters* 108.20–1). Attalus the Stoic, who came perhaps from Pergamum in Asia Minor, introduced Seneca to mental routines of self-examination (ibid. 108.3), a prominent feature of his treatises and letters; he also had an interest in divination, which the Stoics saw not as superstition but as a scientific discipline; according to Seneca's *Natural Questions* (2.84.2, 2.50.1), Attalus undertook a study of the Etruscan art of interpreting sky signs, like lightning. However, what for Seneca might have been an unequivocally happy period of his life was interrupted by frequent and at times dangerous bouts of ill health, notably various respiratory diseases;[5] this eventually caused him to spend some time in Egypt, where the climate was supposed to be conducive to the improvement of his condition. Seneca took the opportunity to write a treatise about local customs and religious practices (*Natural Questions* 4.2.7).[6]

---

[3] By the first century AD it was no longer common for young Romans of Seneca's status to go to Athens and study philosophy there, as it had been in the first century BC.

[4] Seneca said of Sextius' books that they were 'written in Greek, but exhibited Roman morality' (*Letter* 59.7); despite his Stoic leanings, Sextius claimed not to be a Stoic (64.2). On Neo-Pythagoreanism in Rome see C. H. Kahn, *Pythagoras and the Pythagoreans: A Brief History* (Indianapolis, 2001), ch. 7; on Q. Sextius see E. Zeller, *Die Philosophie der Griechen in ihrer geschichtlichen Entwicklung* (Leipzig, 1880–92), vol. 3.1, pp. 675–82.

[5] See M. Griffin, *Seneca: A Philosopher in Politics* (Oxford, 1976), 42–3.

[6] For details on Seneca's biography and intellectual context see ibid. ch. 2, and B. Inwood, *Reading Seneca: Stoic Philosophy at Rome* (Oxford, 2005), ch. 1.

Following his return to Italy in AD 31, Seneca pursued his political career for eleven years; nonetheless he managed to write the *Consolation to Marcia*, as well as scientific treatises on stones, fish, and earthquakes, which are, however, not extant. Seneca also wrote tragedies, and probably started doing so quite early in his career.[7] He became quaestor, a high-ranking financial clerk. But in AD 39 a particularly spectacular performance in court aroused the jealousy of the emperor Gaius (Caligula); on this occasion Seneca seems to have escaped execution only because a courtier pointed out that he would soon die anyway, on account of his bad state of health (at least according to the third-century historian Cassius Dio, at 59.19.7). In AD 41, after Caligula had been murdered and Claudius had become the new emperor, Seneca was accused of adultery with Julia Livilla, a sister of Caligula, and had to go into exile on Corsica until 49. After Claudius' death Seneca wrote a vitriolic satire on the deceased emperor, the *Apocolocyntosis* ('Pumpkinification [of Claudius]'). It has been suggested that the real reason for his exile was that he favoured and promoted a less autocratic style of government than Augustus' successors had adopted. This view is certainly consistent with certain aspects of two dialogues written during his exile: in his *Consolation to Helvia* he praised two high-profile opponents of the dictator Caesar (9.4–8: Marcus Junius Brutus and Marcus Claudius Marcellus), while in the *Consolation to Polybius*, written for a powerful freedman at the imperial court, he devised an image of a mild and reasonable emperor.

In AD 49 Agrippina, mother of the future emperor Nero, managed to secure permission for Seneca to return. He became tutor to Nero as well as praetor, a high judicial office. However, philosophy was excluded from the curriculum, since Agrippina deemed it unsuitable for a future emperor (Suetonius, *Life of Nero* 52). Seneca's teaching was thus restricted to rhetorical instruction. After Claudius' death in AD 54 Seneca, and the well-respected prefect of the Praetorian Guard, Sextus Afranius Burrus, acted as senior advisers to the young emperor, who was just 17 years old on accession. Seneca wrote speeches for Nero and exercised influence in connection with important appointments. In his first declaration in the senate, Nero stated that

---

[7] On the difficulties of dating the tragedies see E. Fantham, *Seneca's Troades* (Princeton, 1982), 9–14.

he would restore some of that body's powers, which had been eroded
over time, thus declaring an intention to return to the situation of
Augustus' principate. Seneca's essay *On Mercy*, written in AD 55–6,
is the political manifesto of this programme. A few years of successful government followed, in which Nero had comparatively little
involvement; notable successes included the quelling of crises at the
margins of the empire without major military operations. But it
turned out that Nero had primarily used his two advisers to moderate the influence his mother had over him, and by AD 59 it was
brought home to Seneca and Burrus that they were not in control of
Nero, when he arranged the murder of Agrippina (already in 55
Nero had had Britannicus, his younger brother since his own adoption by Claudius, poisoned). Seneca's influence declined sharply.
Burrus died in 62, and Seneca retired to private life in the same year,
devoting himself entirely to literary work. It was probably in these
final years that he wrote, among other things, the *Letters to Lucilius*.
In AD 65 the so-called Pisonian conspiracy against Nero, in which
Seneca had no involvement, gave the emperor a pretext to order him
to kill himself. The historian Tacitus (AD 56–after 118) described
the event: according to the *Annals* (15.60–3), Seneca modelled his
suicide on that of Socrates (described in Plato's dialogue *Phaedo*),
who was forced to drink poison by a corrupt and misguided court
and used his final hours to conduct philosophical discussions with his
friends on the immortality of the soul. Tacitus contrasts the somewhat self-conscious manner in which Seneca parted with life (complete with finely wrought last words) with the unpretentious suicide
of another of Nero's courtiers, the writer Petronius (16.18–19), who
committed suicide in the context of a pleasant dinner party, breaking
his seal to make sure that it could not be used by the emperor's
henchmen to implicate his friends.[8]

Stoic Philosophy

The works of Seneca collected in this volume are not philosophical treatises which carefully and rigorously develop philosophical positions,
backing them up with detailed argument. Rather, they are exercises

[8] On Seneca's final years see Griffin, *Seneca*, 66–128.

in practical philosophy, which to some extent already presuppose familiarity with central tenets of Stoic teaching; not unreasonably so, since by Seneca's time the teachings of that school had become part of the intellectual *habitus* of educated Romans. This section, then, begins with an introduction to the main doctrines of Stoicism, then gives a survey of the school, and finally considers why Greek philosophy, and Stoicism in particular, made such a considerable impact in Rome.[9]

In some respects, Stoicism can be seen as a systematized version of views which can be drawn from the argumentative positions Socrates adopts in the various dialogues of Plato (on this 'debt' to Platonic philosophy see also below, p. xv). At its heart lies the notion that the only thing in life that actually matters and is worth caring about is the self, that is, the soul; that whether one has a good life or not crucially depends only on factors which affect the soul; and that in order to have a good life we need wisdom, that is, a certain kind of knowledge of what is good and bad. For the Stoics, this kind of knowledge is virtue, and the various virtues the Greeks traditionally distinguished are aspects of that knowledge.

Given the importance accorded to care for the self, the Stoics treated most of the things that ordinary people either desire or dread in life as 'indifferents' (*adiaphora*), but made a distinction between 'preferred indifferents', which are 'in accordance with nature', and others (see below on the conception of nature at issue here, p. xiii). Thus, while it is preferable to be healthy, not in material need, and to enjoy social prestige, all of these things are external to the good life, in that they do not affect the soul, so that not obtaining them does not make a life bad; likewise, suffering great pain or misfortune, or having one's life cut short in the bloom of youth, while not to be preferred, do nothing to make a life bad; indeed, within a broader context, which places us within the world as a whole, there may even be a sense in which our life is enhanced by such occurrences.

[9] A collection of Stoic fragments, with English translation and commentary, is in A. A. Long and D. N. Sedley, *The Hellenistic Philosophers*, 2 vols. (Cambridge, 1987). See also K. Algra *et al.* (eds.), *The Cambridge History of Hellenistic Philosophy* (Cambridge, 1999); and B. Inwood (ed.), *The Cambridge Companion to the Stoics* (Cambridge, 2003). A philosophical introduction to Stoic ethics is T. Brennan, *The Stoic Life: Emotions, Duties, and Fate* (Oxford, 2005).

Virtue alone is the good for the Stoics, and sufficient for happiness. This is the most extreme conception of virtue to be found in antiquity. To be virtuous means to be perfectly rational and to know both how to act in private life and with respect to one's friends, business associates, fellow citizens or countrymen, or indeed other members of the human race (see below on the notion of the *kosmopolitēs*, p. xv). (There is no clear distinction between proper behaviour in one's private life and social morality.) One way in which the Stoics sought to convert others to their conception of the good life was by accommodating traditional moral concepts, such as the various virtues, and articulating and redefining them in accordance with their other views. Thus, for example, practical wisdom (*phronêsis*) was defined as 'knowledge of what should and should not be done', and was then analysed into a wide range of sub-virtues. Since being virtuous is a condition of perfect rationality, it is not possible to have some virtues but not others; rather, there is a relationship of mutual entailment between the various virtues, and the perfectly rational human being (the sage), however rare he might be,[10] has all virtues simultaneously. But how does one become virtuous, given that the Stoics assume that virtue is not itself innate and that the faculty of conceptual thinking, a necessary condition for virtuous action, is only acquired at around the age of 14? The Stoics specified a goal of life (*telos*), namely 'living in agreement with nature', glossed as 'living in agreement with virtue, since nature leads us to virtue' (Diogenes Laertius 7.87).[11] They assumed that human beings are naturally endowed with inclinations towards virtue,[12] and that humans are naturally conditioned or programmed by what is called 'affinity' (*oikeiôsis*), which helps them acquire patterns of behaviour as well as an understanding of those patterns relating to one's own health and status, the interests of others, and appropriate action.[13] But since many of the factors which need to be taken into account in

[10] See R. Brouwer, 'Sagehood and the Stoics', *Oxford Studies in Ancient Philosophy*, 23 (2002), 181–224.

[11] On these formulae see M. Schofield, 'Stoic Ethics', in Inwood (ed.), *Cambridge Companion*, 233–56, esp. 241–2.

[12] See J. Brunschwig, 'The Cradle Argument in Epicureanism and Stoicism', in M. Schofield and G. Striker (eds.), *The Norms of Nature: Studies in Hellenistic Ethics* (Cambridge, 1986), 113–44.

[13] On 'affinity' see G. Striker, *Essays on Hellenistic Epistemology and Ethics* (Cambridge, 1996), chs. 12 and 13.

order to behave in the right way are external to our exercising our rational faculties, living in accordance with nature and acquiring a notion of the good also require developing a complex understanding of the processes and events in the world and universe as a whole, which itself is conceived as rational and well ordered.[14] Thus, living in agreement with nature both refers to human nature and to nature generally speaking.

A fully rational being cannot exist in an irrational world. Thus, for the Stoics there is a perfect order to the universe, which is governed and organized by a supremely rational intellect, whose influence extends from cosmic events down to minute and trivial occurrences in the world around us. This rational intellect is called nature, or 'god' (sometimes in a way which calls for capitalization), or Zeus, or is referred to by names of other gods, if manifestations of divine input which are traditionally associated with other gods are meant, although it is understood that strictly speaking there is only Zeus. It is on account of him that there is fate, which the Stoics view as a complex, perfectly organized network of causes which extend from the remote past through the present into the future. It is because of their conception of fate that the Stoics do not regard divination as superstition but as a rational means of inquiring into the future, if properly conducted: if this substructure of cause-and-effect relationships exists in the universe, then it provides a solid basis for analysis. If some events seem uncaused, then that just means that their causes are obscure and inaccessible. However, the fact that human beings live in a world that is thus organized does not mean that they do not have the freedom to act as rational agents; rather, nature has constructed them in such a way that they are free agents within the context of a deterministic world governed by providence. It is against this broad background that the formulation of the goal for man is to be seen. That the universe is organized and governed by Zeus' will also accounts for the status of 'indifferents', which are not preferred within the Stoic ethical theory: what may strike the non-Stoic as bad or detrimental for the individual is nonetheless seen as part of the divine plan.

---

[14] See M. Frede, 'On the Stoic Conception of the Good', in K. Ierodiakonou (ed.), *Topics in Stoic Philosophy* (Oxford, 1999), 71–94; on Seneca's views about how we come to acquire the notion of the good see Inwood, *Reading Seneca*, ch. 10.

The Stoic conception of a rationally governed universe is another point of contact with Platonic philosophy; a similar conception is developed in Plato's dialogue *Timaeus*.

Epistemology, or the theory of knowledge, is integral to Stoic ethics. For virtuous behaviour as characterized above to be possible, human beings must not hold any beliefs which are false, for if they did it might be possible for these false beliefs to form the premisses of arguments which lead to the conclusion that another, true belief is false; clearly this cannot be allowed to happen, which is why the sage only holds true beliefs. The Stoics agree again with Socrates that, if we want to have a really good life—a life of the sort that human beings are programmed and constructed to have—we have to have knowledge of certain facts, in the first instance of the world around us; we need to be sure that what we think we know we really do know; and we need to have a theory which explains how all this is possible. Now the Stoics distinguished between opinion, a variable epistemic state characteristic of human beings who are not sages, and knowledge, which only the sage (and the supremely rational being that is god) possesses. Between these two states they recognized a third, cognition (*katalêpsis*), which is different from opinion in that it is guaranteed to be true, and different from knowledge in that one can theoretically still be argued out of it (that to know something amounts to holding that something is the case, and to be so firm in that view that one cannot be reasoned out of it, is also already a Platonic position). Crucially, cognition is a state that is available both to the sage and the non-sage, and hence represents the pivotal route by which someone who is aspiring to become rational and virtuous can become so.

The Stoics analyse emotions as judgements of a certain sort: unlike Platonists, they do not posit an irrational part of the soul, and hold that we experience passions when we misguidedly assent to impressions of a certain sort, 'impulsive' impressions, with assent being a faculty which is within our gift to control.[15] Inappropriate emotional behaviour thus becomes an error of judgement. Morever, since the human soul only has a rational part, which receives different types of impression to which we can then assent or not, there is strictly speaking only one sin,

---

[15] See T. Brennan, 'Stoic Moral Psychology', in Inwood (ed.), *Cambridge Companion*, 257–94.

namely, assenting in cases where it is wrong to give assent. This helps to explain one of the famous Stoic paradoxes: that one is either a sage or a madman.

Accounts of aspects of the Stoic system are not normally ahistorically assembled from views which emerged over centuries.[16] Rather, Stoic orthodoxy is largely coextensive with the teachings of Chrysippus of Soloi (*c*.280–207 BC), who was the third head of the Stoa after Zeno of Citium (335–263 BC), who founded the school in Athens, and Cleanthes. Among the notable writings of Zeno was a treatise called *Republic*, in evident allusion to Plato's *Republic*.[17] But while Plato's work, though idealized, had a realistic side to it, in that two of the three classes he posited for his ideal city were non-philosophers, Zeno's state was exclusively a city of sages. Otherwise Zeno laid the doctrinal groundwork for all aspects of Stoic doctrine. It was, however, Chrysippus who devised most of the positions the Stoics are identified by, and who turned the teachings of the school into a fully integrated system. One innovation by Chrysippus was to promote the notion of a *kosmopolitēs* who lived in the world as a universal city inhabited by rational beings regardless of their nationality. Engagement in society and public life was promoted, but it was seen as the individual's contribution and fitting-in within the workings of the universe. As a consequence, more practical questions, like the place of the individual in the community or the relative worth of different forms of government, did not enter into the picture.[18] The successors of Chrysippus, Diogenes of Babylon and Antipater of Tarsus, did not substantially alter Stoic doctrine, but modified it slightly in the process of defending it against sceptical attacks by Academics, philosophers of the school originally founded by Plato.

The next phase of the school, traditionally called 'Middle Stoa', is represented by Panaetius of Rhodes (*c*.185–110 BC) and Posidonius of Apamea in Syria (*c*.135–50 BC). Panaetius wrote moral treatises

---

[16] On the history of the Stoic school see D. N. Sedley, 'The School, from Zeno to Arius Didymus', and C. Gill, 'The School in the Roman Period', ibid. 7–32 and 33–58, respectively.

[17] Points of contact between Platonic philosophy and Stoicism have been mentioned earlier; Zeno seems to have made a point of stressing this connection. On this issue see A. A. Long, 'Socrates in Hellenistic Philosophy', *Classical Quarterly*, 38 (1988), 1–34.

[18] On Stoic political philosophy see M. Schofield, in C. Rowe and M. Schofield (eds.), *The Cambridge History of Greek and Roman Political Thought* (Cambridge, 2000), ch. 22.

which were no longer geared to the unattainable ideal of the sage but dealt with the situations the *aspiring* sage might find himself in. While this is today no longer interpreted as a fundamental shift in Stoic moral doctrine (the 'sage' and the 'ordinary man' can be seen as literary devices used to induce the same kind of behaviour), this change of perspective does mean that Panaetius and Diogenes did now discuss problems of practical politics and the individual's place, obligations, and rights not in the world as a whole but in this 'second community'. Thus Cicero could use a treatise by Panaetius as the source for Books 1–2 of his *On Obligations* (*De Officiis*), and went some way towards articulating the affinity between traditional Roman morality and Stoic moral doctrine by illustrating the doctrinal framework derived from Panaetius with a wealth of examples drawn from great Romans of the past.[19] Poseidonius had a great interest in science and the accumulation and organization of knowledge, and is often credited with infusing Stoicism with the encyclopedic and empirical approach that is the trademark of the Peripatos, the school founded by Aristotle. The representatives of the 'Roman Stoa', which included Seneca, Musonius Rufus (AD 30–100), Epictetus (AD 55–135), and the emperor Marcus Aurelius (AD 121–80), addressed Romans specifically and offered a popularized version of Stoicism in which ethics overshadowed the two other branches of philosophy; of these, Seneca was the only one to write in Latin.

From the beginning there was, in principle, an affinity between traditional Roman morality and Stoic ethical doctrine. If it is one of the features of morality that it keeps selfishness and blunt utilitarianism in check, and that it encourages the purposeful forgoing of opportunities to dominate opponents or indeed other members of the same community, then of course such attitudes were present in Rome before Greek philosophy arrived. Conventionally, there are three main 'traditional virtues': *fides*, *virtus*, and *pietas*. *Fides* is the trust one puts in others, as well as enjoying from others; it is trust grounded in the assumption that you yourself and others are decent. *Fides* is a key term in Roman jurisprudence, often invoked in connection with legal decisions. *Virtus* was primarily manliness displayed in

---

[19] See A. R. Dyck, *A Commentary on Cicero's* De Officiis (Ann Arbor, Mich., 1996), 17–29.

war, that is, less of a moral term than it later came to be. Romans aspired to it, but did not own it. The early poet Ennius (239–169 BC) is reported as having a character say in a tragedy (frg. 71 Jocelyn): 'the law is better than *virtus*; for bad men often achieve *virtus*; what is right and just stands clearly apart from bad men.' *Pietas* refers to the bond of obligation that exists between ourselves and the gods, our country, and those we are associated with by nature, notably our parents and our children. The historian Livy, engaged in Augustus' project of moral restitution, tells many stories which can be read as evidence for traditional Roman morality.[20] These traditional notions were gradually influenced and transformed by Greek philosophy, but the course of this process is not easy to trace, partly because our main evidence for it comes from Cicero, who had reasons of his own for devising a particular picture of how Greek thought came to exercise an influence on Roman values.

It is one of the recognized patterns of interaction between two cultures that the dominant, but culturally less advanced, culture in the first instance adopts external features of the more sophisticated culture.[21] When Rome came to dominate the Greek-speaking world in the course of the second century BC, Roman aristocrats filled their villas with Greek art and adopted other readily detachable features of Greek culture, but did not engage with it in a thoroughgoing way, let alone wonder what Greek science, scholarship, and philosophy might contribute to genuinely Roman endeavours. This adoption of external features of Greek culture brought with it an anti-Greek sentiment, in evidence, for example, in the way in which the satirist Lucilius, who came from a senatorial family, mocked the philhellenism and penchant for Greek philosophical jargon which members of his class exhibited on occasion. There was an interest in Greek philosophy, but it was seen as an intellectual pastime and pursued without any of the involvement and urgency that we detect in later Roman philosophical writers. Yet there are texts which seem to capture key moments for the deeper appropriation of Greek intellectual culture; these texts, however, pursue goals and objectives of their

---

[20] See the material collected in L. R. Lind, 'The Tradition of Roman Moral Conservatism', in C. Deroux (ed.), *Studies in Latin Literature and Roman History I* (Brussels, 1979), 7–58.

[21] A classic study on the reception of Greek philosophy in Rome is R. Harder, 'Die Einbürgerung der Philosophie in Rom', *Die Antike*, 5 (1929), 291–316.

own and should not be mistaken for independent evidence. In Cicero's *Republic* (1.23) we learn how one general's interest in Greek astronomical inquiry enabled him to furnish a rational explanation for an eclipse, which was terrifying a Roman army just before the battle of Pydna in 168 BC, and enabled him to carry the day. We also hear (1.21–2) that earlier M. Marcellus, the conqueror of Syracuse in 212 BC, dedicated a model of the universe that had been constructed by Archimedes in the Temple of *Virtus*, an event often seen as indicative of the ongoing expansion of the understanding of *virtus*. The Greek historian Polybius (*c*.200–*c*.118 BC) tells a famous story (31.23–4) of how the younger Scipio Africanus revealed to him that he felt unequal to the traditional demands the Roman aristocracy made on young men, and asked Polybius if he was willing to give him instructions on how to show himself worthy of his ancestors. Polybius' point in telling this story is that, in order to meet the high expectations of what a young Roman aristocrat should be like, the young Scipio thought he needed instruction from a cultivated Greek.

The first century BC brought increasing internal turmoil for the Roman state. Various powerful individuals emerged who dominated the Roman politics of their time. One consequence of this was that the conventional career of the upper-class Roman male became a much more precarious endeavour, leading to disillusionment with the system. Although simplistic biographical explanations of complex literary phenomena should be resisted, it is surely not by chance that poets in the first century BC began to devise alternative lifestyles, like the 'life of love' for which the Roman elegists are known. This may be one of the reasons why philosophy became more than a pastime. The didactic poet Lucretius wrote a powerful work, *On the Nature of Things*, in which he, following Epicurean doctrine, identified fear of death as the main blight of the human condition, and explained all sorts of other worries or types of misguided behaviour as ultimately due to this fear.[22] Epicurean philosophy, which is meant to dispel the fear of death, was supposed to be a crucial tool for achieving happiness. It is no coincidence that Lucretius, not Virgil, is the poet most frequently quoted in the *Letters* of Seneca.

[22] See D. and P. Fowler's introduction in R. Melville (tr.), *Lucretius: On the Nature of the Universe* (Oxford, 1997).

The appropriation of Greek philosophical thought for Roman purposes is also key to Cicero's writings. He embarked on an ambitious project of introducing the Romans to the major schools of Hellenistic philosophy and their findings. Being an Academic sceptic himself, who was not firmly committed to any particular doctrines, but who would consider the tenets and theories of the dogmatic philosophers and scrutinize and evaluate them, Cicero covered almost all major areas in philosophical dialogues in which representatives of the various schools are pitted against each other, developing their positions in extended speeches, as opposed to engaging in the sharp question-and-answer format known from Platonic dialogues. However, apart from his desire to introduce his readership to Greek philosophy, Cicero also thought creatively about the way in which Greek ethics and political philosophy can be used to articulate and creatively develop political ideology and attitudes. This concern of his is primarily in evidence in his treatise *On Obligations*. A case can be made that Cicero's own personal background, in particular the fact that he did not come from an old senatorial family, meant that he had less of a sense of ownership of the values of that class; at the same time, he embraced the ideology of the elite he had just entered, and promoted and upheld it staunchly. This combination of alienation and commitment may have prompted him, more than others, to articulate and motivate traditional Roman values in new ways, by using Greek philosophy as a conceptual tool to which he had more claim than almost any of his contemporaries.

Stoicism grew steadily in influence from the time of Cicero onwards. The reasons for this are manifold. On the one hand Athens ceased to be the dominant centre for philosophy, and Rome and Alexandria took its place. On the other, the peculiar nature of the ideology of the Principate was such that it embraced and strengthened the appropriation of Stoic philosophy for the purpose of formulating Roman ideology. Augustus was keen to stress the continuity with the values of the Republic, and elements of Stoic doctrine which had not so far come to the fore were useful for that purpose. The sage could become a vehicle for the notion that political leadership, while in the hands of an individual in contravention of Republican practice, is rational, free of passions, benign, and sees power as an obligation and a commitment (a conception of the powerful politician whose origins can be traced to Cicero's defence speech for Milo, delivered in 52 BC). Poets, chiefly Virgil, would liken Augustus to Jupiter, with clear features of the Stoic Zeus (the image persisted, and is also found at the end of Tacitus' *Dialogue on the Orators*, written around AD 100).[23] Most of Seneca's prose writings can be seen as exercises in practical philosophy in this changed environment. Crucially, he has been called a 'first-order philosopher', in contrast to Cicero, in that he is not so much concerned with communicating doctrine as with engaging with it in an original fashion.[24]

Seneca's Dialogues and Essays

Apart from the tragedies Seneca wrote and the *Letters to Lucilius*, the dialogues and essays represent the third major part of Seneca's work (these treatises are commonly categorized as either dialogues or essays depending upon their manuscript transmission).[25] It has already been mentioned above that Seneca engages with philosophical issues in a free and self-determined way, that is, not with the purpose of merely expounding Greek doctrine which is more characteristic of Cicero. He presents himself as not interested in narrow scholarly or

[23] At the same time, there was the so-called Stoic opposition to the Principate, represented, for instance, by the senators Thrasea Paetus under Nero and Helvidius Priscus under Vespasian. While Stoicism does advise withdrawal to private study rather than active opposition to those who find themselves unable to make a positive contribution in unfavourable political circumstances, it is not difficult to see how, for instance, requests for the Senate's opinion made by a bad emperor could appear to make it incumbent on the Stoic to take a stand. See P. A. Brunt, 'Stoicism and the Principate', *Papers of the British School at Rome*, 43 (1975), 7–35.

[24] One consequence of this fact is that scholars have always been less tempted to construct simplistic theories about how Seneca's works relate to their Greek 'sources' than they have been in the case of Cicero.

[25] Of the treatises, *On Benefits* and *On Mercy* are transmitted through the same MS tradition. The *Natural Questions* have a MS tradition of their own. All other treatises are commonly referred to as 'dialogues', which is what they are called in the MS on which our text of them mainly depends. The term 'dialogue' requires explanation, in that the texts in question are not dialogues in a conventional, e.g. Platonic or Ciceronian, sense. The term 'dialogue' is first used in connection with Seneca's works by the rhetorician Quintilian (*On the Education of the Orator* 10.1.129) towards the end of the first century AD (there, however, the reference seems to be to prose works other than the *Letters* in general, not to a subset of these prose works). This shows that the use of the Latin term *dialogus* is ancient, not an invention by medieval scribes. One plausible solution to the puzzle is that 'dialogue' or *dialogus* could be a technical rhetorical term, which denotes words delivered by a speaker assuming a particular *persona*; thus H. Lausberg, *Handbook of Literary Rhetoric* (Leiden, 1998), secs. 820, 822.9.

doctrinal disputes, and his attitude to the inclusion of non-Stoic material is neatly encapsulated in *On the Shortness of Life* 14: 'We may hold argument with Socrates, feel doubt with Carneades, find tranquillity with Epicurus, conquer human nature with the Stoics, exceed it with the Cynics.'

Seneca's treatises address a variety of philosophical issues. *On Providence* is variously dated to the period of exile and to that of Seneca's retirement (however, since it is used in the *Natural Questions*, it cannot have been written towards the end of his retirement). Seneca argues for the existence of providence and explains that trials are imposed on those whom god loves. Consequently evils are to be seen as part of a grander, well-conceived plan; they are beneficial as steps on the path to true happiness; thus, fate is to be embraced. At the very end suicide is considered as a possibility of coping with trials which are too demanding.[26]

On Anger, of which book 3 is included here, is dedicated to Seneca's brother Novatus. Its date is suggested by two facts: the representation of the tyrant in the work is reminiscent of Caligula, but the work must have been written before 52, since Seneca's brother then changed his name through adoption. Book 3 combines an analysis of the phenomenon with practical advice. Anger is the result of weakness. It cannot exist without our assent to an impulsive impression, and is a misguided expression of reason (so animals cannot experience it); see above, p. xiv. One must avoid anger and try to exercise a calming influence on others. Forethought helps to prevent crises: encounters with irritating contemporaries are to be avoided, and reflection on good as well as bad examples helps. Clemency is to be shown to others, transgressions are to be forgiven. Detrimental feelings like suspicion, jealousy, and unreasonable expectations are to be avoided.

The *Consolation to Marcia*, one of the two representatives of this genre in the present collection, is Seneca's earliest work, written under Caligula.[27] Consolation was a genre which was comparatively fashionable among philosophers in the Hellenistic period; through its attempts to console a grieving addressee, it offered scope for penetrating analyses of what constitutes a human life, what was important in it,

[26] See W. Englert, 'Stoics and Epicureans on the Nature of Suicide', *Proceedings of the Boston Area Colloquium on Ancient Philosophy*, 10 (1994), 67–98.

[27] A short introduction to the genre of consolatory literature is in J. H. D. Scourfield, *Consoling Heliodorus: A Commentary on Jerome, Epistle 60* (Oxford, 1993), 15–33.

and how human beings might conceive of themselves in the wider context of the world as a whole. Marcia has been in mourning for three years over her son Metilius; before that her father, the historian Cremutius Cordus, had committed suicide. Seneca observes that excessive grief is unnatural, and that it is advisable to anticipate mentally any misfortune that might befall us, so as to lessen the impact of the actual event when it occurs (this is one of the psychagogic techniques mentioned below, p. xxv). It is also appropriate to reflect on whether our mourning is a form of selfishness: do we grieve for the deceased or for ourselves? But grief can be healed through reflection on the nature of life and death, and duration is an accidental feature of life, not a criterion for its evaluation.

On the Happy Life must have been written after 52, as the addressee is Seneca's older brother Gallio, who had only adopted this name in that year. The fact that Seneca presents himself as wealthy and well respected makes it unlikely that it was written after his withdrawal from public life in 62. Seneca is here concerned with two factors which are commonly, but wrongly, held to be important for a happy life: enjoyment and wealth. Notably, he defends himself against the charge of hypocrisy: he was one of the wealthiest men of his time, and yet argued for the irrelevance of material goods. Seneca replies that the wise man need not live in poverty; on the contrary, he alone has the right independent attitude to wealth.

On the Tranquillity of the Mind must have been written after Caligula's death, and before 63, when the addressee of the work, Serenus, a high official at Nero's court, died. Serenus begins unusually with a speaking part. He lays before Seneca the result of his mental self-examination: he is troubled by the attraction exercised by external things, especially luxury and fame. Seneca suggests that as a cure for his state of anxiety and restlessness he needs to achieve calmness of mind, which he will bring about by combining the fulfilment of his professional duties with philosophical reflection.

On the Shortness of Life was written between 49 and 55. In it Seneca argues that the alleged shortness of human life depends on a mistaken analysis of what is important in life. Indulging one's pleasures leads to a view in which the success of a life becomes a matter of accumulating pleasant experiences. Rather, one has to learn to find the right attitude to time, and to value and allocate time in the right way.

In the *Consolation to Helvia* Seneca attempts to console his mother, who is lamenting his exile. Seneca's own supposed misfortunes (deportation to a remote place, poverty, loss of social status) are negligible anyway, nor should Helvia grieve on her own account: since she has no ambitions, she is not in need of a supporter or protector. There is thus a glimpse of lives lived in fear under a totalitarian system. Helvia is encouraged to devote herself to her family, in particular her sister, whom Seneca praises at the end of the work.

On Mercy was written between 15 December 55 and 14 December 56; it seems to have been extended and revised by Seneca, and is not transmitted in its entirety (we only have the first two of three books). It reflects the hopes Seneca had for the principate of Nero, to whom it is dedicated. Mercy befits the ruler and is evidence of his greatness. Roman citizens should be treated as the ruler hopes to be treated by the gods. Augustus, who was mild late in life, is cited as an example of this attitude; Nero has the opportunity to show himself so already as a young man. By contrast, cruelty marks the tyrant; it throws the life of the individual into uncertainty. The love of his subjects makes the position of the ruler secure. In Book 2 Seneca argues that mercy is not just opposed to cruelty but also different from pity, which is a vice, according to the Stoic view.

The *Natural Questions*, Seneca's only substantial venture into the field of physics, is an encyclopedic work, covering a wide range of subjects, among them astronomy (Book 2), winds (Book 5), and comets (Book 7); Book 6, included here, is concerned with earthquakes. But beneath the enjoyment and curiosity of choice facts about intriguing natural phenomena, the work has an ethical dimension too, in that it is concerned with the relationship of man and god, whose influence is manifest in the workings of the natural world, and with man's position in the universe.

Style and Literary Form

Seneca is the main representative of so-called Silver Latin prose. The hallmark of his style is a clipped, paratactic way of writing, which depends for its effect on particular stylistic devices like parallelism, antithesis, and the pointed and brilliant one-liner, the epigram or *sententia*. By contrast, the main representatives of late Republican prose, Caesar and Cicero, are renowned for writing long and complex, hypotactically structured sentences, which were suited to expounding

complex, interdependent events like the planning and execution of a
military campaign, or the intricate interplay of accusation and defence,
praise and blame, or cause and effect in public speeches. The reasons for
Seneca's adopting a different mode of writing are multiple. The inter-
locutor Aper in Tacitus' *Dialogue on the Orators* (see above, p. xx)
sketches the development of Roman eloquence from Cicero's youth to
the mid-first century AD, and observes that audiences were tiring of the
expansive, complex style already during Cicero's lifetime, and that
Cicero adjusted accordingly, on the grounds that part of the success of
an orator depended on the aesthetic satisfaction he was able to induce in
his audience. Moreover, the recognition which the stylist Cicero enjoyed
was paradoxically bound to create the desire in some people to write in
a quite different way. And the character of Seneca's works made long,
complex sentences unsuitable for his purpose, because they are not the
right medium for conducting practical philosophical instruction and for
directly engaging with and involving a readership. Finally, the advent of
declamation practice is frequently connected with the emergence of
Silver Latin. From around the middle of the first century BC declamation represented the final stage of rhetorical education, but it also developed into a form of sophisticated entertainment, comparable to
concerts.[28] There were two types of this exercise. The *suasoria*, seen as
the easier one, required the pupil to give advice to a famous character
from myth or history (e.g. 'Should Alexander the Great attempt to cross
the ocean?'). The *controversia* was formally a courtroom speech, often
involving rather unlikely scenarios, including references to fictional laws
('A law decrees that a rapist may either be put to death on his victim's
request or has to marry her. A man has committed two rapes, and one
victim wants to see him dead, the other one wants to be married.').

There was no lack of critics already in antiquity who condemned this
practice, and many modern scholars echo this viewpoint. However, if
properly carried out, the skills pupils could develop through this exercise
are not very different from those one would hope to acquire during many
courses in a modern university; nor is it difficult to see that attractive

---

[28] Extant texts of interest include the works of the elder Seneca (see above, n. 1) and
the so-called lesser declamations ascribed to Quintilian (edited by D. R. Shackleton
Bailey for the Loeb series (Cambridge, Mass., 2006), 2 vols.). See further S. F. Bonner,
Roman Declamation in the Late Republic and Early Empire (Liverpool, 1949);
E. Gunderson, *Declamation, Paternity, and the Roman Self* (Cambridge, 2003).

features of Seneca's treatises can be linked to this practice. A succesful declaimer had to learn to analyse the data pertaining to a complex problem in such a way as to construct arguments relevant to it. A grasp of the psychology of the main characters featuring in a *suasoria* is obviously a transferable skill. After an exercise the instructor would give comments concerning the image a pupil had projected of himself, through the content of his speech, his manner of presentation, and his body language; the relevance of this for public speakers, aspiring politicians, or indeed one particular Stoic philosopher is transparent. Declamations also follow certain patterns of organization, which help to group loosely related topics, allowing for sufficent flexibility to enhance a preconceived point by an unprepared aside; some of these structural features can likewise be discerned in Seneca. Literary devices which Seneca uses with great skill include the colourful anecdote or the example of a great Roman of the past, the latter an archetypal Roman way of dealing with abstract issues which might otherwise be conceptualized, and the vivid metaphor or sustained image, which has a strong Stoic tradition and fully comes to life in the works of Seneca. He also uses imaginary interlocutors, who liven up the discursive exposition, appearing suddenly and voicing their objections in direct speech; Seneca's skill in composing heated and punchy exchanges, in evidence in his tragedies, served him well in his treatises too. Notable also is his use of embedded quotations from a wide range of sources, which often send the reader back to the quoted text to investigate how its original context is considered and modified by Seneca, and a cleverness in applying psychagogic techniques, that is, devices which are calculated to produce a particular response on the part of the reader.

Seneca's Influence[29]

Seneca made no noticeable impact on the Stoics who wrote not long after him for a Roman audience—Musonius, Epictetus, and the emperor Marcus Aurelius. His reputation in the first and second

---

[29] See G. M. Ross, 'Seneca's Philosophical Influence', in C. D. N. Costa (ed.), *Seneca* (London, 1974), 116–65; K. A. Blüher, *Seneca in Spanien: Untersuchungen zur Geschichte der Seneca-Rezeption in Spanien vom 13. bis 17. Jahrhundert* (Munich, 1969). On the transmission of the texts of the treatises in the Middle Ages see the relevant sections in L. D. Reynolds (ed.), *Texts and Transmission: A Survey of the Latin Classics* (Oxford, 1983).

centuries AD was mixed. Pliny the elder admires the *Natural Questions* for the learning on display (*Natural History* 14.5.5), the agricultural writer Columella recognizes his moral quality (*On Agriculture* 3.3), and other Spanish writers claim him as one of their greats (Martial, *Epigrams* 1.61.7–8). Another Spaniard, Quintilian, who is otherwise ambiguous about Seneca, acknowledges his enormous popularity with the young (*On the Education of the Orator* 10.1.125). But there was criticism of Seneca too. He was attacked on moral grounds; the charges—debauchery and hypocrisy among them—seem to have some connection with the fact that he was both powerful and enormously wealthy and a Stoic philosopher. Tacitus relates them in sufficient detail for them to have an effect, but without endorsing them; others, like Cassius Dio, make them their own. Seneca was also criticized as a stylist, although that criticism too had a moral tinge to it; Quintilian, who pursued a neo-Ciceronian ideal of rhetorical style, thought that he was excessive in his striving for brilliance and pointed expression, so much so that he lost both structure and the scope for contrast, which is instrumental for generating variety (10.1.125–31).[30] As an educator, he also felt that the superficial attraction of Seneca's prose taught the young excess where they needed judgement; stylistic imitation was a crucial didactic strategy of rhetorical education. Later writers, like Fronto or Gellius, sometimes called archaizers, rejected Seneca on the same grounds, and also because he had been dismissive of great Roman writers of the early period.[31] While these attitudes to Seneca did not do much to shape perception of him in late antiquity and through the Renaissance (notably, Tacitus and Cassius Dio were only 'rediscovered' by the Italian Renaissance), they did affect scholars' views on him from the nineteenth century onwards. For the remainder of antiquity, and throughout the Middle Ages, Seneca enjoyed a very high reputation. This was due to the fact that the Latin church fathers discovered him for themselves. The reasons for this were the general affinity between Christian doctrine and Stoic philosophy (as well as the absence of other Stoic treatises written in Latin), and the appearance of what was believed to be a correspondence between

[30] See also C. O. Brink, 'Quintilian's *De causis corruptae eloquentiae* and Tacitus' *Dialogus de oratoribus*', *Classical Quarterly*, 39 (1989), 472–503, esp. 480–2.

[31] See L. Holford-Strevens, *Aulus Gellius: An Antonine Scholar and his Achievement*, 2nd edn. (Oxford, 2003), 274–81.

Seneca and the apostle Paul, which eventually led to the claim by early Italian humanists that Seneca was a Christian.[32] Evidence for Senecean influence wanes towards the end of late antiquity, to pick up slightly in the Carolingian renaissance of the ninth century. A practice of creating excerpts from his works had started in late antiquity, encouraged by his epigrammatic style of writing, and the availability of this kind of anthology makes it difficult to detect genuine familiarity with his works. Towards the end of the eleventh century the monastery of Monte Cassino was instrumental in the distribution of the dialogues, as it was for other pagan classics.[33] In the twelfth century Seneca is quoted and admired by Peter Abelard and John of Salisbury. Scholasticism limited the role given to Seneca in the thirteenth and fourteenth centuries, but helped to ensure renewed interest in him in the humanistic period. Petrarch, among others, was attracted both by his philosophical position and his style.[34] Later, Erasmus moved from fervent admiration to qualified appreciation of Seneca, but helped ensure his later influence through two complete editions of his works;[35] and he strongly argued against the authenticity of the correspondence between Seneca and St Paul. The next important stage in his reception is connected with the work of the Flemish scholar and philosopher Justus Lipsius (1547–1606), who worked on the texts of Seneca as a philologist and editor, but more importantly developed his whole philosophical position (moral as well as physical doctrines) into Neo-Stoicism, partly as a means to enable others to live through a difficult, war-stricken period.[36] It is largely due to Lipsius that Seneca's thought and style exercised a crucial influence on the European moralists Montaigne, Francis Bacon, La Rochefoucauld, and Pascal.[37] For much of the twentieth century Seneca was rather neglected, until, in the context of the resurgence of interest which Hellenistic and Roman philosophy have enjoyed over the last thirty years, he too has once more become a central classical author.

[32] See Blüher, *Seneca in Spanien*, 19.

[33] See Reynolds, *Texts and Transmission*, 366.

[34] See A. Bobbio, 'Seneca e la formazione spirituale e culturale del Petrarca', *La Bibliofilia*, 43 (1941), 224–91.

[35] See Ross, 'Seneca's Philosophical Influence', 143–4.

[36] See Jan Papy, 'Justus Lipsius', *Stanford Encyclopedia of Philosophy* (Fall 2004 Edition), Edward N. Zalta (ed.), URL=<http://plato.stanford.edu/archives/fall2004/entries/justus-lipsius/>.

[37] See A. A. Long, 'Stoicism in the Philosophical Tradition: Spinoza, Lipsius, Butler', in Inwood (ed.), *Cambridge Companion*, 365–92.

NOTE ON THE TEXT

The critical edition used as a basis for the translation of all treatises included in this volume except for *Natural Questions*, Book 6, is the Oxford Classical Text of Seneca's *Dialogi* by Leighton D. Reynolds (Oxford, 1977); for *Natural Questions*, Book 6, the Teubner edition by Harry M. Hine (Stuttgart and Leipzig, 1996) has been used.

Seneca wrote in all thirteen treatises, commonly called dialogues or essays, of which seven are here given complete, together with Book 3 of *On Anger* and Book 6 of *Natural Questions*. The selection shows the range of Seneca's philosophical interests in its most accessible form (see pp. xx–xxiii). The full list of treatises is as follows:

On Leisure (*De Otio*)
On Providence (*De Providentia*)
Natural Questions (*Naturales Quaestiones*)
On Anger (*De Ira*)
Consolation to Marcia (*De Consolatione ad Marciam*)
On the Happy Life (*De Vita Beata*)
On Firmness (*De Constantia*)
On the Tranquillity of the Mind (*De Tranquilitate Animi*)
On the Shortness of Life (*De Brevitate Vitae*)
Consolation to Helvia (*De Consolatione ad Helviam*)
On Mercy (*De Clementia*)
On Benefits (*De Beneficiis*)
Consolation to Polybius (*De Consolatione ad Polybium*)

SELECT BIBLIOGRAPHY

Editions

[Quintilian], *The Lesser Declamations*, 2 vols. (Cambridge, Mass., 2006), ed. D. R. Shackleton Bailey (Loeb Classical Library).

The elder Seneca, *Controversiae and Suasoriae*, 2 vols. (Cambridge, Mass., 1974), ed. M. Winterbottom (Loeb Classical Library).

Seneca, *De Vita Beata* (Paris, 1969), ed. P. Grimal.

—— *Dialogi* (Oxford, 1977), ed. L. D. Reynolds (Oxford Classical Texts).

—— *Naturales Quaestiones* (Stuttgart and Leipzig, 1996) (Bibliotheca Teubneriana).

—— *De Otio — De Brevitate Vitae* (Cambridge, 2003), ed. G. D. Williams (Cambridge Greek and Latin Classics).

—— *Troades* (Princeton, 1982), ed. E. Fantham.

Tacitus, *Dialogus de Oratoribus* (Cambridge, 2001), ed. R. Mayer (Cambridge Greek and Latin Classics).

On Seneca

Berno, F. R., *Lo specchio, il vizio e la virtù. Studie sulle Naturales Quaestiones di Seneca* (Bologna, 2003).

Blüher, K. A., *Seneca in Spanien: Untersuchungen zur Geschichte der Seneca-Rezeption in Spanien vom 13. bis 17. Jahrhundert* (Munich, 1969).

Bobbio, A., 'Seneca e la formazione spirituale e culturale del Petrarca', *La Bibliofilia*, 43 (1941), 224–91.

Cooper, J. M., and Procopé, J. F. (eds. and trs.), *Seneca: Moral and Political Essays* (Cambridge, 1995).

Edwards, C., 'Self-scrutiny and Self-transformation in Seneca's Letters', *Greece & Rome*, 44 (1997), 23–38.

Gill, C., 'The School in the Roman Period', in Inwood (ed.), *Cambridge Companion*, 33–58.

Griffin, M., *Seneca: A Philosopher in Politics* (Oxford, 1976).

Inwood, B., *Reading Seneca: Stoic Philosophy at Rome* (Oxford, 2005).

Ross, G. M., 'Seneca's Philosophical Influence', in C. D. N. Costa (ed.), *Seneca* (London, 1974), 116–65.

Background Reading

Algra, K. *et al.* (eds.), *The Cambridge History of Hellenistic Philosophy* (Cambridge, 1999).

Bonner, S. F., *Roman Declamation in the Late Republic and Early Empire* (Liverpool, 1949).

Brennan, T., 'Stoic Moral Psychology', in Inwood (ed.), *Cambridge Companion*, 257–94.

—— *The Stoic Life: Emotions, Duties, and Fate* (Oxford, 2005).

Brink, C. O., 'Quintilian's *De causis corruptae eloquentiae* and Tacitus' *Dialogus de oratoribus*', *Classical Quarterly*, 39 (1989), 472–503.

Brouwer, R., 'Sagehood and the Stoics', *Oxford Studies in Ancient Philosophy*, 23 (2002), 181–224.

Brunschwig, J., 'The Cradle Argument in Epicureanism and Stoicism', in M. Schofield and G. Striker (eds.), *The Norms of Nature: Studies in Hellenistic Ethics* (Cambridge, 1986), 113–44.

Brunt, P. A., 'Stoicism and the Principate', *Papers of the British School at Rome*, 43 (1975), 7–35.

Dyck, A. R., *A Commentary on Cicero's De Officiis* (Ann Arbor, Mich., 1996).

Englert, W., 'Stoics and Epicureans on the Nature of Suicide', *Proceedings of the Boston Area Colloquium in Ancient Philosophy*, 10 (1994), 67–98.

Frede, M., 'On the Stoic Conception of the Good', in Ierodiakonou (ed.), *Topics*, 71–94.

Griffin, M., and Atkins, E. M. (eds. and trs.), *Cicero: On Duties* (Cambridge, 1991).

Gunderson, E., *Declamation, Paternity, and the Roman Self* (Cambridge, 2003).

Harder, R., 'Die Einbürgerung der Philosophie in Rom', *Die Antike*, 5 (1929), 291–316.

Holford-Strevens, L., *Aulus Gellius: An Antonine Scholar and his Achievement*, 2nd edn. (Oxford, 2003).

Ierodiakonou, K. (ed.), *Topics in Stoic Philosophy* (Oxford, 1999).

Inwood, B., *Ethics and Human Action in Early Stoicism* (Oxford, 1985).

—— (ed.), *The Cambridge Companion to the Stoics* (Cambridge, 2003).

Kahn, C. H., *Pythagoras and the Pythagoreans: A Brief History* (Indianapolis, 2001).

Lausberg, H., *Handbook of Literary Rhetoric* (Leiden, 1998).

Lind, L. R., 'The Tradition of Roman Moral Conservatism', in C. Deroux (ed.), *Studies in Latin Literature and Roman History I* (Brussels, 1979), 7–58.

Long, A. A., 'Socrates in Hellenistic Philosophy', *Classical Quarterly*, 38 (1988), 1–34.

—— *Stoic Studies* (Cambridge, 1996).

—— 'Stoicism in the Philosophical Tradition: Spinoza, Lipsius, Butler', in Inwood (ed.), *Cambridge Companion*, 365–92.

—— and Sedley, D. N., *The Hellenistic Philosophers*, 2 vols. (Cambridge, 1987).

Reynolds, L. D. (ed.), *Texts and Transmission: A Survey of the Latin Classics* (Oxford, 1983).

Rowe, C., and Schofield, M. (eds.), *The Cambridge History of Greek and Roman Political Thought* (Cambridge, 2000).

Schofield, M., *The Stoic Idea of the City* (Cambridge, 1991).

—— 'Stoic Ethics', in Inwood (ed.), *Cambridge Companion*, 233–56.

Scourfield, J. H. D., *Consoling Heliodorus: A Commentary on Jerome, Epistle 60* (Oxford, 1993).

Sedley, D. N., 'The School, from Zeno to Arius Didymus', in Inwood (ed.), *Cambridge Companion*, 7–32.

Striker, G., 'Following Nature: A Study of Stoic Ethics', *Oxford Studies in Ancient Philosophy*, 9 (1991), 1–73.

Zeller, E., *Die Philosophie der Griechen in ihrer geschichtlichen Entwicklung*, 3 vols. (Leipzig, 1880–92).

Further Reading in Oxford World's Classics

Aristotle, *The Nicomachean Ethics*, trans. David Ross, rev. J. R. Ackrill and J. O. Urmson.

Cicero, *On Obligations*, trans. P. G. Walsh.

—— *On the Nature of the Gods*, trans. P. G. Walsh.

—— *The Republic and The Laws*, trans. Niall Rudd.

Herodotus, *The Histories*, trans. Robin Waterfield.

Lucan, *Civil War*, trans. Susan H. Braund.

Lucretius, *On the Nature of the Universe*, trans. Ronald Melville.

Marcus Aurelius, *Meditations*, trans. A. S. L. Farquharson and R. B. Rutherford.

Petronius, *The Satyricon*, trans. P. G. Walsh.

Plato, *Phaedo*, trans. David Gallop.

Seneca, *Selected Letters*, trans. Elaine Fantham.

—— *Six Tragedies*, trans. Emily Wilson.

CHRONOLOGY

For most of Seneca's works we are unable to give definite dates; the dialogues and essays are listed here in their probable positions (see the Introduction for further details). All dates are AD unless otherwise indicated.

*c.*138–78 BC	Lucius Cornelius Sulla.
106–43 BC	Marcus Tullius Cicero.
100–44 BC	Gaius Julius Caesar.
55 BC	Seneca's father born in Corduba, Spain.
31 BC	Defeat of Antony at the battle of Actium, end of the Republic.
31 BC–AD 14	Principate of Augustus.
1 BC	Seneca born in Corduba; education in Rome in rhetoric and philosophy.
14–37	Principate of Tiberius; Seneca spends time in Egypt for health reasons.
31	Seneca returns to Italy; pursues a political career, eventually becoming quaestor.
37–41	Principate of Caligula; Seneca writes the *Consolation to Marcia*
39	Seneca arouses the jealousy of Caligula and is threatened with execution.
41	Seneca accused of adultery with Julia Livilla (Caligula's sister); exiled to Corsica until 49. *Consolation to Helvia* and *Consolation to Polybius*.
41–54	Principate of Claudius.
49	Seneca's return to Rome is secured by Agrippina; becomes tutor to her son, the young Nero, as well as praetor. Probable period for *On Anger*, *On the Happy Life*, *On the Tranquillity of the Mind*, and *On the Shortness of Life*.
54–68	Principate of Nero.
54–62	Senior adviser to Nero (together with Burrus, prefect of the Praetorian Guard). *On the Happy Life*.
55	Nero poisons his younger brother, Britannicus.

55–6   *On Mercy*

59   Nero kills his mother, Agrippina. *On Leisure*.

62   Death of Burrus. *On Benefits*. Seneca retires from public
            life. Probably writes *On Providence*, the *Natural Questions*,
            and *Letters to Lucilius* in this period.

65   Seneca commits suicide, on Nero's orders, after being impli-
            cated, wrongly, in the Pisonian conspiracy against the
            emperor.

DIALOGUES AND ESSAYS

ON PROVIDENCE

TO LUCILIUS

Why some misfortunes happen to good men, although there is providence

1. You have asked me, Lucilius,* why, if the world is governed by providence, it is still the case that good men suffer from many misfortunes. This question would receive a more fitting answer in a coherent work that set out to prove that providence does preside over us all and that God concerns himself with us; but since your wish is that a small part be severed from the whole and that I refute a single objection without tackling the main question, I shall turn my hand to a task that is not difficult—it is the gods' cause I shall be pleading.

It is superfluous for present purposes to show that this great edifice of the world does not stand without some power to guard it, or that the stars that assemble and disperse above us are not propelled by chance; that, though bodies whose motion is due to accident frequently become disordered and swiftly collide, our rapidly revolving heavens, governed as they are by eternal law, proceed without hindrance, displaying so many things by land and sea, so many radiant lights in the sky all gleaming in fixed order; that this system is not produced by matter which moves randomly, and that such combinations as do result from chance are not dependent on the great artistry that makes the earth with all its mighty weight remain stationary, observing the swift passage of the heavens as they whirl around it, that makes the seas, flooding the valleys, soften the land, and feel no increase from the rivers, and makes enormous growths arise from the smallest seeds. Not even those natural events which appear capricious and undetermined—I mean showers of rain and clouds, the strokes of crashing thunderbolts and the fires that leap up from shattered mountain peaks, the tremors of the ground when it quakes, and the other motions caused around the earth by the violent element in nature—not even those occur without reason, however suddenly they occur; no, they too have specific causes, in the same way as phenomena which are taken to be miraculous because the setting in which we see them happen is so incongruous—I mean warm waters in the middle of sea waves, and chains of new islands springing up in the vastness of the ocean. Again, if anyone observes how shores are laid bare as the sea withdraws into itself, and yet are covered again in the shortest of time, he will believe it is some unseen fluctuation that causes the waves now to diminish and flow inwards, now to burst forth and with a great surge reclaim their former home; but in fact the waves increase by degrees, approaching to the hour and day proportionately larger or smaller in volume as they are attracted by the star we call the moon, whose power controls the ocean's surge. But let matters such as this be kept for their proper time, all the more so as you do not question the existence of providence but complain of it.

I shall restore you to good relations with the gods, who are best to the best of men. For it is not Nature's way to let good ever do harm to good; between good men and the gods exists a friendship sealed by virtue. Friendship, do I say? No, rather it is a bond of relationship and similarity, since undoubtedly a good man differs from God only in the sphere of time; he is God's pupil and imitator, his true offspring whom that illustrious parent, no gentle trainer in virtue, rears with severity, as strict fathers do. And so, when you see good men of whom the gods approve toiling and sweating, with a steep road to climb, and bad men, on the other hand, enjoying themselves, surrounded by pleasures, consider that our sons please us by their self-control, but our house-slaves by their free spirit, that we restrain the former by tighter discipline and nurture the latter's boldness of manner. It is no different with God, let me assure you: he does not pamper a good man like a favourite slave; he puts him to the test, hardens him, and makes him ready for his service.

2. 'Why do many reversals of fortune happen to good men?' Nothing bad *can* happen to a good man: opposites do not mix. Just as the vast number of rivers, all the rain that falls in showers from above, and the massive volume of mineral springs do not alter the taste of the sea, do not even moderate it, so adversity's onslaughts are powerless to affect the spirit of a brave man: it remains unshaken and makes all events assume its own colour; for it is stronger than all external forces. I do not mean that he is insensible to those forces but that he conquers them, and as a man who in all else is calm and tranquil of mind he rises to face whatever attacks him. All adversity he regards as a training exercise. Who, provided he is a man and intent

on what is right, will shirk reasonable toil or show reluctance to face duties involving danger? What man of energy does not find inactivity a punishment? We see wrestlers, who concern themselves with physical strength, matching themselves with only the strongest opponents, and requiring those who prepare them for a bout to use all their strength against them; they expose themselves to blows and hurt, and if they do not find one man to match them, they take on several at a time. Excellence withers without an adversary: the time for us to see how great it is, how much its force, is when it displays its power through endurance. I assure you, good men should do the same: they should not be afraid to face hardships and difficulties, or complain of fate; whatever happens, good men should take it in good part, and turn it to a good end; it is not what you endure that matters, but how you endure it.

Do you not see how differently fathers and mothers show their love? The father orders his children to be roused early to pursue their studies, not allowing them to be idle even on a holiday, and wrings from them sweat and sometimes tears; but the mother wants to cherish them in her embrace and keep them out of the sun's glare, and wishes them never to know sadness, never to shed tears, never to toil. It is a father's heart that God shows to good men; he loves them in a manly way, and says, 'Let them know the pain of toil, of suffering, of loss, so that they may acquire true strength.' Bodies that have become fat grow sluggish through lack of use, and not effort alone but even movement and their very own weight cause them to fail. Prosperity that is undiminished cannot withstand a single blow; but the man who has struggled constantly against his own ills becomes hardened by suffering and no misfortune makes him yield, indeed, if he falls, he still fights on his knees. Are you surprised if that God who so loves good men and wants them to be as good, as virtuous as possible, assigns to them a fortune that will make them struggle? It causes me no surprise if the gods are sometimes moved by the desire to view great men struggling against some calamity. We humans at times enjoy the sight of a courageous youth meeting the charge of some beast with his spear-point, if without fear he stands up to a charging lion, and the more honourable the young man who does so, the more pleasure we take in the sight. But these are not the kind of actions that can make the gods gaze on us, being merely childish things that amuse frivolous humans; no, here is a spectacle worthy of God's attention as he contemplates his own work, here is a contest worthy of God—a brave man matched against bad fortune, all the more so if he has made the challenge. I cannot, I say, imagine a finer spectacle on earth for Jupiter to view, should he wish to turn his attention there, than that of Cato,* when his cause had been shattered more than once already, yet standing upright amid the ruins of the republic. 'Let all the world fall under one man's sway,' he said, 'let Caesar's legions guard the land and his ships the sea, let his troops blockade the city-gates, Cato has yet a means of escape: with one hand he will open a broad path to freedom. This sword, that even civil war has not sullied or stained with guilt, shall at last render good and noble service: the freedom that it could not give to its country it will give to Cato! Come, my soul, attempt the task you have long planned, set yourself free from the world of men! Already Petreius and Juba* have clashed in combat and lie slain, each by the other's hand, a pact with fate that shows courage and nobility, but would not suit my own greatness: for Cato to ask for death at another's hand is as shameful as to ask for life.' I am in no doubt that the gods looked on with great pleasure, while that man, so fierce in avenging himself, took thought for the safety of others and enabled his departing comrades to make their escape; while he pursued his studies even on that final night; while he drove the sword into his holy breast; while he spilled his guts and with his hand gave passage to that most upright soul, so unworthy of a sword's defilement. This, I would like to believe, is why the wound he dealt himself was not well-aimed or successful: it was not enough for the immortal gods to gaze only once on Cato; his bravery was kept in check and summoned again so that it might reveal itself in a harder role; for it requires greater courage to seek death twice than once. It must have pleased the gods to watch their pupil leaving life in such a distinguished and memorable end. Death consecrates those men whose death wins praise even from the fearful.

3. But as the discussion proceeds, I shall show how true evils are not those which appear to be so: I now make this point, that the things you call hardships, that you call adversities and detestable, actually are of benefit, first to the very persons they happen to, and secondly to the whole human race, which matters more to the gods than individuals do; I also say that good men are willing that such things should happen to them, and that, if they are unwilling, misfortune is what they deserve. I will go further, and say that it is by destiny that

these events occur in this way, and that they happen to good men by the same law which is responsible for their being good. I will proceed to persuade you never to feel pity for a good man; for men can call him wretched, but he can never be so.

The most difficult of the propositions I put forward appears to be the one I made first, that the things which induce fear and loathing in us are of benefit to the very persons to whom they happen. 'Is it to our benefit', you ask, 'to be thrown into exile, to be reduced to poverty, to follow the funeral procession of our children or wife, to suffer public disgrace or be broken in health?' If you are surprised that these things are of benefit to a man, you will be surprised that surgery and cautery, yes, and abstinence from food and drink, sometimes make sick men whole. But if you reflect that, in order to effect a cure, some men have their bones scraped and removed, and their veins extracted, and that sometimes limbs are amputated which could not be left without the whole body being destroyed, you will allow yourself to be convinced also of this fact, some things which are praised and eagerly sought are bad for those who take delight in them, things very like over-eating, drinking too much, and the other activities that kill through pleasure. Among the many splendid sayings of our friend Demetrius* there is this one, which I have recently heard—it still sounds and rings in my ears: 'Nothing', he said, 'seems to me more unhappy than the man who has no experience of adversity.' For he has not been allowed to put himself to the test.

Although everything has flowed in his direction according to his prayer, even before his prayer, yet the gods have passed an unfavourable judgement on him: he was considered unworthy of ever gaining a victory over Fortune, who draws back from all men with cowardly hearts, as though she were saying: 'Why should I select that fellow as my opponent? He will lower his weapons at once; I have no need of all my power against him—an idle threat will send him packing—he cannot bear to look me in the eye. Let me search for another man I can come to blows with: I am ashamed to fight a man who is ready to yield the victory.' A gladiator counts it shameful to be matched against a lesser opponent, and knows that a victory won without danger is won without fame. With Fortune it is the same: she looks for the bravest men to match with her, and passes some men by with scorn. She attacks all who are most unyielding and obdurate, men she can test her strength against: she tried Mucius by fire, Fabricius by poverty,

Rutilius by exile, Regulus by torture, Socrates by poison, Cato by death.* Only bad fortune reveals a great example.

Is Mucius unfortunate because he seizes the fire of the enemy with his right hand and exacts from himself punishment for his mistake, because he routs with scorched hand the enemy he failed to rout with armed hand? Tell me, would he be happier if he were warming his hand in his mistress's bosom?

Is Fabricius unfortunate because he tills his own fields, whenever he gains respite from business of state? Because he wages war as much on wealth as he does on Pyrrhus? Because he dines at his hearth on those very roots and herbs he pulled up while cleaning off his land, he, an old man honoured by a triumph? Tell me, would he be happier if he heaped his belly with fish from a distant shore and fowl from foreign parts, if he stirred his dyspeptic stomach from its torpor with shellfish from the Adriatic and Tuscan seas, if he had wild game of the first rank, taken at the cost of many a hunter's life, served up to him with a huge pile of fruit all around?

Is Rutilius unfortunate because the men who condemned him will be pleading their case in every generation? Because he was more content to endure his country's loss of him than his own loss of exile? Because he alone refused anything to the dictator Sulla and, when he was recalled from banishment, he virtually withdrew and fled to a greater distance? 'Let those whom your "happy age" has caught in Rome', he said, 'enjoy the sight of it: let them see the blood flowing in the forum, the heads of senators placed above Servilius' pool (for that is where Sulla's proscriptions* dispose of their victims), and gangs of assassins roaming all over the city, and many thousands of Roman citizens slaughtered in one place after, or rather because of, a guarantee of security; let those who cannot undergo exile enjoy such sights.' Tell me, is Lucius Sulla fortunate* because men are pushed out of his path at sword-point as he makes his way down to the forum? Because he allows the heads of men of consular rank to be shown to him and makes the treasury official pay for the cost of their murder out of public funds? And these are all the actions of the very man who proposed the Cornelian law!*

Let us come to Regulus:* what harm did Fortune do to him in making him an example of honesty, an example of endurance? His skin is pierced by nails, and wherever he rests his exhausted frame he lies upon a wound; his eyes stare out in unending sleeplessness: yet the greater his torture is, the greater will be his fame. Do you wish to know how little he regrets that he set virtue at such a price? Set him free from the cross and send him back to the senate: he will state the same opinion. Do you, then, consider Maecenas a more fortunate man, who, distressed by affairs of the heart and lamenting the daily rebuffs of a cantankerous wife,* would seek sleep by means of harmonious music playing softly at a distance? Though he steeps his senses in unmixed wine, and diverts his anxious mind with the sound of water falling, beguiling it with a thousand pleasures, he will no more find sleep on his pillow than Regulus on his cross; but while the one has the consolation of enduring hardship for what is right and dwells not on his suffering but on its cause, the other, enervated by pleasures and encumbered with excessive good fortune, is tormented more by the cause of his suffering than by what he suffers. The human race has surely not become so subject to vice that there is any doubt that more men would prefer to be born a Regulus than a Maecenas, if fate permitted them the choice; or should there be anyone bold enough to say he would rather have been born a Maecenas than a Regulus, then that same fellow, though he deny it, would rather have been born a Terentia.

In your opinion was Socrates badly treated because he drank down the well-known drink that the Athenians mixed for him just as if it was the elixir of immortality,* and discoursed on death right up to the point when it claimed him? Was he ill-used because his blood grew cold and gradually stopped pulsing in his veins, as the chill stole over him? How much more should we envy him than those who are served with goblets of gold, whose wine is diluted with snow held above in a golden bowl by a catamite, trained to submit to any treatment, his sexual parts removed or in abeyance! These men will measure out whatever they have drunk in vomit, tasting anew with twisted lips their own bile, but he will drink down poison cheerfully and with a happy heart.

As far as Cato is concerned, enough has been said, and the consensus of men will grant that the fullest measure of happiness fell to that man, whom Nature chose to be the one to confront her dreaded power. 'The enmity of powerful men makes for hardship,' she said: 'let him match himself against all three of Pompey, Caesar, and Crassus.* It is a hardship to be overtaken by inferior men in competing for office: let him come behind Vatinius.* It is a hardship to take part in civil wars: let him fight all the world over for a cause that is just, unsuccessful to the last and stubborn to the last. It is a hardship to do violence to oneself: let him do it. What shall I gain by this? That all may know that these trials I have considered worthy of Cato are not true ills.'

4. Good fortune comes to common men and even to those of inferior talent; but only a great man is able to triumph over the disasters and terrors afflicting mortal life. It is true that to be always happy and to pass through life without any mental distress is to lack knowledge of one half of nature. You are a great man: but on what do I base this if Fortune denies you the opportunity to demonstrate your worth? You have entered the lists at the Olympic Games, but you are the only competitor: you win the crown, but the victory is not yours; I congratulate you, but not as a brave man, rather as one who has gained the office of consul or praetor: it is your personal standing that has been enhanced. I can make the same point also to a good man, if no more difficult circumstance has given him the chance to show his mental strength: 'You are unfortunate in my judgement, for you have never been unfortunate. You have passed through life with no antagonist to face you; no one will know what you were capable of, not even you yourself.' For a man needs to be put to the test if he is to gain self-knowledge; only by trying does he learn what his capacities are. Consequently some men have presented themselves of their own accord to misfortune when it is slow to afflict them, seeking to find an opportunity for their worth to shine out when it is in danger of falling into obscurity. Sometimes great men delight, I say, in adversity, just as brave soldiers delight in warfare; I once heard the gladiator Triumphus in the reign of Tiberius Caesar complaining about the shortage of shows: 'What a splendid age has passed away!' he said.

True worth is eager for danger, and gives thought to its aim, not what it will endure, as even what it will endure is a part of its renown. Warriors glory in their wounds, and delight in displaying the blood that was spilled in better fortune: those who return unscathed from battle may do the same, but the wounded survivor attracts more eyes. God, I say, is favouring those he wants to attain to the highest possible excellence whenever he gives them the means to perform a brave and courageous action, and for this purpose they must encounter some difficulty in life: you would come to know a ship's pilot in a storm and a soldier in the line of battle. How can I know with what strength of mind you would face poverty, if you abound in wealth? How can

I know what fortitude you would show in the face of disgrace, dishonour, and the hatred of the people, if you grow old to the sound of cheers, if you attract an irresistible popularity that falls to you from a certain disposition of men's minds? How do I know how calmly you will bear the loss of children, if you see all the ones you have fathered? I have heard you giving consolation to others: that was when I might have seen your true worth, had you been consoling yourself, or telling yourself not to grieve. Do not, I implore you, live in dread of what the immortal gods apply like spurs to our souls: disaster is the opportunity for true worth. It would be just to describe as wretched those who are dulled by excessive good fortune, who remain at rest, as it were, in dead calm upon an untroubled sea: whatever happens to them will come as a change. The cruelty of Fortune bears harder on the inexperienced; it is the tender neck that finds the yoke oppressive; the raw recruit grows pale at the thought of a wound, but fearlessly the veteran looks at his own gore, knowing that blood has often been the price to pay for victory. And so it is that God hardens, reviews, and disciplines those who have won his approval and love; but those whom he seems to favour, whom he seems to spare, he is keeping soft against the misfortunes that are to come. You are wrong if you think anyone has been exempted from ill; the man who has known happiness for many a year will receive his share some day; whoever seems to have been set free from this has only been granted a delay.

Why does God afflict the best men with bad health, or grief, or other misfortunes? Because in the army the bravest men are ordered to carry out dangerous missions: it is the picked soldiers whom a general sends to take the enemy by surprise in an attack by night, or to reconnoitre a route, or to force a garrison to yield their position. Not one of them as he goes off says, 'the general has done me a bad turn', but rather, 'this is a sign of his favour'. The same should be said by men who are ordered to undergo trials that would make the faint-hearted and cowards weep: 'God has judged us worthy instruments of his purpose to ascertain how much human nature can bear.'

Shun luxury, shun good fortune that makes men weak and causes their minds to grow sodden, and, unless something happens to remind them of their human lot, they waste away, lulled to sleep, as it were, in a drunkenness that has no end. If a man has always been protected from draughts by glazed windows, if his feet have been kept warm by hot compresses, regularly applied, if his dining-rooms have been controlled by hot air passing below the floor and round all the walls, he will run no small risk if he is brushed by a gentle breeze. Although all things in excess bring harm, the greatest danger comes from excessive good fortune: it stirs the brain, invites the mind to entertain idle fancies, and shrouds in thick fog the distinction between falsehood and truth. Would it not be better to endure unending misfortune, having enlisted the help of virtue, than to burst with limitless and extravagant blessings? Men meet a gentler death through starvation, but explode from gorging themselves.

So the gods follow the same rule in the case of good men as teachers do in dealing with their pupils, requiring greater effort from the ones who inspire the surer hope. Surely you don't suppose that Spartans hate their children when they test their character by means of public floggings? Their own fathers encourage them to endure bravely the blows of the lash, and ask them, mangled and half-dead though they are, to continue offering their wounded backs to further wounds. What, then, is remarkable in God testing noble spirits with severity? Never is the proof of virtue mild. Fortune lays into us with the whip and tears our flesh: let us endure it. It is not cruelty but a contest, and the more often we engage in it, the stronger our hearts will be: the sturdiest part of the body is the one that is kept in constant use. We must offer ourselves to Fortune so that in struggling with her we may be hardened by her: little by little she will make us a match for her, and constant exposure to risk will make us despise dangers. So the bodies of mariners are tough from the buffeting of the sea, the hands of farmers calloused, the muscles of soldiers strong to enable them to hurl the javelin, the legs of athletes agile: in each case the part of the body exercised is the strongest. It is by enduring ills that the mind can acquire contempt for enduring them; what this endurance can achieve in our own case you will know if you observe how much toil produces for those destitute peoples whose lack of means makes them the more sturdy. Consider all the nations beyond the scope of Roman civilization, I mean the Germans and all the nomadic tribes that oppose us in the region of the Danube: they are oppressed by unending winter and a gloomy sky, and grudged sustenance by a barren soil; they keep off the rain by means of thatch or leaves, they range over marshes frozen with ice, they catch wild beasts for food. Do you think they are unhappy creatures? There is no unhappiness for those whom habit has brought back to nature; for little by little what they begin from necessity becomes a pleasure. No homes, no resting-places do they have except those that fatigue assigns for the day; their food is fit for beggars and must be gained by hand, the harshness of the climate is fearful, no clothing covers their bodies: this state, which you regard as disastrous, constitutes the life of so many tribes. Why are you surprised that good men are shaken so that they may gain strength? No tree is sturdy or firm-rooted without enduring many an assault from the wind; for the battering itself makes it tighten its grip and fix its roots more securely: trees that have grown in a sunny valley lack strength. Accordingly it is expedient even for good men, in order that they may be fearless, to spend much time in fearful pursuits, and to endure with a patient mind things that are bad only to the one who bears them badly.

5. Take into account the further fact that it is to everyone's benefit that all the best men become soldiers, so to speak, and do service. God's purpose, and the wise man's, too, is to show that what ordinary men desire, and what they fear, are not either goods or evils; but it will appear that there *are* goods, if these are granted only to good men, and that there *are* evils, if these penalize only bad men. Blindness will earn men's curses if no one loses his eyes except the man who merits having them ripped out; therefore let an Appius and a Metellus* be denied the daylight. Wealth is not a good; therefore let even the pimp Elius have wealth, so that men, despite hallowing money in temples, may see it also in a brothel. In no way can God better cast doubt on what we desire than by awarding those things to the most disreputable men and denying them to the best. 'But it is unjust that a good man should be maimed or pierced with weapons or put in fetters, while bad men proceed on their way freely, pampered and quite unscathed.' But consider: is it not unjust that brave men should take up arms and spend all night in camp, standing before the rampart with bandaged wounds, while in the city perverts and those who live on vice have not a care to trouble them? Again, is it not unjust that the noblest maidens are roused each night to perform the sacred rites, while those whose lives are mired in sin enjoy the deepest slumber? Toil summons the best men: the senate often remains in session for the whole day, though all that time the most worthless fellows amuse themselves at the Campus Martius or skulk in an eating-house or fritter away their time in some gathering. It is the same in this great commonwealth of mankind: good men work, spend their

energies and have them spent, and all without complaint; they are not dragged along by Fortune but follow her and match her pace; if they had known how, they would have left her in their wake. Here is a spirited remark of that brave man Demetrius* I remember having heard: 'I can make only this complaint against you, immortal gods,' he said, 'that you did not make your will known to me before now; for all the sooner would I have reached the state I now am in, after your summons. Do you wish to take my children? It was for you I fathered them. Do you wish to take some part of my body? Take it: it is no great thing I offer you, and soon I will leave the whole behind. Do you wish to take my life? Why should I object at all to your taking back what you gave? All that you ask for shall be willingly given. What troubles me, then? I should have preferred to offer than to deliver. What need was there to take by force? You could have had it as a gift; but not even now will you take it so, for nothing is forced from a man's grip unless he seeks to keep it there.'

I am in no way under compulsion, I suffer nothing against my will, and I follow God, not as his slave, but as his pupil, all the more so because I know that everything moves forward according to a law that is fixed and passed for eternity. Fate is our guide, and the amount of time that remains for each of us was determined at the first hour of our birth. Cause is linked with cause, and all matters public and private are directed by a long sequence of events; that is why we should endure everything with courage, because it is not by accident, as we suppose, that everything happens, but by design. Long ago it was decided what should make you happy, what should make you weep, and, although individual men's lives appear to be marked by considerable change, they all end as one thing: we receive what will perish, and will ourselves perish. Why, then, are we resentful? Why do we complain? For this we are prepared. Let Nature make whatever use she pleases of matter, which is her own: let us be cheerful and brave in the face of all, and consider that nothing of our own perishes. What is the duty of a good man? To offer himself to fate. It is no small consolation that we are swept along together with the universe; whatever it is that has ordered us to live like this and to die like this, binds the gods as well by the same necessity. An unchangeable course carries along the affairs of men and gods alike: the great creator and ruler of the universe himself wrote fate's decrees, it is true, but he follows them; he obeys for ever, but made his decrees only once.

'But why was God so unjust in allotting fate that he assigned poverty and wounds and cruel deaths to good men?' The creator cannot alter matter: this is the law to which it has submitted. Certain features cannot be separated from certain others, they cling to one another, and cannot be divided. Natures that are indolent and prone to sleep, or to a state of wakefulness that is virtually sleep, are formed of dull elements: it requires a stronger fate to produce a man who deserves serious mention. For him the road will not be level: uphill and downhill must he go, tossed by waves as he steers his vessel through stormy seas. He must hold his course against the force of Fortune; much will happen that is hard and rough, but the one he will himself soften, the other make even.

As fire tests gold, so misfortune tests brave men. See how high virtue must climb: you will learn the path she must take is fraught with peril:

> Steep is the way at first, which my steeds scarce
> Can climb in morning freshness; in mid-sky
> The altitude is greatest and the sight
> Of land and sea has often struck
> In my own heart an agony of fear.
> The final part drops sheer; then above all
> Control must be assured, and even she
> Whose waters lie below to welcome me,
> Tethys, waits fearful lest I headlong fall.*

When he heard these words, that noble youth replied: 'I like the journey, I shall mount; though I fall, it is worth the risk to soar above such sights.' But his father did not cease from trying to make his bold heart tremble with fear:

> And though you keep your course and steer aright,
> Yet you shall meet the Bull, must brave his horns,
> And face the Archer and the ravening Lion.*

To this he said: 'Harness the chariot you have granted: what you think makes me frightened makes me bold; I want to stand where the Sun himself shakes with fear.' The soul that is earth-bound and sluggish will follow the safe course: virtue takes to the heights.

6. 'But why does God allow something bad to happen to men who are good?' He absolutely does not. He keeps apart from them all manner of evil—crime and sin, wicked thoughts and schemes to foster greed, blind lust and avarice ready to pounce on another's

goods; he guards and rescues from harm the good man himself: surely no one makes the extra demand that God should keep the good man's baggage safe as well? The good man himself spares God any concern for this: he has contempt for external things. Democritus rejected wealth, regarding it as a burden to the virtuous mind: why, then, are you surprised that God allows the good man to experience something that the man sometimes chooses for himself? Good men lose sons: why not, as sometimes they even kill them themselves? They are sent into exile: why not, as sometimes they freely quit their homeland, never to return? They are killed: why not, as sometimes they choose to take their own lives? Why do they suffer certain hardships? The reason is so that they may teach others to endure them; they were born to set an example. Imagine, therefore, God saying: 'What complaint can you make of me, you who have chosen the course of virtue? Other men I have surrounded with false blessings and have mocked their vacant minds, as it were, with a long, deceptive dream: I have adorned them with gold and silver and ivory, but inside there is nothing good. Those you regard as fortunate, could you only see them in their hearts, not as they meet the eye, are wretched, dirty, ugly, and, like the walls of their own homes, decorated only on the outside; such good fortune is not long-lasting or genuine: it is plasterwork, and thinly applied at that. So, as long as they may stand and show themselves as they would wish, they dazzle and deceive; when something happens to disrupt and uncover them, then all may see what depth of true ugliness their borrowed splendour concealed. To you I have given blessings that are sure and destined to last, ones that are better and greater the more someone turns them over and looks at them from every angle; I have allowed you to despise terrors and to scorn desires; outwardly you do not shine, your blessings are directed inwards. In this way the universe despises externals and delights in viewing itself. Inside I have given you every good; your good fortune consists in not needing good fortune.

"Yet many grim events do befall us, terrible and hard to endure." Because I could not remove you from their path, I armed your minds to combat them all: endure with courage. This is where you may surpass God: he is beyond the endurance of evil, you triumph over it. Despise poverty: no one lives as poor as he was born.

'Despise pain: it will either be relieved or will give you relief. Despise death: it either ends you or takes you elsewhere. Despise Fortune: I have given her no weapon for striking your soul. Above all I have taken care that no one may detain you against your will; the way out lies open: if you do not wish to fight, you may run away. That is why, out of all the things I judged necessary for you, I have made nothing easier than dying. I placed life on a downward slope: if it is prolonged, only observe and you will see how short, how easy is the path that leads to freedom. I have not made your departure from life as lingering and tedious as your entrance; otherwise, if men's deaths were as protracted as their births, Fortune would have maintained her great dominion over you. Let every time, every place teach you how easy it is to reject the claims of Nature and to throw her gift back in her face; in the very midst of altars and the customary rites of sacrifice, as you make your prayers for life, acquaint yourself fully with death. The fatted bodies of bulls fall from a slight wound, and creatures of great strength are felled by a blow from one man's hand; a thin blade severs the sutures of the neck, and when that joint which links head and neck has been cut, all that great mass collapses.

'The soul does not lie hidden in a deep recess, no knife at all is needed to root it out; no wound must be planted deep to search for the vital parts: death is close to hand. I have set no definite place for these mortal blows: anywhere you wish, the way lies open. That very thing which is called dying, the soul's departure from the body, is so brief that its swiftness cannot be perceived: whether a knot strangles your throat, or water stops you breathing, or you fall to the hard ground below and it crushes your skull, or flame you inhale cuts off the process of breathing: whatever it is, your end comes fast. Are you not blushing with shame? For so long you have dreaded what happens in a moment!'

ON ANGER

BOOK 3

TO NOVATUS

1. I shall now try to do what you have particularly desired, Novatus,*
to expel anger from the mind, or at least to rein it in and check its
violence. This should be done sometimes openly and plainly, when a
less serious attack of the evil permits, sometimes secretly, when it burns
too fiercely and every obstacle intensifies and increases it; it depends
on how much strength and energy it has, whether we should beat it
back and force its withdrawal, or should give way to it until the initial
storm has spent its fury, in case it carries off with it the very means
of effecting a cure.

Each man will have to adopt a plan of action according to his own
character; for some are won over by appeals, some trample and stamp
on those who submit, some we will win over by making them afraid;
some are deflected from their purpose by being taken to task, others
by an admission of wrong, some by shame, others by delay—a
tedious cure for a swift malady, and only to be undertaken as a last
resort. For though the rest of the passions may be amenable to such
postponement and may be cured at a slower pace, this one, with its
rapid and self-propelled violence, does not proceed gradually but
reaches its full scope the moment it begins; unlike other vices it does
not tempt the mind but carries it off by force, and drives on those
who, lacking self-control, desire the destruction, it may be, of everyone,
spending its rage not only on the targets of its aim but on whatever
happens to cross its path. The other vices drive the mind on, anger
hurls it headlong. Even if a man may not resist his passions, yet at
least his passions themselves may cease: anger intensifies its force
more and more, like lightning and hurricanes and all other phenomena beyond control, as they do not simply move but fall. Other vices
revolt from good sense, this one from sanity; the others come upon
us gently and grow without our noticing: the mind plunges into
anger. Therefore no greater frenzy besets the mind, none so dependent
on its own strength, none so arrogant in success or insane in failure; not
even defeat makes it weary, and when chance has removed its enemy,

it turns its teeth upon itself. And it makes no difference how great the source is from which it springs; for from the most trivial origins it reaches massive proportions.

2. No time of life does it pass by, no breed of men does it leave untouched. Certain peoples, through the blessing of poverty, have no knowledge of luxury; others, because they are active and nomadic, have escaped indolence; those who live in the wilds in an uncivilized state are strangers to trickery and guile and all the evil that is bred in the forum: there is no race that is not stirred by anger, which is as powerful among Greeks as barbarians, and as deadly to those who respect laws as to those who make their strength the measure of their right. In short, the other vices seize individuals, this is the one passion that sometimes takes hold of an entire state. Never has an entire people burned with love for a woman, no state in its entirety has placed its hope in money or profit; ambition seizes men one by one on a personal basis, lack of self-restraint does not afflict a whole people; often they rush to anger in one mass. Men and women, old men and boys, the nobility and the rabble are in accord, and the whole crowd, spurred on by a handful of words, succumbs to a greater passion than the one who spurred them on; they rush at once to weapons and firebrands, declaring war on their neighbours or waging it against fellow citizens; entire houses are consumed by fire, root and branch, and the man who was lately admired for his eloquence and held in high esteem is now the victim of his own followers' anger; legions hurl javelins at their own commander; all the common people are at odds with the nobility; the senate, that takes counsel for the state, does not wait to levy troops or appoint a commander, but chooses extempore leaders to realize its anger, and hunting down its noble victims through the houses of the city enacts punishment by its own hand; international law is broken and embassies treated with outrage, and a madness beyond words sweeps away the state, with no time allowed to let the public tumult subside, as fleets are launched at once and loaded with riotous troops; with no customary preparation, no omens taken, the people, led by their anger, go forth, wielding as weapons whatever they have snatched up as chance provided, until a great disaster makes them atone for the rash boldness of their anger. This is the outcome when barbarians rush into war randomly: whenever their fickle minds are stirred by the thought of wrongs inflicted, they mobilize at once and, where their resentment draws them, they fall like an avalanche on our legions, with no order in their ranks, no fear in their hearts, no thought for the consequences, seeking their own ruin; it is a joy to them to be struck down, to press on with the sword, to launch themselves on our men's spears and perish from a self-inflicted wound.

3. 'There is no doubt', you say, 'that such a force is considerable and deadly: so show how it should be remedied.' And yet, as I said in my earlier books,* Aristotle stands as the defender of anger and forbids that it be cut out of us: it is, he says, the spur to virtue, and, if the mind is robbed of it, it cannot defend itself and becomes lazy and indifferent to great endeavours. And so we must first of all prove how loathsome and savage a thing anger is, and set before the eyes what a monster a man is when he rages against another man, with what violence he rushes on to wreak destruction, while bringing it on himself, and seeks to wreck what can only be sunk if he, too, sinks in the process. So, tell me, will someone call a man sane who, as if caught up in a tempest, does not walk but is driven along, and takes as his master a furious demon, a man who does not entrust his revenge to another but executes it himself, and so becomes a savage in thought and deed, the executioner of those persons he holds most dear and destroyer of the things whose loss will soon make him weep? Is this a passion that anyone can assign as a helper and companion to virtue, when it makes havoc of the resolutions essential to virtue achieving anything?

Fleeting and noxious, and potent only to effect its own harm, is the strength a sick man gains at the height of a fever. There is, therefore, no reason for you to suppose that I am wasting time on unnecessary matters when I denounce anger, on the assumption that men hold different views about its worth; for there is someone, indeed a philosopher of considerable distinction, who assigns to it a function, and, thinking it useful and a supplier of energy, calls upon its aid in warfare, in affairs of business, in any enterprise to be conducted with some zeal. So that no one may be deceived into supposing that there is any time, any place when anger will be of benefit, its unbridled and deranged madness must be revealed, and it must have restored to it the equipment that is its very own—the horse of torture, the cord, the gaol, the cross, the fires that encircle live bodies buried in the ground, the hook that drags along corpses as well, the different kinds of chains and of punishments, the tearing of limbs, branding of the forehead, the pits where monstrous beasts prowl: let anger be set in the midst of these implements, uttering a terrible and horrible shriek, more loathsome than all these instruments that let it vent its fury.

4. Although in other respects there may be doubt about anger, no other passion surely has a worse expression, the one we have pictured in the earlier books: one moment rough and fierce, then pale when the blood has flowed back and been dispersed, then flushed and, it seems, gorged with blood, when all the heat and energy of the body has been directed to the face, with swollen veins, with eyes now rest-less and protruding, now fastened and rooted in one fixed stare; note also the sound of gnashing teeth, as if the owners were eager to eat up someone, like the noise wild boars make when they rub their tusks to sharpen them; and notice the cracking of joints as the hands are violently wrung together, the repeated beating of the breast, the fast breathing and deep groans, the shaking body, the broken speech with sudden outcries, the lips quivering one moment, tight another, as they hiss out some curse. Wild beasts, believe me, present a less ghastly sight than a man on fire with anger, whether they are tormented by hunger or by a weapon that has pierced their innards, even when, half-dead, they attack their huntsman to deliver a final bite. Come, were you free to hear the cries and threats he utters, what manner of language would come from that tortured soul!

Surely every man will want to restrain any impulse towards anger when he realizes that it begins by inflicting harm, firstly, on himself! In the case of those who give full rein to anger and consider it a proof of strength, who think the opportunity for revenge belongs among the great blessings of great fortune, do you not, then, want me to point out to them that a man who is the prisoner of his own anger, so far from being powerful, cannot even be called free? In order that each man may be the more watchful and keep a careful eye on himself, do you not want me to point out that, though other vile passions affect only the worst sort of men, anger creeps up even on enlightened men who are otherwise sane? This is so much the case that some men call anger a proof of frankness, and it is popularly believed that the most obliging people are particularly liable to it.

5. 'What', you say, 'is the point of this?' So that no one may consider himself safe from anger, since it summons even men gentle and peaceful by nature to acts of cruelty and violence. Just as physical robustness and careful attention to health are of no benefit against plague (for it attacks the weak and the strong without discrimination), so men of a calm and relaxed nature are as much at risk from anger as those who are more excitable, and the more it causes a change in these, the more it brings shame and danger upon them. But since the first essential is not to become angry, the second to cease being angry, the third to cure also anger in others, I will state first how to avoid succumbing to anger, then how to free ourselves from it, and lastly, when a man is angry, how we may restrain him, calm him down, and bring him back to sanity.

We shall prevent ourselves from becoming angry if we repeatedly place before our eyes all anger's faults and form a proper judgement of it. It must be tried before the jury of our own hearts and found guilty; its faults must be searched out and dragged into the open; in order to reveal its true nature, it should be compared with the worst evils. Greed procures and amasses wealth for the use of someone who is better: anger spends, few succumb to it without cost. How many slaves have been driven to flight, or to their deaths, by a master's anger! How much more serious was his loss from giving way to anger than the offence that prompted his anger! Anger has brought grief to a father, divorce to a husband, hatred to a magistrate, defeat to a candidate. It is worse than riotous living, as that derives pleasure from its own enjoyment, but anger from another's pain. It outdoes malice and envy; for those wish a man to become unfortunate, anger wishes to make him so; those take delight in misfortune that strikes by chance, anger cannot wait for chance: it wishes to harm the man it hates, not to have him harmed. There is nothing more dangerous than animosity: it is anger that breeds this. Nothing is more deadly than war: it is the anger of powerful men that finds violent expression in this; but also anger among the common people or between private persons is war, though war without weapons or manpower. Besides, leaving aside anger's immediate consequences, such as financial loss, plots, and unending worry caused by mutual strife, it suffers for the penalty it exacts; it repudiates human nature, which encourages men to love, while it incites hatred, and bids a man give help, while it bids him do harm. There is the further fact that, though its resentment stems from excessive self-regard, designed to make it appear spirited, it is, in fact, insignificant and narrow-minded; for no man who regards himself as despised by another can fail to be inferior to his detractor. But the mind that is truly great, that has a just appreciation of its own worth, fails to avenge injury only because it fails to be aware of it. As weapons bounce off a hard surface and the man who strikes a solid object feels the pain of the impact, so no injury causes a great mind to feel its force, since it is more fragile than the object of its attack. How much more splendid it is for the mind, impenetrable, as it were, to any weapon, to reject with disdain all injuries and insults! Revenge is an admission of pain; a mind that is bowed by injury is not a great mind. The man who has done the injury is either stronger than you or weaker: if he is weaker, spare him, if stronger, spare yourself.

6. There is no more reliable proof of greatness than to be in a state where nothing can happen to make you disturbed. The higher part of the universe, being more ordered and near to the stars, is not condensed into cloud, or driven into storms, or spun into any whirlwind; it is free from all disorder: the lower parts are where the lightning flashes. In the same way a lofty mind, always composed and established in a peaceful location, suppresses all that produces anger, and so is moderate, well ordered, and earns respect; none of these things will you find in an angry man. For what man who succumbs to pain and fury does not at once abandon any sense of shame? Who that rages in his violence and rushes to attack someone does not throw away all that he had in him worthy of respect? What man in a state of excitement remembers the number or order of his official engagements? Who restrains his tongue? Who keeps any part of his body in check? Who can control himself once he has let himself go? We shall find that well-grounded doctrine of Democritus* of benefit to us, in which he shows that a tranquil state of mind is only possible if we devote relatively little time to private or public affairs, or at least to those that are too great for our strength. When a man busies himself with many duties, the day never passes so happily for him that he fails to encounter some problem, arising from a person or a situation, which makes his mind ripe for anger. Just as a man hurrying through the busy districts of the city must collide with many people, and will inevitably lose his footing in some places, and be held back in others, and, in others still, be splashed, so in this activity of life, with all its variety and inconstancy, many hindrances, many causes for complaint cross our path. One man cheats our hopes, another postpones them, a third dashes them; our designs do not proceed as we had planned. No man finds Fortune so compliant that she responds on each occasion to his many overtures; it follows, therefore, that when a man finds that some of his plans have fallen out contrary to his wishes, he grows impatient with men and the world, and on the slightest of pretexts becomes angry, now with a person, now with his occupation, now with where he lives, now with his luck, now with himself. And so, in

order that the mind can achieve peace, it must not be tossed about, or, as I said, worn out by activity in many enterprises, or ones that are demanding and place too great a strain on its powers. It is easy to fit light burdens to our shoulders, and to move them from one side to another without their slipping, but what has been placed on us by the hands of others we find hard to support, and, owning defeat, we shed our load onto the next man; even while we stand beneath the baggage, we stagger, finding ourselves unequal to the burden.

7. The same thing happens, be assured, in public and private affairs. Tasks that are straightforward and manageable yield to the control of the doer, but those that are weighty and beyond the doer's capacity are difficult to master; and if they are attempted, they weigh him down and run away with him, and, just when he seems to have them in his grasp, down they fall, bringing him down with them: so it happens that the man who does not attempt easy tasks but wants what he attempts to be easy, is often baffled in his wishes. Whenever you attempt something, measure yourself and at the same time what you are attempting, both the thing you intend and that for which you are intended; for if you fail in the task, the regret this causes will make you bitter. It makes a difference whether a man is of a fiery nature, or a cold and docile one: defeat will drive a man of spirit to anger, but induce sadness in one whose nature is sluggish and passive. Accordingly let our activities be neither trivial nor bold and over-ambitious, let us keep our hopes within sensible bounds, and let us attempt nothing to make us wonder later at our success, even should we succeed.

8. As we do not know how to endure injury, let us take pains not to receive any. We should live with a very calm and compliant person, one not at all given to worry or peevishness; we adopt our habits from our associates, and, as certain bodily diseases spread to others from contact, so the mind passes on its faults to those nearest: the drunkard draws his fellow drinkers into a love of neat wine, shameless company perverts even the strong man who has a will of iron, greed transfers its poison to its neighbours. The same principle is true of the virtues, but to opposite effect, namely that they exert a good influence on all they are in contact with; no suitable location or more healthy climate benefits an invalid as much as association with better company benefits a mind that lacks strength. You will understand what a powerful effect this can have if you note that even wild animals

grow tame through living with us, and that no beast, however savage, keeps its violent nature, if it has known a man's companionship for a long time: all its fierceness is blunted, and little by little forgotten amid peaceful surroundings. It is also the case that the man who lives with peaceful people not only becomes better through example but does not practise his anger because he finds no reasons for his weakness to operate. And so he will have to shun the company of all those he knows are likely to provoke his anger. 'Who are these people?' you say. Many are liable from different causes to produce the same result: a proud person will offend you by his scorn, a sharp wit by an insult, an impertinent one by an offence, a spiteful one by his envy, a pugnacious one by quarrelling, the windbag who tells lies by his emptiness; you will not tolerate being feared by a suspicious man, being defeated by a stubborn one, or being scorned by a fop. Choose men who are honest, easygoing, and have self-control, the sort who will not arouse your anger and yet will tolerate it; more useful still will be men who are amenable, kind, and charming, but not to the point of flattery, for those given to anger are offended by fawning agreement: I, at any rate, had a friend who was a good man, but too quick to feel anger, and it was no more safe to flatter him than to abuse him.

Caelius, it is agreed, was an extremely hot-tempered orator.* The story goes that one of his clients, a particularly tolerant man, was dining with him in his chamber, but was finding it difficult to avoid quarrelling with his table-companion as he was at such close quarters; he decided the best course of action was to agree with whatever the other said, and to play second fiddle. Caelius could not endure this acquiescence and shouted: 'Disagree with me in something, so we may be two people!' But even he, losing his temper because he was not losing his temper, quickly stopped when he had no opponent. Therefore, if we are aware of our own hot temper, let us rather choose men who will take as their guide the look on our face and what we say: they will make us spoilt, it is true, and encourage us in the bad habit of listening to nothing that goes against our wishes, but it will be helpful to give our failing a peaceful interval. Even those of a harsh and unyielding nature will endure gentle treatment: no creature is fierce and frightening if it is stroked. Whenever a discussion becomes protracted and liable to end in blows, let us put a stop to it at the outset, before it gains strength: strife feeds itself and makes prisoners of those who dive too deep into it; it is easier to avoid a dispute than to beat a retreat from it.

9. Hot-tempered people should avoid as well studies that are demanding, or at least engage in ones not liable to end in exhaustion; the mind should not occupy itself with hard tasks, but should be given over to pleasurable arts: let it be calmed by reading poetry and charmed by the tales of history; let it be treated with a measure of gentleness and refinement. Pythagoras* would bring peace to his troubled spirit with the lyre; and who is unaware that the bugle and trumpet stir the mind, just as certain songs have a soothing effect that relaxes the mind? Disordered eyes find benefit in green objects, and weak sight finds certain colours restful but others dazzling, and therefore blinding: in this way pleasant pursuits prove a balm to the troubled mind. We must keep clear of the forum, appearances in court, and trials, and all that exacerbates our failing; equally we must take care to prevent physical exhaustion; for this destroys all that is mild and peaceful in us, and promotes bitterness. That is why those who suspect their digestion control their bile by taking food, if they are going to busy themselves in work of a particularly stressful nature; for bile is especially brought on by exhaustion, either because it drives the heat of the body into the centre, and contaminates the blood and impedes its flow by blocking the veins, or because the mind is weighed down by the body when it is worn and weak; certainly it is for the same reason that those robbed of strength by ill-health or old age are more hot-tempered than others. Hunger, too, and thirst should be avoided for the same reasons; they irritate and inflame the mind. It is an old saying that 'a tired man looks for a quarrel'; but equally so does a man who is hungry, or thirsty, or any man who is vexed by some ailment. For as ulcers are sore at the slightest touch, or even after that at the hint of a touch, so the afflicted mind is offended by mere trifles, so much so that men are summoned to court because of a greeting, a letter, a speech, or a question: never is a painful spot touched without causing complaint.

10. And so the best course is to treat the sickness as soon as it becomes apparent, at that time as well giving oneself the least freedom of speech and curbing emotion. Again, it is easy to detect one's passion, as soon as it arises: diseases have symptoms as their harbingers. Just as the signs of storm and rain precede them, so there are certain messengers that herald anger, love, and all those tempests that batter the soul.

Those who are subject to epileptic attacks realize a fit is coming on if warmth leaves their extremities, if their sight wavers, if their muscles start to twitch, if memory fails and the head begins to swim; accordingly they try the usual remedies to prevent the malady at its beginning, and by smelling or tasting something they drive away whatever it is that makes them unconscious; or apply hot poultices to battle against coldness and stiffness; or, if this treatment has no effect, they separate themselves from the crowd and fall where no one may witness it. It is an advantage to know one's own illness and to destroy its strength before it has scope to grow. Let us take note of what it is that particularly provokes us: one man is roused by insulting language, another by insulting behaviour; this man desires special treatment for his rank, that one for his good looks; this one wishes to be considered a fine gentleman, that one a great scholar; this one cannot bear pride, that one inflexibility; that one does not consider his slaves worthy of his anger, this one is cruel in his own home but mild outside; that one judges it an offence to be put up for office, this one an insult not to be put up. Not all men are wounded in the same place; and so you ought to know what part of you is weak, so you can give it the most protection.

11. It does not serve one's interest to see everything, or to hear everything. Many offences may slip past us, and most fail to strike home when a man is unaware of them. Do you want to avoid losing your temper? Resist the impulse to be curious. The man who tries to find out what has been said against him, who seeks to unearth spiteful gossip, even when engaged in privately, is destroying his own peace of mind. Certain words can be construed in such a way that they appear insulting; some, therefore, should be abandoned, others scorned, others condoned. Anger should be circumvented in many ways; let most affronts be turned into amusement and jest. When Socrates once received a box on the ear, the story goes, he merely said it was a nuisance that men couldn't tell when to wear a helmet when going for a walk. What matters is not how an offence is delivered, but how it is endured; and I fail to see why self-control is difficult, since I know that even tyrants, whose hearts were swollen with the lack of restraint of their privileged position, have suppressed their cruel instincts. The story is certainly handed down about the Athenian tyrant Pisistratus,* that, when a drunken dinner-guest had criticized him at length for his cruelty, and many were willing to

defend their master's honour with their swords, adding fuel to the flame from all over the room, he reacted calmly, replying to those who were urging him on that he felt no more anger against the man than he would if someone wearing a blindfold had charged at him.

12. Very many men manufacture complaints, either by suspecting what is untrue or by exaggerating the unimportant. Anger often comes to us, but more often we come to it. Never should we summon it; even when it falls on us, it should be cast off. No one says to himself, 'I myself have done or could have done the thing that is making me angry now'; no one considers the intention of the person who performs the action, but just the action itself: and yet it is to this person that we should turn our attention, and to the question whether he acted intentionally or by accident, under compulsion or mistakenly, prompted by hatred or by a reward, to please himself or to oblige another. The offender's age is of some account, as is his status, so that it becomes either kindness or expediency to endure his behaviour with patience. Let us put ourselves in the position of the man who is making us angry: in point of fact it is an unjustified estimate of our own worth that causes our anger, and an unwillingness to put up with treatment we would happily inflict on others. No one keeps himself waiting; and yet the greatest cure for anger is to wait, so that the initial passion it engenders may die down, and the fog that shrouds the mind may subside, or become less thick. Some of the affronts that were sweeping you off your feet will lose their edge in an hour, not just in a day, others will disappear altogether; if the delay you sought produces no effect, it will be clear that judgement now rules, not anger. If you want to determine the nature of anything, entrust it to time: when the sea is stormy, you can see nothing clearly. On one occasion Plato was angry with his slave and could not grant himself a delay. He ordered the man to take off his tunic at once and to bare his shoulders to the whip, intending to flog him with his own hand; when he realized he was angry, he held back his hand, upraised as it was, and stood there, as if poised to strike; a friend who happened to walk in asked him what he was doing, and received the reply: 'I am exacting punishment from an angry man.' Like a man stunned he kept that position, unbecoming in a philosopher, of someone about to vent his rage, all memory of the slave now banished, as he had found another man he was more eager to punish.

Accordingly he deprived himself of power over his own household and once, when some offence had particularly upset him, he said,

'Speusippus,* you punish this wretched slave with a whipping; for I am angry.' What caused him not to strike was the very thing that would have prompted another man. 'I am angry,' he said; 'I would do more than I ought, and would take too much satisfaction in it: this slave should not be in the power of one who is his own slave.' Does any man wish to entrust punishment to an angry man, when Plato stripped himself of this power? Grant yourself no licence when angry. Why? Because then you want complete licence.

13. Do battle with yourself: if you have the will to conquer anger, it cannot conquer you. Your conquest has begun if it is hidden away, if it is given no outlet. Let us conceal the signs of it, and as far as is possible let us keep it hidden and secret. This will cost us a great deal of trouble (for it is eager to leap out and inflame the eyes and alter the face), but if it is allowed to display itself outside ourselves, it is then on top of us. In the lowest recess of the heart let it be hidden away, and let it not drive, but be driven. Moreover, let us change all its symptoms into the opposite: let the expression on our faces be relaxed, our voices gentler, our steps more measured; little by little outer features mould inner ones. In the case of Socrates a symptom of anger was the lowering of his voice and speaking fewer words; at such times it was clear that he was struggling with himself. Accordingly he would be detected by close friends and taken to task, but the charge of trying to hide his anger did not displease him. Why would he not be gratified that many realized his anger, but no one felt it? But they would have felt it, if he had not allowed his friends the same privilege of criticizing him as he had assumed in their case. How much greater is the obligation on us to do this! Let us ask all our closest friends to treat us with the most freedom particularly when we are least able to tolerate it, and to show no forbearance to our anger; let us summon help against an evil that is powerful and often wins indulgence from us, while we have our wits and are masters of ourselves. Those who cannot hold their wine, who fear the rashness and rudeness their drunken state may cause, instruct their friends to take them away from banquets; those who have learned that they become unreasonable when ill direct that their instructions be ignored if their health fails. The best course is to look out for obstacles to our known weaknesses, and above all to order the mind in such a way that, even when struck by the most serious and sudden events, either it does not feel anger, or buries deep any anger arising from the gravity of so unforeseen an affront,

or does not acknowledge that it has been hurt. It will be clear that this can be done if I adduce a few examples from the vast array at my disposal; from these one may learn two things: how much evil is inherent in anger when it has at its service all the power of extremely powerful men, and how great is the control it can exert over itself when restrained by the greater force of fear.

14. King Cambyses* was addicted to wine, and one of his dearest friends, Praexaspes, kept advising him to be more moderate in his drinking, pointing out that drunkenness was disgraceful in a king, who attracted the eyes and ears of all men. To this the king replied: 'To make it plain to you that I never lose control of myself, I will now prove to you that my eyes and hands perform their duty after I have taken wine.' He then proceeded to drink more wildly than ever, from cups of unusual depth, and when he was now heavy and intoxicated with wine, he ordered the son of his critic to go beyond the threshold and to stand there with his left hand raised above his head. Then he drew his bow and shot an arrow right through the young man's heart (this was the target he had nominated), and cutting open the breast he showed the arrow-head lodged in the heart itself. He then turned to the father and asked if he had a sufficiently steady hand. But the father replied that Apollo could not have shot with greater accuracy. May the gods blast such a man to perdition, a slave in mind even more than in status! He praised a deed that any man would have found beyond him to look at. When his son's chest had been split in two and his heart was quivering beneath its wound, he considered it an opportunity for flattery: he should have challenged Cambyses to a dispute about his boast and demanded a second shot, to give the king the satisfaction of demonstrating an even steadier hand in the case of the father himself. What a bloodthirsty monarch! How much he deserved to have all his subjects turn their bows on him! We may damn him for concluding a banquet with mortal punishment, but it was a viler action to praise that arrow than to shoot it. We shall see how the father ought to have conducted himself as he stood over his son's corpse, gazing at that murder which he had caused as well as witnessed: the point we are now discussing is clear, that anger is capable of being checked. He did not curse the king, he did not utter one word, even of anguish, though the heart he saw pierced was his own as much as his son's. One can say he was right to swallow his words; for had he said anything as an angry man, he could have

achieved nothing as a father. It is, I say, possible to consider that he showed more wisdom on that occasion than when he urged moderation in drinking on a man who would have done better to drink wine than blood, in whose case peace meant busying his hands with a wine-cup. Accordingly he increased the number of those who have shown through terrible misfortune how much kings value the good advice of friends.

15. I have no doubt that Harpagus* also made some such recommendation to his king, the king of the Persians, which so offended him that he served up the flesh of Harpagus' sons before him as part of a banquet, and continually asked him if the cooking was to his taste; then, when he saw that he had eaten his fill of his own wretched offspring, he gave the order for their heads to be brought in and asked his guest how he rated his entertainment. The wretched man was not lost for words, his lips did find utterance: 'At a royal table', he said, 'every dish is a delight.' What did he gain by this flattery? He escaped an invitation to eat what remained on his plate. I do not say that a father should refrain from condemning an act of his king, I do not say he should not seek to punish so abominable a monster as he deserves, but the conclusion I draw for the moment is that even anger arising from an appalling crime can be concealed and compelled to the use of words that contradict it. Such curbing of grief is necessary, especially for those whom fortune has allotted this kind of life, the kind that makes them share the board of kings: this is the condition of their eating, their drinking, their replying: they have to smile at the deaths of their own family. Whether a life of this sort is worth the price, we shall see: that is a different question. We shall not sympathize with such a pitiful chain-gang, or encourage them to endure the commands of their butchers: we shall show that in every form of slavery the path to liberty lies open. If a man is sick in soul and miserable because of his own imperfection, he may end his sorrows together with his own life. I will say to the man who finds himself the victim of a king who aims his arrows at the breasts of his friends, and to the man whose master feeds fathers full on the flesh of their own children: 'Why these groans, you madman? Why do you wait for some enemy to avenge you by destroying your own nation, or for a powerful monarch to fly to your aid from afar? Wherever you turn your eye, there lies the end of your sufferings. Do you see that precipice? Down that lies the path to liberty. Do you see that sea, that river,

that well? Liberty resides there, at the bottom. Do you see that tree, stunted, blasted, blighted, and bare of foliage? Liberty hangs from its boughs. Do you see your throat, your gullet, your heart? They are routes of escape from slavery. Are the means of departure I show you too troublesome, requiring both courage and strength in great measure? Do you ask what path leads to liberty? Any vein you please in your body.'

16. Now, as long as we feel there is no hardship so unbearable as to force us to give up life, whatever our position in life may be, let us rid ourselves of anger. It is destructive to those of servile status; for every sense of grievance grows to self-torture, and the more resentful the man who submits to orders, the more irksome he finds them. So by struggling a wild beast tightens its noose; so birds smear all their feathers with lime while trying in their panic to free themselves of it. No yoke is so constricting that it does not cause less pain to the one who bears it than to the one who resists it: there is only one relief for great sufferings, and that is to endure and surrender to their compulsion. But while it may be in the interest of those who serve to control their passions, and in particular this mad and unbridled one, it is more in the interest of kings: general destruction is the result when Fortune allows a man free scope for the promptings of his anger, and no power can endure for any length of time when the exercise of it means that many men must suffer; for it finds itself at risk when those who moan in distress separately are united by a common fear. And so many rulers have become the victims of violence, sometimes from individuals, sometimes from a mob, when a general indignation had compelled men to unify their disparate feelings of anger. Yet many kings have used anger like a badge of royal office, for example Darius, who became the first monarch of the Persians and of a great part of the east after the dethronement of the Magian.* For when he had declared war on the Scythians who threatened his eastern borders, he was asked by a nobleman, Oeobazus, to leave behind one of the old man's three sons to be a comfort to his father, and to use the services of the remaining two. Darius promised more than he was asked, and, telling him he would relieve all three of duty, he had them killed and thrown down before their father's eyes, as it would have been cruelty, he said, to take them all away. How much more reasonable Xerxes was! When Pythius, the father of five sons, asked that one be exempted from service, he allowed him to choose the one he wanted, and then he had the chosen son torn in two, and placing each half of him on either side of the road, offered him as a sacrifice to win the gods' favour for his army. Therefore it met the end that was its due: conquered, scattered far and wide in defeat, and witnessing its own destruction on all sides, it tramped along between the two lines of corpses formed by its own soldiers.

17. This was the savagery shown in anger by barbarian kings, men who had enjoyed no contact with learning or literary culture: but I will give you the instance of a king tutored by Aristotle, Alexander, who during a banquet stabbed with his own hand one of his closest friends, Clitus, with whom he had grown up, for refusing to flatter him and being reluctant to make the transition from freeborn Macedonian to Persian slave. Lysimachus* was no less intimate a friend and yet he threw him to a lion. Now did the fact that this Lysimachus by some stroke of fortune escaped the lion's teeth make him any kinder when he became a king? Indeed not: he completely mutilated his friend, Telesphorus of Rhodes, and after cutting off his ears and nose, he kept him in a cage like some strange and unfamiliar animal, living for a long time in terror of him, since the hideousness of his maimed and mutilated face had destroyed all appearance of a human being; there was also the fact that he endured starvation and squalor, his body encrusted with filth and left to wallow in its own excrement; on top of this, his knees and palms grew calloused, as the cramped conditions compelled him to use them as feet, and his sides were covered in ulcers from the rubbing, so that the sight he presented to onlookers aroused as much disgust as fear, and, as his punishment had turned him into a monster, he had forfeited even pity. Nonetheless, although the man who underwent this suffering was not at all like a human being, the man who caused it was even less like one.

18. How I wish that examples of such savagery had been confined to foreign races, and that the barbarism of torture and anger had not been imported into our Roman customs, together with other vicious practices from abroad! The people had set up statues in honour of Marcus Marius* in every street, and were honouring him as a god with offerings of frankincense and wine, when Lucius Sulla gave the order for the man's ankles to be broken, his eyes gouged out, his tongue and hands to be cut off, and, as though he could kill him with each wound he dealt, little by little and one limb after another, he tore him to shreds. Who was the one who carried out this command?

Was it not Catiline,* who already was training his hands for every kind of crime? He butchered his victim before the tomb of Quintus Catulus, profaning the ashes of that gentlest of men, as drop by drop on top of them the hero shed his blood, a man of evil influence, it may be, but dear to the people, who loved him, not without cause but without measure. It was fitting that a Marius should suffer such punishment, that a Sulla should order it, that a Catiline should inflict it, but not fitting that Rome should receive in her breast at the same time the swords of her enemies and of her defenders.

Why do I delve into early times for crimes? In recent years Gaius Caesar flogged with the whip and tortured on a single day Sextus Papinius,* whose father had held the consulship, Betilienus Bassus,* his own quaestor and the son of his own praetor, and others, both senators and knights, not for the purpose of seeking evidence but to gratify his anger; then he was so reluctant to postpone his pleasure, a pleasure so enormous that his cruelty was demanding it without delay, that, as he strolled with some ladies and other senators on the terrace of his mother's gardens (which runs between the colonnade and riverbank), he decapitated some of them by the light of torches. Why was he in such a hurry? What danger, either private or public, was threatened by a single night? How little would it have cost him to wait just until daybreak, to avoid killing senators of the Roman people in his dinner shoes!

19. It is not irrelevant to observe the arrogance that informed his cruelty, though someone may consider that we are straying from the point and launching into a digression; but this arrogance will be a contributing factor in cruelty when it assumes an unwonted savagery. He had flogged senators with the whip; he himself made it possible for people to say of this, 'an ordinary enough event'. He had tortured them in all the direst ways known to man—by the cord, by knotted bones, by the rack, by fire, by his own face. But even then he will receive the answer: 'No light matter indeed! Three senators maimed by the whip and fire as though they were worthless slaves by a man who considered murdering the entire senate, who kept praying that the Roman people might have one neck, so that he could concentrate his crimes spread over so many places and times in a single blow and a single day.' What was ever so unheard of as an execution by night? It may be that acts of robbery are usually concealed by darkness, but punishments serve to warn and admonish men, the more publicity they are given. Here, too, I will be given the answer: 'What makes you so surprised is the daily practice of that creature; for this he lives, for this he stays awake, for this he makes the night his day.' Certainly no one else will be found who has given the command that those to be executed by his orders should have their mouths crammed with sponges to give them no opportunity to utter a cry. What man condemned to death was ever prevented by lack of breath from uttering a groan? The emperor feared that the man might speak out too frankly in his final agony, that he himself might hear something he would rather not; and he knew that there were countless offences that no one would dare accuse him of unless on the point of death. When sponges could not be found, he gave the order for the wretches' clothes to be torn and the strips stuffed into their mouths. What savagery is this? Allow a man to draw his last breath, grant his departing soul a passage, allow him to send it on its way through a different aperture from his wound. It would be a lengthy business to add further details, how he sent centurions round the homes of the men he had executed and despatched their fathers that same night; that is, as a man of compassion he set them free from their grief. For my purpose is to draw a picture, not of Gaius' savagery, but of anger's, which not only vents its fury on individual men but lacerates whole nations, lashing with its whip cities and rivers and inanimate things not liable to any sense of pain.

20. In such fashion did the king of the Persians cut off the noses of an entire people in Syria, from which the place gets its name, 'Land of the Stub-Nosed'. Do you judge this to have been an act of mercy because he did not cut off their whole heads? Rather he derived pleasure from a novel form of punishment. Some such fate might also have befallen the Ethiopians, who because of their extreme longevity are called 'The Long-Livers'; for Cambyses* became incensed against them because, rather than submitting to slavery with outstretched arms, they had dispatched envoys and replied with the independent words that kings call insulting language; therefore, without making provision for supplies or reconnoitring routes, he hurried his entire fighting force through a pathless tract of desert. In the course of the first day's march his supplies began to fail, and nothing was provided by that barren and uncultivated region where no man's foot had trodden before; at first their hunger was satisfied by the most tender parts of leaves and tree-shoots, then by skins which fire had softened and anything that necessity had required them to eat; after even roots and herbage had failed them amid the desert sands, and what met their eyes was a wilderness empty also of animal life, they chose by lot every tenth man and resorted to a form of nourishment more savage than hunger. The king was still being driven headlong onwards by his anger, until, after losing part of his army and eating another part, he became afraid that he himself might also be called to selection by lot: only then did he give the signal for retreat. All this while birds of noble stock were being kept for him, and supplies for his banqueting were being transported by camels, though his troops were drawing lots to see who should meet a horrible end, and who should continue a more horrible existence.

21. This monarch was angry with a nation that was not known to him and did not deserve punishment, yet was able to feel it: Cyrus' anger was directed at a river. For when, with the intention of attacking Babylon, he was hurrying to war, in which opportunity plays the most important part, he tried to ford the river Gyndes* which was in full flood, though it is scarcely safe to do this even when it has felt the summer's heat and has sunk to its lowest level. On this occasion one of those white horses that were accustomed to pull the king's chariot was swept away, to the intense annoyance of the king; he therefore swore that he would so reduce that river which was robbing a king of his retinue that even women could cross it and crush it under their feet. To this operation he then transferred all the preparations for his war, and he delayed at this task long enough to cut 180 wedges across the riverbed, diverting its water into 360 little streams that flowed in different directions and so left the channel dry. Accordingly both time was sacrificed, no minor loss in major undertakings, and the enthusiasm of his troops, which was crushed by the pointless effort, and the chance to attack the enemy off guard, while he waged against a river the war he had declared on his foes. This madness—for what else would you call it?—has affected Romans as well. For Gaius Caesar levelled a very beautiful villa in the neighbourhood of Herculaneum because his mother had at one time been kept a prisoner inside it, by his very action drawing everyone's attention to her misfortune; for while the villa was standing we would sail past it, but now that it has been destroyed we ask the reason why.

22. These should be considered as examples to be avoided, but the following, on the other hand, as ones to imitate, as they show behaviour that is restrained and mild, on the part of men who had every reason for anger and every opportunity for revenge. Nothing indeed would have been easier for Antigonus* than to order the execution of the two ordinary soldiers who, as they leaned against their king's tent, were voicing their low opinion of him, something that men do with great enjoyment and equal risk. Antigonus had heard the entire conversation, since only a canvas was between the speakers and listener; he shook this gently and said: 'Move further away, in case the king should hear you.' The same ruler one night, on overhearing some of his soldiers heaping all manner of curses on their king's head for leading them on to such a road with its inextricable mud, went up to those in the greatest difficulty and, after he had pulled them clear without telling them the name of their helper, said: 'Now curse Antigonus, whose folly has led you into this misery; but bless the man who has got you out of this morass.' He also showed as much forbearance in tolerating the curses of his enemies as those of his countrymen. Accordingly, when he was besieging some Greeks in a small fortress and their confidence in their position was making them scorn their enemy, constantly poking fun at Antigonus' ugliness and mocking now his lack of height, now his snub nose, he said: 'I am delighted, and hope for some good luck, if I have Silenus* in my camp.' When he had tamed these abusive wits by hunger and taken them prisoner, he treated them in the following way: the ones who were fit for service he enrolled in his regiments, the remainder he auctioned as slaves, saying that he would not have done this if it was not a good idea for men with such wicked tongues to find themselves a master.

23. This man's grandson was Alexander, who used to hurl a spear at his dinner-guests, and, of the two friends whom I described earlier, exposed one to the rage of a wild beast, the other to that of himself. But of these two men it was the one who was thrown to the lion who survived. This was a fault he did not inherit from his grandfather, or even from his father; for if Philip* had any other virtues, they included a capacity to tolerate insults, an enormous benefit in keeping a throne secure. Demochares, who was called 'The Outspoken' because of his uncontrolled and audacious tongue, had paid Philip a visit in the company of other envoys of the Athenians. After he had given the embassy a friendly hearing, Philip said, 'Tell me what I can do to please the people of Athens.' Demochares, taking his cue from this, said, 'Hang yourself.' The bystanders had reacted indignantly to so

impolite a reply, but Philip told them to be quiet and to send that Thersites* on his way safe and unharmed. 'But you remaining ambassadors', he said, 'take the message to the Athenians that men who say such things are far more arrogant than those who listen to them without retaliating.'

The deified Augustus also said and did many things worthy of memory, which demonstrate that he was not governed by anger. Timagenes, a writer of history, had made certain derogatory remarks about the emperor himself, about his wife, and his entire family, and these remarks had not been lost; for indiscreet witticisms have greater currency and are widely quoted by people. On several occasions the emperor warned him to use his tongue more responsibly, finally banning him from his home when he persisted. Afterwards Timagenes lived to an old age under the roof of Asinius Pollio,* celebrated by all of Rome: he was denied access to the emperor's palace but all other houses opened their doors to him. He gave readings of the histories he wrote after the event, but threw on the flames the books which detailed the actions of Augustus Caesar; he continued his enmity with the emperor, but no one shrank from being his friend, no one shunned him as a pariah, and though he fell so low in favour, one man took him to his hearth and home. As I said, the emperor tolerated this patiently, not even upset by the fact that his fame and exploits had been impugned by this man; never did he complain to him who gave hospitality to his enemy. All that he said to Asinius Pollio was, 'Another beast for your menagerie, I see'; then, when Pollio was about to defend his attitude, he stopped him, saying, 'Enjoy yourself, my dear Pollio, enjoy yourself!' And when Pollio said, 'If you tell me to, Caesar, I will immediately deny him the use of my house,' he said, 'Do you suppose I would do this, when it was I who made the two of you friends again?' For Pollio had at one time quarrelled with Timagenes, and his only reason for becoming his friend was that the emperor had become that man's enemy.

24. Therefore, whenever any man is provoked, let him say to himself: 'Am I any more powerful than Philip? But he had his name taken in vain without retaliating. Am I more powerful in my own home than the deified Augustus was in the whole world? But he was content simply to avoid the company of the man who maligned him.' What justifies my making my slave pay with a whipping and manacles for replying too loudly, or looking at me too stubbornly, or muttering too low for

me to hear? Who am I that it should be a criminal offence to offend my ears? Many have pardoned their enemies: should I not pardon laziness, carelessness, or chattering? A child should be excused by his age, a woman by her sex, a stranger by his independence, a servant by the bond of familiarity. Someone gives offence now for the first time: let us consider how long he has given pleasure; someone has given offence at other times and often: let us tolerate what we have tolerated for a long time. He is a friend: he acted against his better judgement; he is an enemy: he acted within his rights. Let us put our trust in one who is sensible, and show understanding towards a fool; whoever the man is, let us say to ourselves on his behalf that the wisest men have many faults, that no one is so observant that his attention to detail does not occasionally falter, that no one is so ripe in judgement that his self-possession is not driven by misfortune into some heated action, that no one is so afraid of giving offence that he does not stumble into it while seeking to avoid it.

25. As it has brought comfort to a humble man in misfortune that the fortune even of great men is precarious, and as the man in a shack feels the pain of mourning a son less acutely if he has seen a miserable funeral procession leaving a palace as well, so a man more easily bears being harmed by one man or scorned by another, if he has reflected that no power exists so great that it is beyond the reach of harm. But if even the wisest men do wrong, what man will not have a good excuse for his offence? Let us consider how many times when we were young men we did not show enough care in duty, or enough control in speech, or enough restraint in drinking. If a man is angry, let us give him time to come to realize what he has done: he will be his own critic. Suppose in the end he deserves punishment: that is no reason for us to offend on an equal scale. There will be no doubt that whoever regards his tormentors with scorn separates himself from ordinary humanity and towers above his fellow men: it is the mark of true greatness not to feel when you have received a blow. So the huge wild beast calmly turns to survey barking dogs, so the wave dashes to no effect on a great cliff. The man who does not become angry maintains his stance, unshaken by harm; the man who does become angry loses his balance. But the man whom I have just placed beyond the scope of all damage holds in his embrace, as it were, the highest good, and not only to man but to Fortune herself makes this response: 'Do whatever you will, you are not capable of undermining my serenity.

This is forbidden by reason, to which I have entrusted the guidance of my life. The anger I feel is more likely to do me harm than any wrong you may do me. And why should it not do more? Because its limit is fixed, whereas there is no telling to what lengths anger may carry me.'

26. 'I am not able', you say, 'to show tolerance; it is no easy matter to put up with a wrong.' You are not being honest; for who is unable to tolerate wrong that is able to tolerate anger? Moreover, what you are now proposing is to tolerate both anger and wrong. Why do you tolerate a sick man's lunatic behaviour, a madman's crazed words, or children's petulant blows? Because, of course, they appear not to know what they are doing. What difference does it make what fault it is that makes a person behave irresponsibly? Irresponsibility can be used to defend anyone's conduct. 'Well, then,' you say, 'shall that man go unpunished?' Allowing for the fact that this is your wish, it will still not happen; for the greatest punishment of wrongdoing is having done it, and no one is punished more severely than the man who submits to the torture of contrition. Again, one should take into account the boundaries of our human condition, if we are to be fair judges of all that happens; and there is no justice in blaming the individual for a failing shared by all men. Among his own countrymen the Ethiopian's colouring is not remarkable, and among the Germans hair of reddish colour that is tied in a knot becomes a man: you are to judge no feature peculiar or shameful in one man, if it is common to his whole race. Even those instances I have mentioned can be defended by the custom of a particular portion or corner of the world: consider now how much more justice consists in pardoning those qualities that are common to the entire human race. All of us are inconsiderate and imprudent, all unreliable, dissatisfied, ambitious—why disguise with euphemism this sore that infects us all?—all of us are corrupt. Therefore, whatever fault he censures in another man, every man will find residing in his own heart. Why do you find fault with that man's pale skin, or this man's leanness? These qualities spread like plague. So let us show greater kindness to one another: we live among wicked men through our own wickedness. One thing alone can bring us peace, an agreement to treat one another with kindness. 'That man has already harmed me, but I haven't yet paid him back.' But already perhaps you have harmed a man, and will harm another. Do not take just this hour or this day into account, examine the whole

cast of your mind: even if you have committed no wrong, you are capable of it.

27. How much better it is to heal a wrong than to avenge one! Vengeance takes considerable time, and it exposes a man to many injuries while only one causes him resentment; we always feel anger longer than we feel hurt. How much better it is to change our tack and not to match fault with fault! No man would consider himself well balanced if he returned the kick of a mule or the bite of a dog. 'Those animals', you say, 'do not know they are doing wrong.' In the first place, how unjust is the man who thinks that being a human debars one from forgiveness! Secondly, if the fact of their lacking judgement exempts all other creatures from your anger, you should place in the same category every man who lacks judgement; for what does it matter that he does not resemble dumb animals in his other qualities, if he does resemble them in the one respect that excuses dumb creatures however they offend, a mind shrouded in darkness? He did wrong: well, was it his first offence? Will it be his last? There is no reason for you to believe him, even if he says 'I will not do it again': not only will he offend but another will offend against him, and the whole of life will be a cycle of error. Unkind behaviour should bring out our kindness. Words that usually prove most salutary in time of grief will have the same effect also when a man is angry: 'Will you cease at some time or never? If at some time, how much better is it to abandon anger than to wait until it abandons you! Or will this inner tumult continue for ever? Do you see how troubled a life you are condemning yourself to? For what will a man's life be like if he is constantly swollen with anger? Moreover, once you have truly inflamed yourself with rage and repeatedly renewed the causes that give impetus to your passion, of its own accord anger will take its leave and time will reduce its strength: how much better it is that you defeat anger than that it defeats itself!'

28. First this man will make you angry, then that one; first slaves, then freedmen; first parents, then children; first acquaintances, then strangers: for motives exist in plenty everywhere, unless the mind intervenes to arbitrate. Rage will sweep you here and there, from one man to another, and time and again fresh provocations will surface to prolong your madness: come, you poor fellow, will you ever find time for love? Oh, what valuable time you waste on something that is worthless! How much better would it now be to win friends, pacify

enemies, serve your country, turn your attention to private affairs, than to look around to see what harm you can do to some individual, what wound you can inflict on his good name, or his finances, or his person, though you cannot achieve this end without a dangerous struggle, even if your opponent is lower-born than you! Let us grant that he falls into your hands in chains and you have the power to make him submit to every form of endurance: many times too much force in the man administering a flogging has dislocated a joint or left a sinew lodged in the teeth it had broken; many men have been incapacitated by their anger, many disabled, even when their victims have yielded to such treatment. In addition, no creature exists so weak that it presents no risk of harm to its destroyer: sometimes pain, sometimes an accident puts the weakest creature on the same footing as the strongest. There is also the consideration that most of the things that make us angry cause us more offence than actual harm. But it makes a big difference whether someone goes against my wishes or fails to implement them, whether he robs me or simply fails to give. And yet we regard them no differently—the man who steals something from us or simply refuses to give it, the man who cuts off our hope or simply postpones it, the man who acts against us or simply in his own interest, out of love for another or from hatred of us. Some men, it is true, have not only just but honourable reasons for standing against us: one is protecting a father, another a brother, another his country, another a friend; however, we do not pardon these for doing the very thing which we would blame them for not doing; in fact, though it is hard to believe, we often think well of the deed, and badly of the doer. But beyond question the man who is great and just looks up to all the bravest of his enemies, who labour unstintingly to gain the freedom and security of their country, and prays that it may be his fortune to have such men as fellow citizens and fellow soldiers.

29. It is shameful to hate a person who deserves your praise; but how much more shameful it is to hate someone for the very cause that makes him deserve your pity. If a prisoner, suddenly reduced to slavery, still retains traces of his freedom and does not run promptly to carry out demeaning and laborious tasks, if his former inaction has made him sluggish and he fails to keep pace with his master's horse and carriage as he runs along, if he is worn out by his daily vigils and succumbs to sleep, if he refuses the work of the farm or undergoes it

without energy after being transferred to hard labour from the life of a slave in the city with its holidays—if such is the case, let us make a distinction, determining first whether he cannot or will not serve: we shall release many from constraint, if we begin to exercise judgement before anger. But as it is we follow our first impulse, then, although quite unimportant things have stirred our passion, we persist in our anger, so we may not give the impression of having had no reason for our initial loss of temper, and, most unjustly of all, the injustice of our anger makes us more stubborn; for we hold on to it and foster it, as if the intensity of our anger were proof of its justice.

30. How much better it is to examine its first beginnings—how trivial, how harmless they are! What you see happening in the case of dumb animals you will find at work also with humans: we are disturbed by idle, foolish things. A bull is roused by a red colour, an asp strikes at a shadow, bears and lions are provoked by a handkerchief: all creatures that are savage and wild by nature are startled by petty things. The same effect is seen in men, whether their natures are excitable or phlegmatic: they are struck by suspicious thoughts, so much so that sometimes they call moderate acts of kindness wrongs, and these are the most frequent, certainly the most painful, source of anger. For we become angry with those we love most because they have given us smaller gifts than we anticipated or than others gave, although for both difficulties a cure lies ready to hand. Another man has been treated more generously: let us take pleasure in what we have received and make no comparison; no man will ever be happy if tortured by the greater happiness of another. I have less than I hoped for: but perhaps I hoped for more than I deserved. This is the attitude we have most to fear from; this gives birth to the anger that is most deadly, that will profane all that is most sacred.

Among the killers of the deified Julius* more were friends than enemies, men whose insatiable hopes he had not satisfied. He wanted indeed to do this—for no man was more generous in his use of victory, from which he claimed nothing for himself except the power to bestow gifts—but how could he gratify such inordinate desires, since every one of them was eager to win as much as any one of them could possibly desire? And so he saw his fellow soldiers gathered round his chair with their swords drawn, Tillius Cimber, a short while ago the most vigorous advocate of his cause, and others who had finally declared for Pompey when Pompey was no more. It is this that turns their own

weapons against kings, and drives the most loyal of followers to
contemplate the deaths of men for whom they had vowed, before
their very eyes, to give their lives.

31. No one who looks at another man's possessions takes pleasure
in his own: for this reason we grow angry even with the gods, because
someone is in front of us, forgetting how many men are behind us
and what a massive load of envy follows at the back of those who envy
a few. But so arrogant are humans that, however much they have
received, they take offence if they might have received more. 'He gave
me the praetorship, but I had hoped for the consulship; he gave me
the twelve fasces,* but he did not make me a regular consul; he was
willing to have the year named after me, but let me down over the
priesthood; I was elected as a member of the college, but why just of
one? He crowned me with honour before all Rome, but contributed
nothing to my finances; he gave me what he was obliged to give to
someone, he took nothing from his own pocket.' Rather show gratitude for what you have received; wait for the remainder, and be happy
that your cup is not yet full: it is a form of pleasure to have something
left to hope for. You have outstripped all others: rejoice in coming
first in the judgement of your friend. Many outstrip you: reflect on
the fact that more are behind you on the course than in front of you.
You ask what is the greatest failing in you? You keep accounts
badly: you rate high what you have paid out, but low what you have
been paid.`

32. We should let different reflections restrain us in different cases:
with some men let us refrain from anger out of fear, with others out
of respect, with others out of pride. An impressive act it would be on
our part, no doubt, if we packed off some wretched slave to prison!
Why are we in a hurry to flog him on the spot, then promptly to break
his legs? We will not lose the power to do this, if we postpone it. Wait
for the time to arrive when it will be our own order: at the moment
we shall be speaking under anger's command; when it disappears,
then we shall see how much value to set on the damage. For in this
we are particularly liable to error: we have recourse to the sword, to
capital punishment, and with chains, imprisonment, and starvation
we punish an offence that should be chastised by a light whipping.
'How', you say, 'do you tell us to discover how paltry, wretched and
childish are all the offences we imagine we suffer?' For my part I would
truly recommend no more than that you assume a genuinely great

spirit and realize how trivial and worthless are all these things which drive us to employ lawyers, to run here, there, and everywhere, to lose our breath; no man with any lofty or noble purpose should give a thought to such as these.

33. The greatest outcry surrounds money: this is what brings exhaustion to the courts, sets fathers against children, concocts poisons, hands out swords to assassins and the legions alike; this is what wears the stain of our blood; this that makes the nights of wives and husbands noisy with quarrelling, and the crowd surge against the benches where the magistrates arbitrate; because of money, again, kings grow savage and engage in plunder, overthrowing states built by the long toil of centuries so they can rummage for gold and silver amid the ashes of cities. It gives pleasure to look at money-bags lying in the corner; but these are what make men shout until their eyeballs start, that cause the lawcourts to ring out with the din of trials, and jurors to be summoned from distant parts to sit in judgement over which man's greed has the greater claim to justice. What if it is not even a bag of money but just a handful of copper, or a silver coin entered into the account by a slave, that makes an old man who is about to die without an heir split with rage? What if it is merely interest of a trivial 1 per cent that causes a moneylender, for all his poor health and crippled feet and hands no longer strong enough to count money, to shout out, and even as he is racked by his illness, to demand securities for his pennies? If you were to offer me all the money from all the mines we work so energetically at this time, if you were to throw down at my feet all the money that lies in buried treasure, as greed restores once more to the earth what it once wickedly extracted, I would not think all that gathered hoard worthy even of a good man's frown. How loudly we should greet with laughter the things that now make our tears run!

34. Come, now, make a tally of the other causes of anger—food, drink, and the elegant occasions we have contrived for them to bolster our standing, insulting words, disparaging gestures, stubborn beasts of burden, idle slaves, suspicion and the spiteful misconstruing of another's remark, causing man's gift of speech to be counted among the wrongs of nature: believe me, the things that incense us to no small degree are small indeed in importance, like the frivolous reasons for children quarrelling and coming to blows. None of these things which we pursue so intensely is serious, none is of any importance: this, I say,

the fact that you attach great value to trivia, is the source of your anger and madness. This man wished to rob me of my inheritance; this one falsely accused me to a man I had long cultivated in the hope of becoming his heir; this one wanted to bed my mistress: wanting the same thing, which ought to be a bond of love, becomes the reason for alienation and hatred. When a road is narrow, it drives passers-by to blows, but a broad and open thoroughfare can be used even by a large crowd without friction: since the things you are eager to acquire are insignificant and yet cannot be passed on to one man without robbing the other, they stir those who desire the same things to fighting and contention.

35. It makes you angry that a slave has answered you back, or a freedman, or your wife, or a client: you then go on to complain that the state has been deprived of the freedom of which you have deprived those under your own roof. Again, you call it wilfulness, if a man has said nothing when questioned. Let him speak, or remain silent, or laugh! 'In front of his master?' you say. Yes, in front of the head of the household, too. Why do you shout? Why do you rant? Why do you call for a whip in the middle of dinner, just because slaves are talking, just because in a room with a crowd of guests big enough for an assembly there is not the silence of the desert? Your ears are not simply for hearing tuneful sounds, mellow and sweetly played in harmony: you should also listen to laughter and weeping, to words flattering and acrimonious, to merriment and distress, to the language of men and to the roars and barking of animals. Why do you shake, you wretch, at the shout of a slave, at the clashing of bronze, or the slamming of a door? For all your sensitivity, you have to listen to thunderclaps. Apply what has been said about your ears to your eyes, which suffer from just as many qualms, if they have been badly trained: a stain offends them, or dirt, or tarnished silver, or a pool whose water is not clear to the bottom. These same eyes, in fact, which do not tolerate marble that is not variegated and shining from recent rubbing, or a table that is not marked by many veins, that will only have under foot at home floors more precious than gold—these eyes out of doors observe quite calmly overgrown and muddy paths, and the majority of people they encounter in a state of dirtiness, and the walls of tenements cracked and full of holes and out of line. What reason is there, then, other than this for those people not being offended out of doors but annoyed in their own homes: that on the

street our state of mind is calm and accommodating, while under our own roof it is churlish and critical?

36. All our senses should be trained to acquire strength; they are by nature capable of endurance, provided that the mind, which should be called daily to account for itself, does not persist in undermining them. This was the habit of Sextius, so that at the day's end, when he had retired to his nightly rest, he questioned his mind: 'What bad habit have you put right today? Which fault did you take a stand against? In what respect are you better?' Anger will abate and become more controlled when it knows it must come before a judge each day. Is anything more admirable than this custom of examining the whole day? How sound the sleep that follows such self-appraisal, how peaceful, how deep and free, when the mind has either praised or taken itself to task, and this secret investigator and critic of itself has made judgement of its own character! This is a privilege I take advantage of, and every day I plead my case before myself as judge. When the lamp has been removed from my sight, and my wife, no stranger now to my habit, has fallen silent, I examine the whole of my day and retrace my actions and words; I hide nothing from myself, pass over nothing. For why should I be afraid of any of my mistakes, when I can say: 'Beware of doing that again, and this time I pardon you. In that discussion you spoke too aggressively: do not, after this, clash with people of no experience; those who have never learned make unwilling pupils. You were more outspoken in criticizing that man than you should have been, and so you offended, rather than improved him: in the future have regard not only for the truth of what you say but for the question whether the man you are addressing can accept the truth: a good man welcomes criticism, but the worse a man is, the fiercer his resentment of the person correcting him'?

37. At a feast the wit of certain men and their words, aimed to cause you distress, reached their target: remember to avoid low-born entertainments; their freedom from constraint becomes too lax after drinking wine, because they had no sense of shame even when sober. You saw a friend of yours angry with the doorkeeper of some petty advocate or rich man, because the fellow had pushed him out as he tried to enter the house, and on your friend's behalf you became angry yourself with this lowest form of slave: will you, then, become angry with his chained watchdog? Even he, after his sustained barking, is pacified by food thrown to him. Step back some distance and laugh!

For the moment the fellow thinks he is important because he guards a threshold besieged by a crowd of litigants; for the moment the one who lies at ease indoors is happy and enjoys good fortune, and judges that the sign of a prosperous and powerful man is to make access to one's home difficult: he does not know that the hardest door to open is that of a prison. Accept in your mind that there are many things you must endure: does anyone regard it as surprising if he is chilled by winter, or suffers nausea at sea, or is jolted on the highroad? The mind that has been prepared for things meets them with courage. You were assigned a less honourable place at table and so began to feel anger against your host, against the man who wrote your invitation, against even the man who was preferred to you: madman, what difference does it make which part of the couch bears your weight? Can a cushion confer greater honour or disgrace on you? You looked with unfair eyes on a man because he spoke disparagingly about your talent: do you accept this as a principle? On such grounds Ennius,* whose poetry you do not enjoy, would hate you, and Hortensius* would declare his enmity towards you, and Cicero, if you laughed at his poetry, would not be your friend. Are you willing to endure the votes calmly when you are standing for office?

38. Someone has insulted you: was it greater than the insult done to Diogenes the Stoic philosopher,* when an arrogant young man spat in his face at the very moment he was discoursing on anger? He endured this affront mildly and wisely: 'I am not, in fact, angry,' he said, 'but just the same, I am inclined to think I ought to be angry.' But how much better the course adopted by our own Cato! When he was pleading a case, Lentulus,* that seditious and turbulent man, as our fathers remember him, gathered as much thick saliva as he could and spat it in the middle of Cato's forehead. He wiped it off and said, 'If anyone says you have no cheek, Lentulus, I'll tell him he's mistaken.'

39. It is now our achievement, Novatus, that we have brought composure to the mind: either it does not feel anger or it rises above it. Let us see how we are to mitigate the anger of others; for we wish not only to be cured but to cure.

We will not dare to pacify the first burst of anger with speech: it is deaf and without reason; we will give it room. Cures have an effect when the illness subsides; we do not attempt to treat eyes that are swollen, as we are likely to cause irritation by trying to move them in their stiff condition, or to heal the other parts of the body while they are inflamed: the early stages of illness are best treated by rest. 'How poor a remedy you propose,' you say, 'if it calms anger when it is subsiding of its own accord!' In the first place it ensures that it comes to a speedy end; secondly, it guards against its recurrence; it will frustrate as well even the first outburst, which it does not dare to mitigate: it will remove all the means of carrying out revenge, it will affect anger so that, under the guise of a helper and companion in resentment, it may enjoy more influence in counsel, it will invent a web of delays, and, while it looks for a heavier punishment, it will defer an immediate one. By means of every skill it will give respite to the frenzy: if the sufferer becomes more violent, it will stamp on him a feeling of shame or fear that he cannot resist; if he grows calmer, it will introduce conversation that is either welcome or novel, and will distract him by encouraging a thirst for knowledge. The story is told of a doctor who had to treat the daughter of a king and yet could only do so by the use of a knife. While he was gently dressing one of her swollen breasts, he inserted a scalpel hidden in a sponge: the girl would have fought against this cure if it had been openly administered, but because she did not expect it, she put up with the pain. Some cures are only effected through deception.

40. To one man you will say, 'Mind you don't let your anger give pleasure to your enemies,' to another, 'Take care not to lose your greatness of mind and the reputation you have among many people for strength. I am angry myself, believe me, and my vexation knows no limits, but I must wait for my time; he will not escape punishment. Keep that thought in your mind: when you can, you will make him pay for the delay also.' But reprimanding a man when he is angry and getting angry with him into the bargain will only provoke him further: you will approach him with a variety of methods, complimenting him, unless perhaps you have so much influence as a person that you can deflate anger, as the deified Augustus did when he was having dinner with Vedius Pollio.* One of that man's slaves had broken a crystal cup; Vedius ordered that he be seized and executed in no ordinary fashion: the sentence was that he be thrown to the giant lampreys which Vedius kept in his fishpond. Who would not conclude that he was doing this to demonstrate his wealth? It was simply cruelty. The slave escaped the clutches of his captors and flung himself at the emperor's feet, begging only that he might be given a different manner of death, that he should not become food for fish. The unique form of cruelty disgusted the emperor, who ordered that the slave be let off, and, besides, that all Vedius' crystal cups be smashed in front of their owner's eyes and his fishpool be filled in. This was how it was appropriate for Caesar to reprimand his friend; he made good use of his powers: 'Do you order men to be hurried away from a banquet to their death and to be torn apart in an unheard-of form of punishment? If your cup has been broken, will a man's innards be torn apart? Will you be so self-indulgent as to order some man's execution in the presence of your own emperor?' In such fashion, if a man has so much power that he can attack anger from a position of eminence, let him treat it harshly, but only the kind of anger that I have just described, savage, brutal, and bloodthirsty, and now past cure, unless it is faced with the terror of something mightier.

41. Let us grant to our soul that peace which will be provided by constant study of beneficial instruction, by noble actions, and a mind fixed on desire only for what is honourable. Let us satisfy our conscience, and take no thought for reputation; let us even accept a bad name, provided that in reality we merit a good one. 'But the people admire courageous actions, and men of daring win honour, while those who are reserved are thought to be feeble.' At first sight, perhaps; but at the same time, when those men have proved by the even course of their lives that it is peace of mind, not idleness, that they show, the same public will feel reverence and respect for them. So there is not a single useful quality to be found in this monstrous and dangerous passion, but on the contrary every sort of evil, fire and sword. Trampling shame underfoot, it defiles men's hands with murder, casts wide the limbs of children, and leaves no place free from crime, disregarding fame and unafraid of disgrace, beyond remedy once it has hardened from anger to hate.

42. Let us be free of this evil, let us clear it from our minds and tear it up by its roots, as it will grow again if the slightest traces should linger anywhere, and let us not seek to control our anger but rid ourselves of it entirely—for what control can be exerted over anything that is evil? Besides, we will succeed in this, if only we exert ourselves. And nothing will help us more in this task than reflecting on our mortality. Let each man say to himself, and to his fellow: 'Why do we enjoy proclaiming our anger as though we were born to live for ever, and squandering our short span of years? Why do we enjoy using days we might spend on honourable pleasure for the purpose of causing some man anguish and torture? The benefits of life are not to be squandered, and you have no excess time for wasting. Why do we rush into conflict? Why do we court troubles? Why do we shoulder the huge burden of hate, forgetting how weak we are, and rise up to break things, when we are ourselves so easy to break? Soon that war of hatred we wage so relentlessly will be cancelled by a fever or some other sickness of the body; soon the fiercest pair of fighters will be separated by death. Why do we riot and make havoc of our lives by embracing discord? Fate stands above our heads and numbers our days as they go by, drawing nearer and nearer to us; that hour you mark down for another man's death is perhaps near your own.'

43. Why do you not instead gather up your short life and present it in a peaceful state to yourself and to everyone else? Why not instead make yourself lovable to all men while you live, and someone they will miss when you die? Why do you desire to drag down that man who treats you so condescendingly? Why try with all your strength to crush that man who shouts insults at you, a lowborn and worthless enough fellow, but caustic in his tongue and troublesome? Why are you angry with your slave, with your master, with your patron, with your client? Endure for a little: look, death is coming to make you equals. We are accustomed to see in the morning shows of the arena a fight between a bull and a bear that are tied together. When they have savaged one another, their appointed killer waits for them: it is the same with us, we make life unpleasant for someone bound closely to us, although the end, all too swift, hangs over winner and loser alike. Let us rather spend the brief span we have left in rest and peace; let no man regard us with hatred when we lie a corpse. Often the shout of fire in the neighbourhood brings a quarrel to an end, often the arrival of a wild animal saves the traveller from the robber: there is no time to struggle with lesser evils when a more serious fear appears. Why do we bother with fighting and laying traps? Is there any evil greater than death that you wish for the man who has made you angry? He shall still die, even if you lose your rage. You waste your effort if you wish to do what will happen anyway. 'I do not wish to kill him at all,' you say, 'but to punish him with exile, with loss of reputation, with financial ruin.' I have more sympathy with the man who desires to give his enemy a wound than with the one who wants to give him a blister; for this fellow has a mind that is not only wicked but cowardly into the bargain. Whether tortures of the severest kind occupy your thoughts or less drastic ones, how little time there is either for him to experience the agony of his punishment, or for you to derive a wicked pleasure from another's torment! Soon we shall spit out this little spirit. In the meantime, while we have breath, while we are among our fellow men, let us behave as men should; let us not be a cause of fear or danger to anyone; let us despise losses, wrongs, insult, and criticism, and let us tolerate with a great mind our short-lived misfortunes: while we look back, as the saying goes, and turn round, that moment death will be on us.

CONSOLATION TO MARCIA

1. If I was not aware, Marcia,* that you were as much a stranger to female weakness of mind as to all other vices, and that your character was regarded as a pattern of ancient virtue, I should not be bold enough to presume on your grief, the emotion that even men gladly embrace and brood over, nor would I have entertained the hope of being able to make you acquit Fortune of your loss, at a time so unfavourable, when her judge is so opposed, and the accusation she faces such an odious one. But your strength of mind, tested before now, has given me confidence, together with your bravery that has been endorsed by a severe trial.

It is well known how you conducted yourself in relation to your father, showing no less love for him than for your children, except that you had no wish for him to outlive you. And yet I am inclined to think you may have had even that desire; for great familial love can at times transgress the law of nature. The death of your father, Aulus Cremutius Cordus,* you kept at bay for as long as you were able; after it became apparent to you that, finding himself in the midst of Sejanus'* toadies, that was his only means of escape from slavery, you did not favour his plan but nonetheless acknowledged defeat, putting your tears to flight in public and swallowing your sighs, but despite your cheerful face you did not conceal them, and all this in an age when simply avoiding an unfilial act constituted the height of filial affection. But when a change in the times gave you an opportunity, you recovered for men's use the genius of your father which had brought him to his death, and so rescued him from the only true death, restoring to the memorials of the state the books which that heroic man had written in his own blood. It was an outstanding service you rendered to Roman scholarship: a great part of his work had been consumed in flames; an outstanding service also to the men of the future, who will receive a historical account of complete integrity that cost its great author dear; and an outstanding service to the man himself, whose memory flourishes and shall flourish as long as a value is set on learning the history of Rome, as long as there is anyone who wishes to go back to the deeds of our ancestors, as long as there is anyone who wishes to know what it is to be a Roman hero, what it is to hold one's own head high when all men's are bent and compelled to bear the yoke of a man like Sejanus, what it is to be a free man in mind, in spirit, and in action. What a great loss, believe me, our country would have sustained, if you had not rescued that man who had been consigned to oblivion because of two of the world's most noble gifts, eloquence and liberty: he is read, he flourishes, and, taken into the hands and hearts of his fellow men, he fears no passing of time; but as for those butchers, in the shortest of time even their wicked acts, by which alone they deserved to be known, will die on men's lips.

This greatness of spirit of yours forbade me to have regard for your sex, or indeed for your face, that for so many years, ever since sorrow first clouded it, has worn a constant veil of sadness. And note how I do not creep up on you, or plan to rob you of any of your unhappy feelings: I have reminded you of misfortunes long past, and, so that you may know that even the wound of this lash-stroke will surely heal, I have shown you the scar of a wound no less deep. Accordingly, let others deal with you gently, massaging you with soft words, my resolve is to do battle with your grief; I mean to check those eyes so weary and drained of tears, now weeping, if you want the truth, more out of habit than bereavement, by a treatment that, if so it happens, you will welcome, if not, even against your will, though you hold on to your grief and clasp it to your bosom, keeping it alive in place of your son. For what end will it have? Every way has been tried to no purpose: friends' words of consolation have been exhausted, as have the weighty counsels of great men who are your relatives; the reading of books, a delightful benefit passed on to you by your father, now makes its appeal to deaf ears, as this consolation proves fruitless, scarcely serving to provide a brief moment of interest; even time itself, the remedy of nature, which lays to rest the most dire of tribulations, in your case alone has lost its power. Three years have now passed, but the initial storm of your grief continues to blow unabated: your sorrow renews itself and takes fresh strength every day, discovering through delay a justification for continuing, and it has now arrived at the stage where it considers it disgraceful to cease. Just as all vices become deeply implanted unless they are crushed as they spring up, so this state of unhappiness and misery, with its self-inflicted anguish, feeds finally on its own bitterness, and the pain felt by an unhappy mind becomes an unhealthy pleasure. Therefore I should have wished to begin treating your grief in its earliest stages;

while it was still undeveloped, its vigour might have been checked by means of a gentler remedy: a more forceful attack is necessary against ills that have had time to fester. For this is also true of wounds: while they are still freshly inflicted and bloody, they can be easily treated: the time when they are subjected to cautery and opened up to the bottom and investigated by probing fingers is when they have turned septic and become dangerous sores. As it is, I am unable to tackle such hardened sorrow in a kind or gentle manner: it must be shattered.

2. I am aware that all who wish to give advice to someone start with instruction and end with example. But there are times when it is salutary to change this custom; for different people should be treated in different ways: some are guided by reason, some require to be confronted with famous names and the authority that takes away a man's independence of mind, if he is held in thrall by outwardly impressive actions. Let me put just two examples before your eyes, the greatest ones of your sex and age: the first, of a woman who allowed grief to sweep her away; the second, of one who was afflicted by a similar misfortune but a greater loss, and yet did not allow her ills to hold sway over her for long but swiftly brought her mind back to its normal state. Octavia and Livia, the one the sister of Augustus, the other his wife, lost their sons when they were young men, both with the certain hope of becoming emperor: Octavia lost Marcellus,* on whom Augustus, both uncle and father-in-law to him, had begun to lean, transferring to his back the burden of empire, a young man of keen intelligence and powerful ability, yet, together with this, possessing a sense of economy and moderation much to be admired in one so young and rich, who submitted patiently to labours and gave no time to pleasures, but was prepared to shoulder whatever his uncle might want to place, or, so to speak, build upon him; he had chosen well a foundation that no weight would crush. Throughout her entire life she never ceased to weep and sigh, refusing to hear any words of healthy counsel or even to allow herself to be distracted; concentrating on one thing alone, with her whole mind fixed on it, she remained all her life as she was at his funeral, I do not say lacking the resolve to rise, but allowing no one to raise her spirits, and regarding any cessation in weeping as a second bereavement. She refused to have a single portrait of her darling son and would not permit any mention of him. She hated all mothers, directing her rage at Livia in particular, as the good fortune once held out to her seemed to have

passed to that woman's son. She became the intimate of darkness and solitude, and gave no thought even to her brother, disdaining the poems that were written to glorify Marcellus' memory and other literary honours, and closing her ears to every consolation. She withdrew from all customary duties, and, hating even the good fortune that shone too brightly around her because of her brother's greatness, she buried herself in seclusion. Although seated among children and grandchildren, she did not cease to wear clothes of mourning, treating all her family insultingly by thinking of herself as childless when they were still living.

3. Livia had lost her son Drusus,* who was likely to be a great emperor and was already a great general; he had penetrated deep into Germany and had planted Roman standards in a place where it was barely known that any Romans existed. He had died on campaign, and even the enemy had shown reverence towards him when he fell sick by maintaining the peace that we observed and not daring to hope for what their interests dictated. This death, which he had met in the service of his country, aroused an overwhelming sense of loss among his fellow citizens and the provinces, and indeed in all of Italy, throughout which people poured from the townships and colonies to pay their sad respects, escorting him right into the capital in what appeared to resemble a triumph far more than a funeral procession. His mother had not been permitted to receive her son's last kisses or to absorb the loving words from his dying lips; on the long journey on which she followed the remains of her beloved Drusus she was tormented by the great number of funeral pyres burning throughout all Italy, as with the sight of each she felt she was losing him again, but, from the moment she had placed him in his tomb, she laid aside her sorrow together with her son, and grieved no more than was honourable or just to the emperor, considering he still lived. And finally, she never ceased to extol the name of her own dear Drusus, or to have his likeness portrayed everywhere, in public places and in private, and her greatest joy was to speak about him and to hear others do the same: she lived with his memory, but no one can cherish and keep alive a memory that he has turned into a source of personal woe.

Choose, therefore, which of the two examples you consider the more praiseworthy. If you wish to follow the first one, you will remove yourself from the number of the living: you will turn your back on

other people's children as well as your own, and even on the very one
you mourn; mothers will see in you a grim omen; you will spurn
decent, permissible pleasures as not sufficiently in keeping with your
misfortune; you will linger in the daylight that you have come to
loathe, and regard your age as your greatest enemy for not bundling
you away and making an end of you with all possible speed; you will
be guilty of something most shameful and utterly foreign to your
character, which is known to favour the better course of action, namely,
of showing yourself unwilling to live but unable to die. If, however, you
show a more reasoned and gentler spirit by embracing the example of
the second, most impressive, lady, you will not become the partner
of grief or rack yourself with torture: for what lunacy, indeed, what
evil it is, to punish oneself for misfortune and to increase one's own
sorrows! You will demonstrate in this situation also that virtuous and
restrained character that you have maintained all your life; for even
in expressing grief there is such a thing as moderation. As for that
young man himself, so deserving of bringing you happiness by the
constant mention of his name and remembrance in your thoughts,
you will put him in a more worthy place, if he greets his mother's eye
as the same cheerful and joyful son he always used to be in life.

4. And I will not direct your thoughts to instructions of the sterner
sort, so that I tell you to endure your human lot in inhuman fashion,
so that I dry a mother's tears on the very day she buries her son. I will
come with you before an arbitrator: this shall be the point at issue
between us, whether grief should be great or everlasting. I have no
doubt that you will be more impressed by the example of Julia
Augusta,* with whom you formed a close friendship: she is the woman
who summons you to follow her behaviour. She, when her grief was
in its first passion, the time when feelings of misery are particularly
savage and hard to control, made herself accessible to the consoling
words of the philosopher Areus,* a friend of her husband, and subsequently admitted that she had received considerable benefit from
that experience, more than she had from the people of Rome, whom
she had no wish to sadden with her own sadness, more than she
had from Augustus, who was reeling from the loss of one of his major
supports, and not fit to be bowed down by the grief of his loved ones,
more than she had from her son Tiberius, who by his devotion to
her at that poignant funeral that drew tears from nations made her
feel that only in the number of her sons had she suffered any loss.

This, I imagine, was the form Areus' approach to her took, this the way he began to speak to a woman who had always been most reluctant to abandon her own opinion: 'Right up to this day, Julia, as far as I am aware—and, as a constant companion of your husband, I have known not only all those matters made public but also all the more secret thoughts in your minds—you have taken pains to ensure that no one had any grounds for criticizing you; and this conduct you have observed not just in more important matters but also in quite trivial ones, so that you should do nothing which you would wish to be excused by popular feeling, that most outspoken judge of emperors. And there is nothing I judge more impressive than the principle that those who have been placed in a position of eminence should give pardon for many offences but ask for pardon for none; accordingly, in this situation as well you ought to preserve this habit of yours of doing nothing which you might wish you had not done, or had done differently.

5. 'Again, I beg and implore you not to show yourself as difficult to your friends and unwilling to talk to them. For you must be well aware that not one of them knows how to conduct himself, whether he should say something about Drusus in your presence or nothing at all, in case by failing to recall Drusus he may wrong that distinguished young man, or by speaking his name he may wrong you. When we have left your company and are gathered together, we commend his actions and words with all the admiration he merited; in your presence we maintain a deep silence about him. And so you lack the greatest of pleasures, hearing the praises of your son, which I have no doubt you would extend to the end of time itself if you had the power, even at the cost of your life. Therefore permit, or rather invite talk in which his actions may be told, and open your ears to the name and the memory of your son; and do not consider this behaviour offensive in the manner of some others, who think it wicked to listen to consolation. As things are, you have inclined entirely to the other side, and forgetting the better aspects of your fortune, you have regard only for its worse side. You do not turn your thoughts to the pleasant occasions when you met your son and shared his company, or to his boyish and loving endearments, or to the ways in which his studies advanced: you insist on remembering only that final appearance of Fortune; to this, as though it were not quite horrible enough in itself, you add as much horror as you can muster. Do not, I beg you,

set your heart on achieving that most perverted form of renown, that of being regarded as the unhappiest of womankind. At the same time reflect that greatness does not consist in showing courage in prosperous times when life sails on in a tranquil course: a peaceful sea and compliant wind do not show a steersman's skill either; some hardship must be faced to test his resolve. And so do not bow yourself down, but on the contrary plant your feet firmly and support whatever burden falls from above, showing fear only at the noise of its onset. Nothing displays a greater contempt for Fortune than an untroubled spirit.' After these words he showed her the son she had still living, he showed her the children of the son she had lost

6. In that instance, Marcia, it was your problem that was met, it was at your side that Areus sat; change the role—it was you he attempted to console. But consider, Marcia, that you had snatched from you more than any mother ever lost—I am not trying to bring you ease and I do not seek to minimize the disaster you have suffered: if fate is conquered by tears, let us muster them to shed; let every day pass amid grief, let sleepless melancholy consume the night; let blows rain down on our bleeding chests and our very faces feel their violence, if it will serve our purpose, let grief practise every kind of savagery. But if no amount of wailing recalls the dead, if all distress is powerless to alter a fate that is unchangeable and fixed for ever, if death holds fast whatever it has carried away, let sorrow, which runs its course, cease. Let us, therefore, steer our own vessel, and not allow this force to drive us off course. It is a poor ship's pilot who lets the waves wrest the helm from his hands, or abandons his sails to the strength of the wind, leaving his craft to the mercy of the storm; but even in the case of shipwreck we should extol the helmsman whom the sea overwhelms as he still grips the rudder and does battle with the elements.

7. 'But it is natural to mourn for our loved ones.' Who denies this, provided it is done in moderation? For even when our dearest ones merely part from us, far less when we lose them, we feel an inevitable pang, and even the strongest of hearts is wrung. But what opinion adds to our grief exceeds Nature's prescription. Consider the mourning we see in dumb animals, how intense it is and yet how short-lived: the sad lowing of cows is heard for one day, or two, and the frenzied and aimless galloping of mares we see lasts no longer; beasts of the wild, after following the tracks of their stolen young, after roving through the forests and returning many times to their pillaged lairs,

quench their fury within a short time; birds circle noisily around their empty nests with loud shrieks, but in no time they calmly resume their accustomed flight; and no creature spends a long time in mourning for its offspring except man, who nourishes his grief and has as the measure of his affliction not what he feels but what he has decided to feel.

Again, so that you may know that it is not Nature's will that we be broken by grief, note in the first place that, despite suffering the same bereavement, women are wounded more deeply than men, barbarian people more deeply than members of a peaceful and enlightened race, the uneducated more deeply than the educated. And yet the emotions that take their force from Nature exercise the same control over all; it is clear that emotion which exhibits variety is not prescribed by Nature. Fire will burn people of all ages and inhabitants of every country, men and women alike; steel will show its power to cut all manner of flesh. Why? Because they have been given their strength by Nature, which draws no distinction between persons. Poverty, however, sorrow, and ambition are felt differently by different people, depending on the colour imparted to their minds by habit, and preconceived opinion, which makes men fear things they should not, reduces them to weakness and apathy.

8. Secondly, whatever derives from Nature is not diminished by its own duration: grief, however, is erased by the long passage of time. It may be very stubborn, rising up every day and boiling over despite our attempts to calm it, but time robs it of its strength, time that has no equal in taming savagery. Even now there remains in your heart, Marcia, a profound sadness, and already it seems to have grown calloused, not the passionate sorrow of the early days, but stubborn and unyielding; but even this time will take from you little by little: whenever you are engaged in some other pursuit, your mind will feel relief. For the moment you are your own guardian; but it makes a considerable difference whether you permit or order yourself to grieve. How much more would it suit the elegance of your character to bring, rather than to anticipate, an end to your grief, and not to wait for that day when against your wishes your grief comes to an end! Of your own will renounce it now.

9. 'Why, then, do we show such persistence in mourning for one we loved, if it does not come about at Nature's bidding?' Because we fail to anticipate any evil before it actually befalls us, but rather, as

though we are privileged and have set foot on a path less dangerous than others, we fail to learn from the mishaps of others that such things affect us all. So many funeral processions go past our doors: we do not reflect on death; so many deaths are premature: we give thought to our young children's future—the day they will assume the toga, begin military service, become heirs to their father's property; we see before our eyes how so many men of wealth are afflicted by sudden poverty: and never does it enter our heads that our own wealth rests on ground just as treacherous. It follows necessarily, then, that we are more liable to collapse: we are struck, as it were, off guard; an attack we foresee in plenty of time hits us with less impact. Do you want to be told that you stand exposed to every kind of blow, and that the arrows that have pierced others have quivered round you? Just as though you were making an assault on some city wall or climbing up, half-armed, against a lofty position defended by great numbers of the enemy, expect a wound and take it that those rocks flying down from above, together with the arrows and javelins, have been aimed at your own body. Whenever someone falls at your side or in your rear, shout out: 'You will not deceive me, Fortune, or over-power me by taking me when I am confident and careless. I know what plans you are making: you may have struck another man, but your target was myself.' Who ever regarded his property, thinking he would die? Which one of you ever dared to think about exile, about poverty, about grief? Who, if urged to contemplate such things, would not spurn the notion as an unlucky omen, and wish those curses to fall instead on the heads of his enemies or even of that man with his inopportune advice? 'I did not think it would happen.' Is there anything you think will not happen, when you know that it can happen, and your own eyes show it has happened already to many? This is an outstanding verse,* better than I would have expected in any play:

> Whatever fate one man can strike can come to all of us alike.

That man lost his children: you, too, can lose yours; that man received sentence of death: your innocence, too, stands under the hammer. This is the fallacy that takes us in and makes us weak while we suffer misfortunes that we never foresaw that we could suffer. The man who has anticipated the coming of troubles takes away their power when they arrive.

10. All these gifts from above that shine about us, Marcia—children, honours, wealth, vast halls, forecourts crammed with a crowd of unadmitted clients, a famous name, a wife who is beautiful or well-born, and all other things that depend on the uncertainty and fickleness of chance—they are borrowed ornaments, not our own; not one of them is given to us as a gift. We occupy a stage decorated with various properties that are on loan and must be restored to their owners; some of these will be returned on the first day, others on the second, a few only will remain until the final curtain. And so we have no grounds for self-admiration, as though we were surrounded by our own possessions; they have been loaned to us. We may use and enjoy them, but the one who allotted his gift decides how long we are to be tenants; our duty is to keep ready the gifts we have been given for an indefinite time and to return them when called upon, making no complaint: it is a sorry debtor who abuses his creditor. Therefore we ought to love all our dear ones, both those we desire to outlive us by condition of their birth, and those who themselves pray most justly to pass away before us, but always in the realization that we have received no promise that they will be ours for ever, no, not even ours for a length of time. Many times must the heart be reminded, it must not forget that those we love will leave, indeed are already leaving: you should take whatever Fortune has given but realize its security is not guaranteed. Seize the pleasures your children bring, let them in turn take enjoyment in you, and drink the cup of happiness dry without delay: you have been given no promise about tonight—I have granted too long an adjournment—no promise about this very hour. We must make haste, the enemy marches on our rear: soon these companions will all be scattered, soon the cry of battle raised and ties of comradeship severed. Everything is plundered: wretched men, as you join the rout you do not know how to live.

If you grieve for your son's death, it is an accusation of the time when he was born; for at birth his death was proclaimed; into this condition he was fathered, this was the fate that accompanied him immediately from the womb. We have entered the kingdom of Fortune, whose rule is harsh and unconquerable, and at her whim we will endure suffering deserved and undeserved. She will waste our bodies by violent, cruel, and insulting means: some she will burn with fire, applied to punish us, or, perhaps, to work a cure; some she will put in chains, giving this power now to an enemy, now to a fellow citizen; some she will toss naked onto the shifting sea, and after their struggle with the waves she will not even cast them upon the sand or the shore, but will conceal them in the belly of some gigantic monster; others she will keep for a long time hovering between life and death, wasted by diseases of various kinds. Like an unpredictable and wilful mistress who takes no thought for her slaves, she will show no consistency either in punishments or rewards.

11. What is the need to weep at parts of life? All life is worthy of our tears: fresh problems will press upon you before you have done with the old ones. Accordingly, you women especially, so uncontrolled in grieving, should practise moderation, and bring the power of the human heart to bear against your many sorrows. Furthermore, what is this failure to remember what is the individual, and what the common, lot? You were born mortal and gave birth to mortals: did you, who are yourself a crumbling and decaying body, and often attacked by the causes of disease, expect to produce from such weak matter something sturdy and everlasting? Your son has died, that is, he has run his course and reached that goal towards which those you consider more fortunate than your offspring now hasten. To this end proceeds, at a different pace, all this crowd that now engages in disputes in the forum, applauds in the theatre, prays in the temples: those you love, or revere, and those you despise will be made equal by a single quantity of ash. This is evidently the meaning of the well-known saying ascribed to the oracle at Delphi: Know Yourself. What is man? A vessel that the slightest shaking, the slightest buffet, will break. It does not require a great storm for you to be driven off course: wherever you batter against something, it will be your undoing. What is man? A weak and fragile body, naked, in its natural state without defence, in need of another's assistance, exposed to all the insults of Fortune, and, once it has given its muscles a good exercise, food for the first wild beast, prey to everyone; a patchwork of feeble and changing elements that pleases the eye only in its external features, unable to endure cold, heat, or toil, and yet doomed to decay from mere corrosion and idleness; afraid of the sustenance that nourishes it, it perishes now from lack of this, and now splits apart from superfluity; anxious and fearful for its own safety, drawing its breath fitfully and maintaining it with difficulty, as sudden fear or the unexpected sound of a loud noise assailing the ears drives it out, it constantly nurtures its own anxiety, a flawed and useless thing. Do we wonder that this thing

has in it death, which requires only a single sigh? Is it so formidable an undertaking to bring about its ruin? Smell, taste, fatigue, lack of sleep, drink, food, and the things without which it cannot live can all bring death to it; wherever it moves, it is at once aware of its own frailty and does not tolerate every climate, but, as a result of strange waters, or a blast of unaccustomed air, from the most trivial causes and complaints, it falls ill and rots with disease; it began life with tears, and what a commotion meanwhile this despicable creature makes, what great thoughts it entertains, forgetting the end to which it must come! Man ponders on matters immortal and eternal, forming plans for his grandchildren and great-grandchildren, while in the meantime death surprises him amidst his far-reaching designs, and even this period that we call old age is only the circling of a handful of years.

12. This grief you feel, assuming it has some rational basis, does it look to your own misfortune or that of the one who has died? In the loss of your son are you influenced by the notion that you derived no pleasures from him, or is it that you might have known greater ones, had he lived longer? If you say you derived no pleasures, you will make your loss easier to bear; for people miss less the things which gave them no joy or happiness. If you admit to having derived great pleasures, your duty is not to complain about what has been taken away but to be thankful for what you have been given; for simply the act of rearing him has provided you with great enough rewards for your efforts, unless perhaps those who lavish every care on raising puppies and birds and other foolish pets take some pleasure in the sight and touch and fawning caresses of these dumb animals, whereas those who raise children do not experience the reward of the rearer, which is the act of rearing itself. And so, although you have gained nothing from his effort, although you have been saved nothing by his carefulness, although you have learned nothing from his good sense, you have your reward in having had him and in having loved him. 'But it could have lasted longer, it could have been greater.' Yes, but you have been treated more kindly than if you had never had a son; for, if we were given the choice whether it is preferable to be happy for a short time or never to be happy, it is better for us to have blessings that will depart than to have none at all. Would you rather have had a son who was unworthy of his family, who was going to make up merely the name and number of a son, or one with as fine a nature

as your own, a young man who early displayed discretion and early a sense of duty, who early became a husband and early a father, who early was assiduous in every public office and early became a priest, as though he never stopped to draw breath? It is hardly ever a man's lot to be given blessings which are both great and long-lasting, and only the happiness that comes slowly continues and accompanies us to the end: the immortal gods, not intending to give you a son for a long time, gave you from the outset one such as only length of time can bestow.

Even this you cannot say: that you were chosen by the gods in order to be denied the enjoyment of a son. Look around you at all the throng of those you know and those you do not, you will find everywhere men whose sufferings have been greater; legend has not granted exemption from misfortune even to the gods, so that, I imagine, our sorrow for the dead may be eased by the knowledge that even gods can perish. Look around, I say, at everyone: not one home will you mention so wretched that it cannot be comforted by looking at one more wretched. But I do not think so badly of your character— heaven forbid!—that I think you can endure your own misfortune more easily if I produce for you a lengthy list of mourners: it is a peevish form of consolation to make you join a company of misery. I will, however, cite certain ones, not so that you may know that this disaster commonly befalls mankind—for it would be ludicrous to gather together the examples of human mortality—but to show you that there have been many who sweetened the bitterness of their lot by enduring it calmly.

I shall begin with the most fortunate of men. Lucius Sulla lost a son, but that event served neither to blunt his spite and the fierce energy of his resolve in opposing enemies and fellow citizens, nor to make it seem he had wrongly claimed his well-known title; for he assumed this after losing his son, fearing neither men's hatred, though that inordinate prosperity of his was bought by their misfortune, nor the envy of the gods, though they were blamed that Sulla was so much 'The Fortunate'.* But let us leave the question of Sulla's character among matters not yet decided upon—even his enemies will admit he acted well in taking up arms, and well in laying them down: this point we are examining will be undisputed, that an evil which comes to even the most fortunate men is not the greatest of evils.

13. Greece could not bestow too much admiration on the famous father who, when his son's death was announced as he was in the very act of holding sacrifice, merely told the flautist to stop playing and, having removed the wreath from his head, duly performed the rest of the rites. This is due to a Roman priest, Pulvillus, who received the news of his son's death while he was dedicating the temple on the Capitoline and was still grasping the doorpost. He pretended not to have heard the news, and repeated the ritual words of the priest's invocation, not letting a single moan interrupt his prayer and entreating Jupiter's favour with the name of his son sounding in his ears. Do you not consider that grief such as that should have some end, when the first day and first onslaught of it failed to remove him, father as he was, from his responsibility at the public altar and an auspicious pronouncement of his address to the god? He was worthy, indeed most worthy, of that remarkable dedication, worthy of holding the most distinguished priesthood, that man who did not cease from worshipping the gods even when they showed anger. The same man, however, on returning home, had eyes filled with tears and gave way to some mournful cries; but once he had performed the rites prescribed by custom for the dead, he assumed once more the expression he had worn on the Capitol. Paulus,* during those days of his celebrated triumph when he drove Perses in chains before his chariot, gave two of his sons to be adopted and buried the two he had kept for himself. What calibre of men were those he kept, do you suppose, when one of the sons he gave away was Scipio? With considerable emotion the people of Rome viewed Paulus' chariot, now empty. However, he gave a public speech thanking the gods for having granted his prayer; for he had prayed that, if he should have to render some payment to envy because of his great victory, a loss to himself rather than to the people should discharge this debt. Do you observe the nobility of spirit with which he behaved? He congratulated himself on losing his children. And what man would have been more entitled to be shaken by such a reversal of fortune? He lost at one and the same time both his source of comfort and means of support. But Perses was not allowed to see Paulus sad.

14. Why should I now lead you through countless examples of great men, searching for those who were wretched, as if it were not more difficult to find ones who were happy? For how few households have survived right to the end with all members intact? How few have avoided some disastrous occurrence? Take any one year you wish and summon its magistrates, Lucius Bibulus, if you like, and Gaius Caesar:* you will see that, however much hatred these colleagues had for one another, their fortunes were in perfect accord. In the case of Lucius Bibulus, a man whose principles were stronger than his actions, his two sons were killed at the same time, and at the hands of Egyptian troops who had mocked them beforehand, so that the cause of the bereavement was as much a matter worthy of tears as the bereavement itself. Bibulus, however, whom jealousy of his colleague had kept at home for the whole year of his consulship, emerged the day after receiving the news of the double murder, and turned his attention to the customary duties of a proconsul. Who can spare less than one day for his two sons? So swiftly did he conclude his mourning for his children, the man who had mourned a year for the consulship.

When Gaius Caesar was traversing Britain and could not let the ocean itself set limits on his success, he heard that his daughter had passed away, so sealing the doom of the Republic as well. He now saw plainly that Gnaeus Pompey would not calmly tolerate any other man becoming 'great' in the Republic, and was likely to check his own progress, which he appeared to resent even when it increased to the advantage of them both. Three days did not pass, however, before he returned to his duties as a commander, conquering his grief as swiftly as he was accustomed to conquer everything.

15. Why should I remind you of the deaths of the other Caesars? It strikes me that Fortune seems at times to commit outrage on them in order that in this way also they may benefit the human race, by showing that not even those who are said to be born from the gods and destined to father gods have the power over their own fortune that they exercise over other men's. After losing his children and grandchildren, after the store of Caesars had been emptied, the deified Augustus used adoption to replenish his exhausted house: he endured this loss, however, with the strength of mind of one who already viewed it as a personal matter and was particularly concerned that no man should complain about the gods. Tiberius Caesar lost both the son he had fathered and the one he had adopted;* nonetheless he himself delivered the funeral oration for his son from the Rostra,* standing there with the body in full view, and, letting only a veil intervene between them, so that a high-priest's eyes might be shielded from death, he kept his features unchanged as the Roman

people gave way to tears; to Sejanus, who was standing at his side, he presented an example of how patiently he could bear the loss of loved ones.

Do you see how rich is the supply of men who were of the greatest distinction but not exempted from this misfortune that devastates all, men who had been generously endowed with so many mental gifts, so many decorations in public and private life? But anyone can see that this storm goes on its round, bringing destruction to everything without distinction, and driving everything before it as booty. Tell all men individually to compare their accounts: not one has the luck to be born without paying the penalty for it.

16. I am aware of what you are saying: 'You have forgotten that you are consoling a woman, and you are citing examples of men.' But who has stated that Nature has been ungenerous to women's natures and has tightly restricted their virtues? They have just as much energy, believe me, just as much aptitude for noble actions, should they wish; they endure pain and toil as well as we do, if they have grown accustomed to them. Good gods, in what city are we speaking of this? The city which saw Lucretia and Brutus* tear a king's yoke from the necks of Romans: to Brutus we owe our freedom, but to Lucretia we owe Brutus; the city which saw Cloelia* show contempt for the enemy and the river, a woman whose remarkable bravery has made us virtually transfer her to our roll of heroes: the statue of Cloelia, mounted on horseback in the Sacred Way where Rome is at its busiest, mocks our young men as they climb into their cushioned litters, that they journey in such fashion in the city where we have presented even women with a horse. But if you want me to cite examples of women who have shown courage in mourning their loved ones, I shall not seek them from door to door; from one family I shall give you two women, the Cornelias: the first Scipio's daughter, and mother of the Gracchi.* Twelve births did she recall by as many deaths; it matters little about the others, whom the state did not know as either born or lost: Tiberius and Gaius, whose greatness will be admitted even by a man who denies them goodness, she saw not only murdered but also refused burial. But to those who sought to comfort her, calling her unfortunate, she said: 'Never shall I call myself less than fortunate, I who gave birth to the Gracchi.' Cornelia, the wife of Livius Drusus,* had lost a son, a youth of great renown and conspicuous ability, who, while he followed in the footsteps of the Gracchi and still had so many measures to put forward, was cut down by an unknown assassin in the sanctity of his own home. But she displayed as much fortitude in bearing the loss of her son, untimely and unavenged as it was, as he had shown in proposing his laws. Will you now end your hostility towards Fortune, Marcia, if she has not withheld even from you the arrows with which already she wounded the Scipios and the mothers and daughters of the Scipios, and attacked the Caesars?

Life is full of various misfortunes that plague it, and no man enjoys a lasting peace from them, indeed scarcely a truce. You had brought four children into the world, Marcia. Not one javelin, they say, that is flung into the thick of the enemy line falls without a casualty: is it remarkable that a company as great as yours has not been able to pass through life without incurring envy or loss? 'But Fortune was even less fair in not only snatching my sons away but also selecting them.' But if you are forced to share equally with one more powerful, you should never describe it as unfair: she has left you two daughters and their children; and she has not completely robbed you even of the son whom you especially mourn, forgetting your earlier loss: you have still the two daughters he fathered, great burdens if you show weakness, great comforts if you show strength. Frame your mind so that, whenever you see them, you are reminded of your son, not of your grief. When a farmer's fruit-trees are destroyed—either completely uprooted by the wind, or twisted and broken by the sudden onslaught of a hurricane—he nurtures the young stock they have left and loses no time in planting seeds and cuttings to replace his lost trees; and in a moment (for time is as swift and speedy in promoting growth as in causing destruction) they grow up more flourishing than the ones he lost. So now put these daughters of your own Metilius in his place, filling the space he has left, and lighten the burden of grief you feel for one by the comfort you draw from two. It is true that our mortal nature makes us desire nothing so much as what we have lost: our longing for what we have lost makes us less than fair towards what is left. But if you wish to calculate how kindly Fortune has treated you, even in her savage moods, you will discover that she has left you more than consolation: look at your grandchildren, look at your two daughters. Say this as well to yourself, Marcia: 'I would be shaken, if everyone's fortune accorded with his behaviour, and good people never met with misfortune: as it is, I see that this storm buffets the good and the bad without distinction.'

17. 'But it is a heavy blow to lose the young man you have raised, just when he was becoming a source of protection and pride to his mother and his father.' Who maintains that it is not a heavy blow? But it is part of being human. To this end you were born, to experience loss and to perish, to feel hope and fear, to disturb others and yourself, to dread and yet to long for death, and, worst of all, never to know under what terms you exist.

If someone said to a man setting out for Sicily: 'Discover beforehand all the disadvantages and all the pleasures of the journey you are about to make, and then put to sea. These are the things that may excite your wonder: first, you will see the island itself, cut off from Italy by a narrow strait and once, it is agreed, joined to the mainland; the sea suddenly burst in there and

> From Hesperia's side Sicily did sever.*

Then you will see Charybdis,* made famous by legend (for it will be possible to skirt that most greedy of whirlpools), lying peacefully as long as it is untroubled by the south wind, but, if any heavy squalls blow up from that quarter, sucking ships down into its huge, deep throat. You will see Arethusa's fountain,* made so famous in poetry, a shining pool crystal-clear to its depths, pouring out its icy waters, whether it discovered them where they were first born, or it returned a river that had plunged under the earth, and, flowing intact under so many seas, had been kept uncontaminated by waters less pure. You will see the most peaceful of all harbours that Nature has established or the hand of man assisted for ships to find shelter in, so secure from harm that not even the most terrible storms can find access there to spend their fury. You will see where the power of Athens was shattered, where so many thousands of prisoners were enclosed in that natural prison* hewn out of rock to a vast depth; you will see the mighty city itself, spreading over an area wider than many a city's boundaries, where winters are most benign and not a day passes without sunshine. But when you have discovered all these blessings, the benefits of the winter climate will be spoiled by the oppressive and unwholesome heat of the summer. There too will be the tyrant, Dionysius,* destroyer of freedom, of justice, of the laws, whom not even Plato could rid of his appetite for power, or exile of his appetite for life: some men he will burn, some he will flog, some will have limbs chopped off on his orders to answer for some petty offence; he will summon male and female victims to gratify his lust, and among the revolting accoutrements of his royal excesses it will not be enough to enjoy the bodies of two partners at the same time. You have heard what can attract, and what deter, you: and so either set sail or do not leave port.' After this warning if a man expressed a wish to enter Syracuse, is there anyone he could complain more justly about than himself, as he would not have found this state of affairs by accident but come upon it forewarned and with full knowledge?

Nature says to all of us: 'I deceive no one. If you father children, perhaps you will have handsome ones, perhaps ugly ones. It may be that many will be born: it is possible that one of these will save his country, just as possible that he will betray it. There is no reason for you to cease hoping that they will be so highly esteemed that no one out of respect for them will dare to speak ill of you; imagine, however, that they may also acquire such infamy that they themselves prove a curse to you. Nothing stands in the way of their performing the last rites at your funeral, there is no reason why your own children should not be the ones who deliver the eulogy over you; but, equally, keep yourself in readiness for placing your son on the funeral pyre, whether he be a lad, a man, or one of advanced years; for years are of no relevance to this matter, since every funeral where the parent walks behind the bier marks an untimely end.' If, after these terms have been set out, you go on to father children, you must exonerate the gods from all blame: they made you no definite promise.

18. Now come, apply this picture to your entrance into the whole of life. All that could delight you and repel you if you were debating whether to visit Sicily I have placed before your eyes: suppose that I am coming now to give you counsel at your birth. 'You are about to enter a city shared by gods and men, one that embraces the whole world and is bound by fixed and everlasting laws, watching as overhead the heavenly bodies whirl untiringly on their rounds. You will see there the glitter of numberless stars, you will see all of them filled with the radiance of one star, the sun, that distinguishes the intervals of day and night on his daily course, and in his annual course assigns more regularly still the times of summer and winter. You will see the moon inheriting his place by night, and, as she meets her brother, borrowing from him a gentle, reflected light, sometimes hiding herself from our eyes, sometimes hanging over the earth with all her face unveiled, always changing as she waxes and wanes, always different

from her last form. You will see the five planets hurrying on their differing courses and endeavouring to check the headlong whirl of heaven: on the slightest motions of these depend the fortunes of nations, and the greatest and smallest events take shape in accordance with the movement of a friendly or unfriendly star. You will marvel at gathered clouds and falling waters, at slanting strokes of lightning and the crashing din of heaven. When you have gazed your fill on things above and lower your eyes to the earth, a different form of things will greet you, wonderful in a different way: on the one side you will see flat plains stretching out boundlessly, on the other, mountains soaring in great, snow-capped ridges, their peaks rising to heaven; cascading streams and rivers that flow both east and west, though deriving from a single source, and groves of trees swaying on the tops of mountains, and mighty forests with the creatures that inhabit them, and birds singing in discordant harmony; cities in different locations, and nations that dwell apart because of natural barriers, some of them withdrawn to lofty mountains, others in their fear living close to river-banks, lakes, and valleys; fields of corn assisted by cultivation, and orchards with no one to train their wildness; streams gently meandering between meadows, lovely bays, and shores that bend inwards to form a harbour; islands scattered in profusion over the deep, that give definition to its expanse as they break up the seas.

'And what of the precious stones and jewels that gleam, and the gold that flows down amid the sands of rushing streams, and the flaming torches that burst out in the midst of the land and sometimes in the midst of the sea, and the ocean that binds the lands together, dividing the nations' continuous mass by its three gulfs and swelling up in mighty rage? You will see here monstrous beasts, of dimension exceeding all creatures of land, that stir up the waters as they swim, creating waves without wind, some of them of great weight and moving under another's guidance, some swift and faster than a vessel at full oar, others that drink in the sea's waters and blow them out to the great danger of those sailing past; you will see here ships in search of lands they do not know. You will see nothing that the boldness of man does not attempt to master, and you will yourself be a spectator and a partner in their great ventures: you will teach and be taught the arts, some of which provide for life, some which adorn it, and others which direct it. But there will be found a thousand things to plague the body and the mind, wars, robberies, poisons, shipwrecks, unhealthy conditions of climate and of body, untimely grief at the loss of one's dearest, and death, whether free from distress or the result of painful torture, no one can say. Ponder the question in your mind and weigh up what it is that you want: to arrive at those marvels, you must pass through these dangers.' Your reply will be that you want to live. Of course you do. But no, I imagine, you will shun a course that means the suffering of any loss results in pain! Therefore live on the conditions accepted by you. 'No one has consulted us,' you say. Our parents were consulted about us; they knew the terms of life and raised us to comply with them.

19. But to return to the matter of consolation, let us consider, first, what wound it is that must be healed, and then how it is to be done. One who mourns is swayed by longing for the one he loved. This is clearly, in itself, bearable; for while they are alive, we do not shed tears for those who are not with us, or soon will not be with us, although it is not just the sight of them we are robbed of, but all enjoyment of them; it is an opinion, therefore, that puts us on the rack, and every evil is merely as great as we have estimated it to be. We have the cure in our own power: let us suppose that the dead are merely absent, so deceiving ourselves; we have sent them away, or, rather, we have sent them ahead and we will join them soon. This also has an influence on the mourner: 'There will be no one to protect me, to save me from scornful treatment.' To resort to a consolation that is far from plausible but nonetheless true, in this city of ours more influence is gained than lost by not having children, and loneliness, which used to undermine old age, now confers so much power that some men pretend to hate their sons and disown their children, by their own act rendering themselves childless.

I know what your response will be: 'It is not my losses that upset me; indeed, no parent merits consolation who laments the loss of a son as he would that of a slave, who in a son's case finds time to reflect on anything other than the son.' What, then, is upsetting you, Marcia? Is it that your son has died or that he did not have a long life? If it is his death, then you always had cause to mourn; for you always knew he would die. Reflect that no evils afflict one who has died, that the accounts which make the underworld a place of terror to us are mere tales, that no darkness threatens the dead, no prison, or rivers blazing with fire, no river of Forgetfulness, or seats of judgement, no sinners answering for their crimes, or tyrants a second time in that freedom which so lacks fetters: these are the imaginings of poets, who have tormented us with groundless fears. Death is a release from all pains, and a boundary beyond which our sufferings cannot go; it returns us to that state of peacefulness in which we lay before we were born. If someone pities those who have died, let him pity also those who have not been born. Death is neither a good nor an evil; for only that which is something can be a good or an evil; but what is itself nothing and reduces everything to nothingness, delivers us to no category of fortune. For evils and goods operate around something material: Fortune cannot hold on to what nature has let go, and someone who has no existence cannot be unhappy. Your son has gone beyond the boundaries of slavery and has found welcome in a peace that is great and everlasting: he is not a prey to fear of poverty, to anxiety from wealth, to the pricks of lust that through the body's pleasure harrow the soul, he is not touched by envy of another's happiness, or oppressed by envy of his own, no words of reproach beat upon his innocent ears; no ruinous event threatening his country or his home looms up before his eyes; he is not in suspense about the future and does not hang upon the outcome which always repays with increasing uncertainty. Finally, he has come to rest in a place where nothing can drive him away, where nothing can make him afraid.

20. Oh, how little they understand their ills, those men who do not praise death as Nature's finest discovery and look forward to it! Whether it shuts off prosperity, or brings an end to the old man's satiety and fatigue, or takes away the young man in the bloom of life while he hopes for better things, or recalls the boy before he launches on life's harder steps, it is to all an end, to many a cure, to some the answer to a prayer, and none are more favoured than those to whom it comes before being asked. Death frees a man from slavery though his master is unwilling; it makes light the chains of prisoners; it leads out of prison those forbidden to leave by a tyrant's power; it shows to exiles, whose eyes and minds turn always to their homeland, that it does not matter beneath whose soil a man may lie; when Fortune has unjustly distributed common goods, and has given one man into the power of another, though they were born with equal rights, death makes all things equal; after its coming no man ever does anything again at another's bidding; it is death that makes no man aware of his humble condition; it is death that lies open to all; it is death, Marcia, that your father longed for; it is death, I say, that prevents being born

from being a punishment, that keeps me from collapsing under the threats of misfortune, that enables me to keep my soul free from harm and master of itself: I have one final argument to call upon. I see there instruments of torture, not indeed of one kind, but fashioned differently by different people: some hang their victims upside down, some drive stakes through their private parts, others stretch their arms out on a fork-shaped yoke; I see cords, I see whips, and contraptions designed to torture every joint and limb: but I see death as well. There also are bloodthirsty enemies and arrogant fellow citizens: but there, too, I see death. It is no hardship to be a slave, if, when a man can no longer bear his master's yoke, he may with a single step pass to freedom. Life, it is thanks to death that you are precious in my eyes.

Reflect on how great a blessing a timely death provides, on how many have been harmed by too long a life. If Gnaeus Pompey,* that glory and pillar of our rule, had been carried off by illness at Naples, he would surely have ended his life as the foremost representative of the Roman people, with none to challenge him: but, as it is, the addition of a few years cast him down from that pinnacle. He saw his legions cut down before his own eyes, and from that battle where the front line was the senate he saw—how unfortunate a remnant!—the commander himself left as a survivor; he saw an Egyptian as his murderer and gave up to a minion his body that had been decreed inviolable by the victors, though, even if he had escaped with his life, he would have regretted his good fortune; for what greater shame might Pompey endure than to live by the goodwill of a king? If Marcus Cicero had fallen at the time he escaped the daggers of Catiline,* which threatened his country no less than himself, if he had died as the saviour of the country he had liberated, shortly after witnessing the burial of his daughter, even then he could have died a fortunate man. He would not have seen swords drawn to end the lives of Roman citizens, or assassins dividing up the goods of their victims so that they might pay even for their own murders, or a consul's spoils being put up for public auction, or murders officially put out to tender, or robbery, war, and looting, more and more Catilines. If the sea had swallowed up Marcus Cato as he was returning from Cyprus where he had administered the king's bequest,* and together with him those very funds he was bringing to pay the troops in the civil war, would he not have been blessed by Fortune? He would have taken with him this much at least, the knowledge that no one would dare to offend before the eyes of Cato: as it is, because he was granted a handful of years more, this great man, who was born to bring freedom, not just to himself but to his countrymen as well, was forced to flee from Caesar and to become a follower of Pompey.

A premature death, therefore, brought no ill to your son: in fact, it brought him deliverance from suffering all manner of ills.

21. 'But he died too soon, and before his time.' Imagine in the first place that he had survived—assign to him as many years in a long life that a man may have: how many, after all, do they comprise? Brought into the world for the briefest of spans, and destined shortly to give up our place to the next person who comes, we view our life like an enforced stop at an inn. 'Our' life do I say, when Time drives it on with such incredible speed? Consider the centuries allotted to cities: you will see how short an existence is given even to those that boast of their longevity. All things human are doomed to a short life and perishable, and in the boundlessness of time they take up no part at all. If we apply the scale of the universe, this earth with its cities and peoples, its rivers and surrounding sea, we may regard as a pinprick: if compared with all time, our life occupies less space than a pinprick, for eternity has a greater scale than that of the world, which, of course, renews itself* so often throughout the passing of time. What difference, then, does it make to prolong something that, however much is added to its size, will still amount to little more than nothing? In one way only is the time we live considerable: if it is enough. You may quote me the names of men who had long lives, whose old age has passed into memory, you may count up a hundred and ten years for each of them: when you turn to the contemplation of eternity, that distinction between the shortest and longest of lives will count for nothing, if, having examined the number of years a man has lived, you compare these with the number he has not lived.

Secondly, he died when he was ripe for death; for he lived as long as he needed to live, and there remained nothing further for him to do. Humans do not have one uniform time for old age, any more than animals have: exhaustion overtakes certain animals in fourteen years, and for them the first stage of a man's life represents the longest of lives; a different capacity for living has been granted to each. No one meets his death too quickly, since it was not his destiny to live longer than he did. For each the boundary post stands fixed: it will stay for ever where it has been put, and no amount of care or influence will move it further on. Consider it in this way: you lost your son because it was so ordained: he met his fate

> And reached the goal of his allotted span.*

There is, therefore, no reason for you to tax yourself in this way: 'He could have lived longer.' His life has not been cut short, and it is never the way of chance to block the tide of years. Whatever promise is made to each man, it is discharged; the Fates go their way, adding nothing to what has once been promised, and taking nothing away from it. We offer prayers and exert ourselves in vain: each of us will have the span that was marked down for him by his first day on earth. From that moment when he first saw the light of day he entered upon a journey towards death and drew nearer to his appointed end, and even those years that were added to his youth were subtracted from his life. We are all liable to the mistake of thinking that only the old and those already on life's downward slope are inclining towards death, whereas the earliest days of childhood, middle age, indeed any time of life takes us in that direction. The Fates perform the task that is theirs: they deprive us of the realization that we are dying, and the more easily to creep up on us, death lurks under the very name of life; childhood is transformed into boyhood, boyhood into manhood, and the man of middle years is replaced by the greybeard. Should you calculate them accurately, our very gains are losses.

22. You complain, do you, Marcia, that your son's life was not as long as it might have been? For how do you know it was in his interest to have a longer life, or if this death came as a benefit to him? Is there anyone you can find today whose fortunes are so well placed and so securely established that he has nothing to fear from the advance of time? Human affairs have no stability and are in a state of flux, and no part of our life is so delicate and liable to harm as that which causes us the greatest pleasure; it follows from this that the most fortunate men ought to pray for death, since in the great confusion and unpredictability of human life all that we can feel certain about is what has passed. In the case of your son, who was so physically handsome, whose strict adherence to virtuous conduct in a profligate city where every eye was on him had kept him free from corruption, there is no assurance you have that he could have escaped life's host of diseases, so maintaining unimpaired right to old age that remarkable physical beauty. Reflect on the thousand blemishes that disfigure the soul; for

men of upright character do not continuously sustain into old age the fine hopes they had inspired in their youth, but for the most part are lured into other paths: they either fall a prey to excess, which coming late is all the more disgraceful, and begins to discolour the lovely picture of their early years, or they stoop entirely to the level of the eating-house and their stomachs, concerning themselves exclusively with what to eat and what to drink. Add to this fires, collapsing houses, shipwrecks, the torments we suffer from doctors as they remove bones from living bodies, plunging their hands into our innards, right up to the wrist, and inflicting all manner of pain as they treat our private parts; and after these there is exile (your son was no more blameless than Rutilius),* imprisonment (he was no wiser than Socrates), and the suicide's dagger that stabs the heart (he was not more virtuous than Cato): when you consider these possibilities, you will discover that the men most generously treated by Nature are those whom she quickly takes back into a place of safety, since this was the kind of penalty life had in store for them. Nothing is so deceptive as the life of man, nothing is so treacherous: no one, I swear, would have accepted it as a present, if it were not given to us in a state of ignorance. Accordingly, if the greatest fortune is not to be born, the next best, I think, is to die after a short life and be restored to one's original state.

Remind yourself of that time which caused you so much pain, when Sejanus made a gift of your father to his client Satrius Secundus. He was angry with him because he had made one or two rather outspoken remarks, finding it impossible to tolerate in silence that a Sejanus should not only climb onto our necks but actually be set there. The honour of a statue to Sejanus was being voted, to be set up in Pompey's Theatre, which the emperor was restoring after a fire: this drew from Cordus the outburst: 'That's really the end for the Theatre now.' Well, would it not make a man burst with fury, the idea that a Sejanus should be set up over the ashes of Gnaeus Pompey, a disloyal soldier revered by a statue in a place dedicated to the memory of an outstanding general? His signature, too, was revered, and those savage dogs that he used to feed on human blood, to keep them well-disposed to him alone and ferocious to all others, began to bark around that great man, even then undismayed by his predicament. What was he to do? If he wanted to live, he would have to win Sejanus round; if he wanted to die, he would have to win his daughter round, and both were deaf to any appeal: he decided to deceive his daughter. And so he took a bath, and, to reduce his strength further, he retired to his bedroom on the pretext of taking a meal there, and, sending the slaves away, he threw some of the food out of the window to give the impression of having eaten it; afterwards he refused to have dinner, pretending that he had already eaten enough in his bedroom. The next day, also, he did the same thing, and the day after that; the truth was disclosed on the fourth day by the very weakness of his body. Therefore he held you close and said: 'My darling daughter, this is the only thing I have ever kept secret from you in all my life: I have begun my journey towards death and now am almost halfway there; you must not, and you cannot, call me back.' And thus he gave the order that every lamp be doused, and shut himself up in darkness. When his plan became known, there was general delight that their prey was being snatched from the jaws of those bloodthirsty wolves. Prompted by Sejanus, accusers of Cordus presented themselves at the consuls' tribunal, complaining that Cordus was dying and entreating them to stop what they themselves had forced upon him: so strong was their feeling that Cordus was eluding their clutches. It was no minor point that was in dispute, whether a man on trial should forfeit his right to die; while the debate continued, while his accusers made a second appeal, that man had gained his own acquittal. Do you see, Marcia, what great changes of fortune afflict us unexpectedly in wicked times? Do you weep because it was necessary for one of your loved ones to die? One of them was almost not granted this right.

23. Apart from the fact that all in the future is uncertain, and more certain to be worse than the present, it is true that souls which gain a swift release from human society have the easiest journey to the powers above; for they are burdened by the least weight of earthly impurity. Set free before they might grow hardened and become too deeply tainted by earthly matter, they fly back to their source more lightly and wash away more easily all defilement and pollution. And great souls are never happy to linger in the body: they long to depart and to burst forth, and feel resentment at their narrow confines, accustomed as they are to roving on high over the universe and to looking down with scorn from their lofty seat on the world of men. This is what lies behind Plato's cry that the man of wisdom makes death the focus of his whole mind, desires it and dwells on it in his thoughts, and, because he yearns for it, passes through life striving for what lies beyond.

Again, Marcia, when you saw in one who was young the discretion of an old man, when you saw a mind that had conquered all pleasures of the body, uncontaminated, free from fault, pursuing wealth without greed, honours without display, pleasures without dissipation, did you suppose you could have the good fortune to keep him safe from harm for long? All that reaches the highest state is close to its end; consummate virtue rushes away, sweeping from our sight, and fruits that ripen in the early days do not wait for their last ones. The more brightly a fire glows, the more swiftly it dies: the fire kindled with tough and unyielding wood, and buried in smoke, shines with a murky light but has a longer life; for what provides it so grudgingly with sustenance also keeps it burning. So it is with men: the more brilliant their spirits, the briefer their lives; for when there is no room for growth, the end is near. Fabianus recounts—and our parents actually saw him—that there was at Rome a boy as tall as a man of considerable height; but he quickly died, and every sensible person said it would not be long before he died; for he could not reach a time of life that he had already anticipated. This is the way it is: excessive maturity spells impending ruin; when growth is no longer possible, the end draws near.

24. Begin to judge him, not by his years, but by his qualities: he had a life that was long enough. Left as a ward, he was under the care of guardians up to his fourteenth year, but his mother was his guardian for all his life. Although he had his own home, he did not want to leave yours, and he persisted in living under his mother's roof at a time when children can scarcely bear to share the home of their father. In his youth his height, handsome bearing, and assured physical strength made him someone born for the camp, but he refused military service, unwilling to leave you. Consider, Marcia, how seldom women who live in separate houses set eyes on their children; reflect on all the many years that mothers lose and spend in anxiety, when they have sons in the army: you will realize that this time throughout which you suffered no loss was very extended. At no time did he leave your sight; under your eyes he moulded his studies with an intelligence that was outstanding and would have put him on a par with his grandfather, if modesty had not stood in his way, that quality which through silence impedes the advancement of many. Though a young man of striking physical charm, and surrounded by such a great crowd of women, who can lead men astray, he gave

none cause for hope, and, when some of them actually had the effrontery to make advances to him, he blushed, as though he had done wrong by pleasing their eyes. This purity in his morals made men consider him worthy of election to a priesthood, even though he was still a boy, a proposal without doubt supported by his mother, but not even his mother's influence would have carried enough weight, if the candidate had not been a good one. By reflecting upon these qualities you will once more be clasping your son in your arms. Now he has the more leisure to bestow on you, now he has nothing to call him from your side; never henceforth will he give you cause for worry, never cause for grief. You have experienced the only sorrow a son so good could have brought you: everything else is now beyond the reach of chance and is full of delight, if only you know how to enjoy your son, if only you understand what was most to be valued in him.

It is only a likeness of your son that has perished, an image that bears little resemblance to him, whereas he himself is everlasting and has now reached a happier state, stripped of external impediments and left just as himself. These trappings you see which envelop us, bones, sinews, the overlay of skin, the face, the hands that are our servants, and the rest of our human vesture, they only serve to fetter our souls and shroud them in darkness; by these the soul is crushed, choked, tainted, imprisoned in falsehood and cut off from its true and natural element. It struggles perpetually against this weight of flesh we bear, to avoid being dragged back and sinking down; it strives to reach that place from which it once fell. There everlasting rest awaits it, once it has left the earth's disordered dullness to view a realm of translucent purity.

25. There is, therefore, no reason for you to rush off to your son's tomb: his worst elements lie there, those that troubled him most in life, bones and ashes that are no more parts of him than were the clothes and other things that gave his body protection. He is whole, and leaving on earth nothing of himself, he has fled and completely departed; and for a short while he lingered above us, while he was being cleansed and was getting rid of all the flaws and blemishes that clung to him in his mortal life, then, soaring on high, he raced to join the company of blessed souls. He was welcomed by a sacred band, the Scipios and Catos, and, in the number of those who held life in contempt and won freedom through the boon of death, by your own

father, Marcia. He keeps his grandson at his side—although there kinship exists among all men—as the youth delights in the strange light, and teaches him the pathways of the neighbouring stars, introducing him gladly to Nature's secrets, not by guesswork but by experience, as he truly knows them all; and as a stranger appreciates having someone to guide him through an unfamiliar city, so the youth, as he inquires into the causes of heavenly things, listens gratefully to a kinsman's instruction. He also tells him to direct his gaze on the things of earth that lie far below; for it is gratifying to look down from on high on what one has left behind. It is, therefore, for you, Marcia, to act always as though you were under the eyes of your father and son, not as once you knew them, but as so much more exalted beings, now residing in heaven's height. Blush to permit yourself any mean or common thought, and to shed tears for your loved ones who have been transformed for the better. They are travellers in the boundless and free spaces of eternity, with no intervening seas to limit their wanderings, no lofty mountains, or trackless valleys, or shoals of the changing Syrtes:* all there is level, and, in their speed of movement and freedom from encumbrance, they are easily permeated by the stars and in turn mingle with them.

26. Imagine, therefore, Marcia, that your father, who possessed as much authority in your eyes as you did in your son's, no longer using those accents in which he lamented the civil wars and himself laid an eternal proscription on the proscribers, but more exalted ones, consonant with his more sublime condition, speaks these words from that citadel in the heavens: 'Daughter, why do you remain a prisoner of such lengthy sorrow? Why do you dwell in such ignorance of the truth that you judge your son to have been ill-treated because he left his family's fortunes whole and healthy, and, whole and healthy himself, returned to his ancestors? Do you not know how massive are the storms of Fortune that throw all things into turmoil, how she only shows herself kind and compliant to those who have crossed her path as little as possible? Should I name for you the kings who would have been most fortunate, if death had removed them sooner from the ills that threatened them? Or the generals of Rome whose greatness will in no way be diminished, if you subtract some years from their tally? Or those men of noblest birth and greatest renown who staunchly presented their necks to the blow of a soldier's sword?

Reflect on your father and grandfather: the latter fell under the power of a foreign assassin; I allowed no man any power over me, and, letting no food pass my lips, I showed that I lived with as much courage as I wrote. Why in our family is the one who met the happiest death mourned the longest? We are all united in one place, and, enveloped no longer in murky night, we see among you nothing that is desirable, as you imagine, nothing that is sublime, nothing glorious, but everything is poor, burdened, and agitated, seeing so small a fraction of our light! Why should I say there are no opposed armies here, charging one another in frenzied rivalry, or fleets smashing against fleets, no murders of fathers thought up or planned, no forums resounding with noisy disputes for days on end, no concealment of truth, but minds are uncovered and hearts disclosed, and lives are open for all to see, while every age and things to come present themselves to our sight?

'It once gave me pleasure to write an account of events which took place in a single period of history in a part of the universe most distant from here and among a mere handful of men: here my eyes may range over so many centuries, the continuous succession of so many ages, all the revolving years; I may witness the rise and collapse of kingdoms, the ruin of great cities, and fresh incursions of the sea. For if the fate that all share can bring comfort to your sense of loss, realize that nothing will remain where now it stands, that time will bring all things to ruin and take all things with it. And not only humankind will be its plaything (for how trifling a part of Fortune's realm is man?) but places, countries, and areas of the universe. Whole mountains it will level and, elsewhere, it will force up new rocks into soaring crags; it will drink up seas, divert rivers, and, destroying communication between nations, it will overthrow the association and commerce of the human race; elsewhere it will swallow cities in enormous chasms, shake them with earthquakes, and from the depths below send up pestilential vapours; it will overwhelm with floods the inhabited world and, deluging the earth, will kill all creatures, and in mighty conflagration will scorch and burn everything mortal. And when the time comes for the world to be destroyed so that it may assume new life, these things by their own strength will bring destruction on themselves, and stars will clash with stars, and all that now shines in orderly arrangement will burn in a single fire, as all matter is consumed in flames.

'We, too, we happy souls that have gained the lot of eternal life, when God shall decide to build the universe anew, shall constitute a tiny addition to this huge destruction, as all things collapse in ruin, and shall be transformed once more into our previous elements.'

How happy is your son, Marcia, who already knows these things!

ON THE HAPPY LIFE

TO GALLIO

1. It is the wish of all men, Gallio my brother,* to live happily, but, when it comes to seeing clearly what it is that makes life happy, they grope for the light; indeed, a measure of the difficulty of achieving the happy life is that the greater a man's energy in striving for it, the further he goes away from it if he has taken a wrong turning on the road; once this starts leading him in the opposite direction, his very swiftness separates him increasingly from his goal.

And so we must first establish what it is that we seek to gain; then we must search for the road to take us there most speedily, and during the journey itself, provided we are on the correct path, we shall come to know how many miles we put behind us each day, and how much closer we are to the goal our natural desire compels us to attain. Now, as long as we wander at large, having no guide and following only the din and jarring cries of men calling us in different directions, our life will be spent in making errors, a life of little enough span even if we should work night and day for a sound understanding. So let us determine both the goal and the road we will take, and let us have, besides, an experienced guide who has reconnoitred the territory we are entering, since this journey will have different conditions from those of most travel.

On such journeys you are prevented from going astray by some recognized road and by questions put to local people, but on this one all the most well-trodden and frequented paths prove the most deceptive. Accordingly, the most important point to stress is that we should not, like sheep, follow the herd of creatures in front of us, making our way where others go, not where we ought to go. And yet there is nothing that brings greater trouble on us than the fact that we conform to rumour, thinking that what has won widespread approval is best, and that, as we have so many to follow as good, we live by the principle, not of reason, but of imitation. What follows from this is that men are piled high, one on top of another, as they rush to their ruin. Just as it happens that in a great crowd of humanity that is crushed together, when the people jostle against each other, no one falls without dragging someone else down with him, and the ones in front bring destruction on the ones behind, so you may see the same thing happening throughout all of life. No one who goes astray affects himself alone, but rather will be the cause and instigator of someone else going astray; it is harmful to attach oneself to the people in front, and, so long as each one of us prefers to trust someone else's judgement rather than relying on his own, we never exercise judgement in our lives but constantly resort to trust, and a mistake that has been passed down from one hand to another takes us over and spins our ruin. It is the example of others that destroys us: we will regain our health, if only we distance ourselves from the crowd. But as things are, the people, defending their own wickedness, set themselves up against reason. And so the same thing happens as at election meetings, when the very people who chose the praetors wonder that those men were chosen, once the shifting breeze of public favour has changed direction: we show approval for something one moment, then criticize it the next; every decision following the majority's wishes ends this way.

2. When we discuss the happy life, there is no reason for you to give me the well-known reply familiar from vote-counting:* 'This side seems to be in the majority.' For that is why it is the worse side. Human concerns are not so happily arranged that the majority favours the better things: evidence of the worst choice is the crowd. So let us enquire what is the best, not what is the most customary, thing to do, and what establishes our claim to unending happiness, not what the rabble, that worst of truth's exponents, has set its stamp of approval on. But by rabble I mean grand people just as much as ordinary folk; for I have no regard for the colour of clothing that adorns the body. In judging a man I do not trust my eyes, I have a better and more reliable light* by which to distinguish truth from falsehood: let the soul's goodness be discovered by the soul. If the soul ever has a moment to draw breath and to withdraw into itself, ah, what self-torture it will know, how it will admit the truth to itself, saying: 'Whatever I have done before this hour, I would wish to be undone; when I recollect all that I have spoken, I envy the dumb; all that I have prayed for I regard as my enemies' curses; all that I have feared, you kindly gods, how much less a burden were they than the weight of my cravings! I made enemies of many men, and returned from hatred to friendship with them, assuming there can be any friendship between the wicked: to myself I remain an enemy still. I took every care to withdraw from

the masses and by means of some bequest to make myself renowned; all I did was to expose myself to the shafts of malice and show it where to wound me. Do you see the men who praise your eloquence, who follow on your riches, who seek to curry favour with you, who sing the praises of your power? All of them either are your enemies, or, what amounts to the same thing, are able to be; behind every admiring stare in the crowd lies the face of envy. Why do I not instead look for some real good, one that I could feel, not just exhibit? Those things that attract men's eyes, that make them stand still, that they point out to each other, open-mouthed, shine brightly on the outside but have no value within.'*

3. Let us seek something that is good not merely in outward appearance, something that is solid, balanced, and more beautiful in that part which is more hidden; let this be what we try to unearth. And it is not situated far away: it will be found, you need only know where to stretch out your hand; as it is, we pass by things that are near us, as though we are in darkness, and stumble over the very objects of our desire.

But not wishing to haul you through circuitous details, I will pass over without comment the opinions of other thinkers—for it would be a tedious business to number and refute them all—and ask you to listen to my own. But when I say 'my own', I do not bind myself to one particular member of the Stoic elite; I also am entitled to hold an opinion. And so I shall follow one individual, I will invite some other one to divide the question, perhaps also, when I have been summoned to speak after all the rest, I shall not attack a single one of the opinions put forward by my predecessors, and I will say, 'I have this further observation to make'. In the meantime, as is agreed among all Stoics, Nature is the guide I choose;* wisdom lies in not wandering from her path and in moulding oneself in accordance with her law and example.

Accordingly, the happy life is the one that is in harmony with its own nature, and the only way it can be achieved is if, first, the mind is sound and constantly in possession of its sanity, and secondly, if it is brave and vigorous, and, in addition, capable of the noblest endurance, adapting to every new situation, attentive to the body and to all that affects it, but not in an anxious way, and, finally, if it concerns itself with all the things that enhance life, without showing undue respect for any one of them, taking advantage of Fortune's gifts, but not becoming their slave.

You understand, even if I were not to make this further point, that, once the things that either exasperate or scare us are banished, there follows a state of peace,* of freedom, that knows no end; for once pleasures and pains have been scorned, then, in place of those things that are trivial and fragile and, because of their noxious effects, harmful, we experience a great joy that is steadfast and constant, then peace and harmony of mind and the greatness that goes with benevolence; for every impulse to cruelty is born from weakness.*

4. There is another way in which this good of ours can be defined, that is, the same notion can be expressed in different words. Just as an army remains the same, though at one time it deploys with an extended line, at another it contracts into a narrow area and either stands with wings curved and centre hollowed, or stretches out with straightened front, and, whatever formation it adopts, it maintains the same energy and same resolve to fight for the same cause, so the definition of the highest good can at one time be made in a lengthy and protracted form, at another concisely and succinctly. It will, then, be the same thing, if I say, 'The highest good is a mind* that despises the operations of chance, rejoicing in virtue,' or 'The power of the mind* resides in being unconquerable, experienced in life, calm in action, and possessed of much kindness and concern for those with whom it has dealings.' We may also offer the following definition, that of calling that man happy who recognizes no good and evil apart from a good and an evil mind, who holds honour dear and is content with virtue, who is not the sort of person to let the workings of chance go to his head or crush his spirit, who does not recognize any good greater than the one he alone can confer upon himself, and who will find true pleasure in despising pleasures. It is also possible, should you wish to take a wider view, to transfer the same notion to other, different forms of expression without impairing or detracting from its meaning; for what prevents us from saying that the happy life is to have a mind that is independent, elevated, fearless, and unshakeable, a mind that exists beyond the reach of fear and of desire, that regards honour as the only good and infamy as the only evil, and everything else as a trivial collection of things,* which come and go, neither subtracting anything from the happy life nor adding anything to it, and do not increase or diminish the highest good? It is inevitable that a man with such a grounding, whether he wills it or not, will be accompanied by continuous cheerfulness and a profound happiness

that comes from deep inside him, since he is one who takes pleasure in his own resources and wishes for no joys greater than those of his own heart. Would he not be justified in matching these joys against the petty and worthless and transitory sensations of that thing, the body? That day a man triumphs over pleasure, he will triumph also over pain; but you observe how wicked and harmful is the servitude to which a man will submit when he is enslaved in turn by pleasures and pains, those tyrants who wield their powers with such wilful cruelty: accordingly, we must escape to freedom. This is won only by showing indifference to Fortune: then will arise that priceless blessing, the peace and eleva-tion of a mind that has found a secure anchorage, and, once all error has been driven out, the great and unalterable joy that springs from discov-ering the truth, together with benevolence and blitheness of spirit, and a man's delight in all of these will come from knowing, not that they are good, but that they derive from a good which is his own.

5. Since I have begun to treat this topic somewhat freely, one may describe the happy man as someone who is free from desire and fear thanks to the gift of reason, inasmuch as even rocks are without fear and sadness, and no less are farm animals; however, this would not be a reason for anyone to call these things 'happy', when they have no understanding of happiness. Assign to the same category those people whose dull nature and lack of self-awareness have brought them down to the level of beasts of the field and animals. There is no difference between these people and those creatures, since the latter have no reason, while the former have reason that is warped, and, because it expends its energy in the wrong direction, detrimental to themselves; for no one can be called happy if he has been cast beyond the border of truth. Accordingly, the happy life has been based on judgement that is reliable and right, and it is not subject to change. For that is the time when the mind is unclouded and released from all ills, as it has escaped not only serious wounds but even scratches, and, determined to hold to the end whatever position it has taken, it will defend its post, however angrily Fortune makes her assault. For as far as pleasure is concerned,* though it pours itself all around us and flows in through every channel, charming our minds with its blandishments, and applying one means after another to captivate us wholly or partly, who on earth, who has any trace of humanity left in him, would wish to have his senses tickled day and night and, aban-doning the mind, to devote himself to the body?

6. 'But', he says, 'the mind, too, will have its own pleasures.' Let it have them by all means, and let it preside as a judge over luxury and pleasures; let it cram itself with all the things that are accustomed to delight the senses, then let it look back to the past* and, recollecting vanished pleasures, let it revel in experiences of the past and eagerly anticipate now those to come, laying its plans, and, while the body lies supine from cramming itself in the present, let it turn its thoughts to future indulgences: yet all this, it seems to me, will bring the mind greater misery, since it is insanity to choose bad things rather than good. And no one attains happiness who has lost his sanity, just as no one can be sane if he sets his heart on future pleasures in preference to what is best. The happy man, therefore, possesses sound judgement; the happy man is satisfied with his present situation, no matter what it is, and eyes his fortune with contentment; the happy man is the one who permits reason to evaluate every condition of his existence.

7. Even those who have stated that the highest good is located in the belly see in how dishonourable a place they have placed it. Accordingly, they say that pleasure cannot be separated from virtue, and they claim that no one can live honourably unless he also lives pleasantly, or pleasantly unless he also lives honourably. I fail to see how things so different from each other belong to the same potter's wheel. What is the reason, I beg you, why pleasure cannot be separated from virtue? Is your argument that, as every good originates in virtue, even the things you love and aspire to spring from virtue's roots? But if these two were inseparable, we would not see certain things that are pleasant but not honourable, and certain things that are indeed most honourable but fraught with pain and only to be won through suffering. There is the further consideration that pleasure makes its way into even the most disreputable life, whereas virtue does not permit a life to be bad, and people exist who are unhappy, not without pleasure, but as a result of pleasure itself; this could not happen if pleasure were an integral part of virtue, as virtue often lacks pleasure, but never needs it. Why do you seek to join two things that are not alike, indeed opposites? Virtue is something lofty, elevated, regal, unconquerable, and untiring: pleasure is something lowly and slavish, weak and destructible, whose haunt and living-quarters are brothels and taverns. Virtue you will find in a temple, in the forum, in the senate house, standing in front of the city walls, dusty and stained, with hands that are calloused: pleasure you will find more often lurking out of sight and searching for dark-ness around the baths and sweating-rooms and places that fear the aedile,* soft and drained of strength, soaked with wine and perfume, with features that are pale or painted and tricked out with cosmetics like a corpse. The highest good is untouched by death, it knows no ending,* it tolerates neither excess nor regret; for the upright mind never turns from its course, or succumbs to self-loathing or alters anything, being perfect. But pleasure is extinguished at the very moment it gives delight; it occupies only a small place, and therefore speedily fills it, and, becoming weary, loses its energy after the first assault. And nothing whose nature resides in motion is certain: thus it is not even possible that there should be any substance in what comes and goes on its way at great speed and is destined to perish in the very exercise of its power; for it toils to reach the point where it may cease, and in its beginning it looks to its end.

8. There is also the fact that pleasure exists as much in the good as in the bad, and that disreputable persons take no less pleasure in their disgrace than honourable ones do in their fine reputation. And this is why the men of earlier days have instructed us to follow, not the most pleasant, but the best life, in order that pleasure should not guide but accompany a right and worthy desire. For we must employ Nature as our guide; it is she whom reason looks to, she whose counsel it takes.* It is, therefore, one and the same thing, to live happily and to live in accordance with Nature. What this is, I will now reveal: if we preserve with care and bravery the body's endowments and Nature's requisites, regarding them as transitory and given us only for a day,* if we avoid becoming their slaves, and do not let these alien things take possession of us, if we assign to the unimportant things that gratify the body the same position that auxiliaries and light-armed troops are given in camp—that of obeying orders, not issuing them—then and only then will these things be of benefit to the mind. Let a man not be corrupted by externals, let him be invincible and an admirer of himself alone,

confident in spirit and for either end prepared*

one who shapes his own life; let his assurance not lack knowledge, and his knowledge not lack resolution; let his decisions, once made, stand firm, and let there be no alteration in his decrees. It is understood, even if I do not add it, that such a man will be balanced and well ordered, and will exhibit a kindly nature together with great dignity in all his actions. Let reason, prompted by the senses, investigate external matters, and, while it derives first principles from these—for it has no other means of making the attempt or launching its assault on the truth—let it have recourse to itself. For God as well,* the world that embraces all things and ruler of the universe, reaches out to external things but nonetheless, disengaging from all sides, returns into himself. Let our mind do the same: when it has followed the senses that do its bidding and through them reached out to external things, let it be master both of them and of itself. In this way a single energy will be created and a power that harmonizes with itself, and that reliable reason which is not at variance with itself, nor doubtful in its opinions or perceptions, or in its beliefs; and this reason, once it has ordered itself and reached harmony among all its parts, and is, so to speak, in tune, has achieved the highest good. For nothing crooked, nothing slippery survives to threaten it, nothing that will make it stumble or fall over; it will do everything by its own authority and nothing will happen to it unexpectedly, but its every action will have a good result, easily and readily, and without subterfuge on the doer's part; for unwillingness and hesitancy indicate conflict and a lack of resolution. Accordingly, you may be bold in declaring that the highest good is harmony of the spirit; for virtues must reside where harmony and unity exist: discord is attendant on the vices.

9. 'But even you,' comes the objection, 'practise virtue purely and simply because you hope to derive some pleasure from it.' In the first place, if virtue is sure to produce pleasure, that is not the reason why we seek virtue; for it is not this, but something more than this, that she provides, and it is not for this that she labours, but her labour, despite having a different goal, attains this also. Just as in a field which has been broken up for corn, some flowers grow here and there, but it was not for these little plants, though they gladden the eye, that so much work was undertaken—the sower had a different purpose, and this came as a bonus—so pleasure is not the reward or the cause of virtue but a by-product, and virtue does not give pleasure because it delights but, if it gives pleasure, it also delights. The highest good is found in the very act of choosing it, and in the condition of a mind that has been made perfect, and when the mind has finished its course and surrounded itself by its own boundaries, the highest good has been perfected and it requires nothing more; for nothing can exist beyond the complete form, any more than a point can exist beyond

the end. Consequently you are mistaken when you ask what my reason is for seeking virtue; for you are seeking something beyond what is in its highest form. You ask what I seek from virtue? Virtue herself. For she has nothing better, she is herself her own reward. Is this not sufficiently impressive a return? When I say to you, 'The highest good is the unyielding nature of a resolute mind, its foresight, its loftiness, its soundness, its freedom, its harmony, its beauty,' do you still require something greater to which these qualities may be attributed? Why do you mention pleasure to me? I seek the good of a man, not of his belly,* which has greater room in cattle and wild beasts.

10. 'You are distorting what I am saying,' comes the reply; 'for my point is that no one can live pleasantly if he does not at the same time live honourably as well, which is an impossibility for dumb animals and for those who measure their own good simply by food. Clearly, I say, and openly I testify that this life which I call pleasant is an impossible attainment without the addition of virtue.' And yet who does not know that those who cram themselves with your kind of pleasure are all the greatest of fools, and that wickedness teems with enjoyments, and that the mind itself provides many vicious kinds of pleasure? In the vanguard of these are arrogance and an excessive opinion of one's own merits, a swollen pride that looks down on others, a blind and thoughtless devotion to one's own interests, exorbitant delight springing from trivial and childish causes, and, in addition, a caustic tongue and haughty manner that takes pleasure in insults, idleness, and the decadence of a slothful mind that is enervated by luxury and falls asleep over itself. All these things virtue shatters, and she plucks the ear,* evaluating pleasures before she allows them, and she attaches small importance to those she approves or even just permits them, taking pleasure, not in her use of them, but her restraint.* But since restraint diminishes our pleasures, it is detrimental to your highest good. You embrace pleasure, I curb her; you enjoy pleasure, I use her; you regard her as the highest good, I do not even consider her a good; you do everything for the sake of pleasure, I nothing.

11. When I say that *I* do nothing for the sake of pleasure, I am speaking of the ideal wise man, to whom alone we grant pleasure. But I do not call any man wise who is subservient to anything, still less to pleasure. And yet, if this takes him over, how will he stand up to toil and danger, to poverty and all the threats that beset the life of man with their clamour? How will he endure the sight of death, how grief,

how the crashes of the universe and all the savage enemies that face him, if he has yielded the victory to so soft an opponent? 'He will act however pleasure prompts him to.' Come, do you not see how many things it will prompt him to do? 'It will not be able to prompt him to a shameful act,' comes the reply, 'because it is associated with virtue.' Do you not see, again, what kind of a highest good it is that needs a guardian in order to be good? And how will virtue rule pleasure if she follows her, since it is the function of one who obeys to follow, and of one who commands to rule? Do you place one that commands in the rear? What a distinguished role virtue performs in your world, that of tasting your pleasures before you try them! But we will see shortly whether virtue still remains virtue to those who have treated her with such contempt, for, once she has yielded her place, she cannot keep her name; meanwhile, on our present theme, I shall show that there are many men who are besieged by pleasures, on whom fortune has showered all her gifts, who are yet, as you are bound to admit, of a wicked nature. Consider Nomentanus and Apicius,* eagerly seeking out, as they say, the blessings of land and sea, and reviewing the produce of every nation on their dining-room tables; see the same fellows reclining on a bed of roses, surveying their own rich fare, their ears delighting in the sound of singing, their eyes in spectacles, their palates in tastes; all the length of their bodies are caressed by soft and gentle cloths that apply warmth, and, to stimulate their nostrils meanwhile, the very room where sacrifice is being offered to luxury is filled with different scents. You will say that these men were in the midst of pleasures, but it will not do them good, as what they delight in is not good.

12. 'They will suffer,' comes the response, 'because many things will encroach that disturb the soul, and opinions at variance with each other will make the mind restless.' I admit the truth of this; but nonetheless, those very men, for all their stupidity and inconsistency and liability to the throes of remorse, will experience great pleasures, so that it must be admitted that at such a time they are as far removed from all discomfort as they are from a sound mind, and that, as happens with many people, they are cheerful in their moments of lunacy and rave with a smile on their lips. But against this, the pleasures of wise men are relaxed, moderate, virtually lacking in energy, and subdued, of such a kind that they come unsummoned, and, despite drawing near of their own accord, they are not held in any honour or received

with any joy on the part of those who experience them; for they allow them only occasionally to mix with life, as we do amusements and jokes with matters of consequence.

Accordingly, let them stop joining things that are incompatible and connecting pleasure with virtue, a flawed course of action that panders to the worst sort of men. The man who has poured himself into pleasures, constantly belching in his drunken state, because he knows he is living with pleasure, imagines he lives also with virtue (for he hears that pleasure cannot be separated from virtue); then he gives to his own vices the name of wisdom and publicly displays what should be hidden from view. And so Epicurus has not driven them to this dissolute behaviour, rather their addiction to vice makes them cloak their profligacy in the garb of philosophy, and they rush as one to the place where they may hear pleasure's praises being sung. And they have no idea of how sober and self-denying the 'pleasure' of Epicurus is, for so, I am entirely convinced, it is, but they fly to the name itself, seeking a measure of justification and concealment for their base urges. Therefore, they lose the single good that remained to them in their wicked state, a sense of shame at doing wrong; for they praise what used to make them blush with embarrassment, and they exult in their vicious ways; and for this reason they may not even rediscover their youthful aspirations, once their disgraceful idleness has found an honourable name. The reason why the praise you bestow on pleasure is ruinous is this: the decent part of the teaching you embrace lies hidden within, the part that corrupts is plain to see.

13. My own view—I shall state it, though it may give offence to members of our school—is that the teachings of Epicurus are holy and upright, and, if examined closely, rigorous; for his well-known doctrine of pleasure is reduced to small and slender proportions, and the rule that we prescribe for virtue he prescribes for pleasure. He bids it obey Nature; but little enough luxury is enough to satisfy Nature. So where does the truth lie? Whoever applies the term 'happiness' to slothful inactivity and to the gratification of gluttony followed by that of lust, is looking for a good sponsor for his wicked conduct, and when he comes along with that persuasive name he has found attractive, he pursues the pleasure he has brought, not the one he has been taught, and, once he begins to think his vices resemble his teacher's instruction, he shows no fear or shame in indulging them, but from that time on he actually revels in them in full view of men's eyes. I will not, then, follow

most of my school in saying that the sect of Epicurus teaches men to practise vice, but this I do say: it has a bad name, it is disreputable. 'But without justification.' Who can know this without gaining admission to the inner circle? Its very exterior gives scope for slander and prompts debased hopes. It is like the situation of a sturdy man dressed in a woman's clothes: your decency remains unimpaired, your virility unharmed, your person is free from any degrading submission, but in your hand is a tambourine.* You should, therefore, select some honourable motto and a title that in itself inspires the mind: the one that exists has merely attracted the vices.

Whoever has joined the ranks of virtue, has given proof of an honourable nature: the man who pursues pleasure is seen to be enervated, broken, no longer a true man, likely to descend into shameful practices, unless someone helps him to distinguish between pleasures, so that he knows which of them reside within the bounds of natural desire, and which rush headlong onwards, transcending all limits and proving the more insatiable, the more they are satisfied. Come, then, let virtue lead the way, and every step we take will be safe. It is, moreover, excess that makes pleasure harmful: in the case of virtue excess should not be feared, since in virtue resides moderation; something that is afflicted by its own magnitude cannot be a good. Furthermore, what better guide can be offered to creatures blessed with a rational nature than reason? Even if such a combination appeals to you, if you think it a good idea to travel towards the happy life in such company as this, let virtue lead the way and pleasure attend her, hovering around the body like its shadow: only a man who can conceive of nothing great in his soul would be prepared to hand over virtue, noblest of mistresses, to be the maidservant of pleasure.

14. Let virtue go first, let her carry the standard: we will nonetheless have pleasure, but we shall be her master and control her; sometimes we will accede to her entreaty, never to her compulsion. But those who have yielded first place to pleasure lack both; for they lose virtue, and yet they do not possess pleasure but are themselves possessed by pleasure, being tortured by the lack of it or choked by its excess, miserable if it abandons them, more miserable if it overwhelms them; they are like men caught in the waters off the Syrtes,* one moment left on dry land, the next tossed in the swirling waves. But this is the result of an excessive lack of self-control and blind love for some commodity; for when a man seeks bad things instead of good it is dangerous for him to attain his ambition. As we face toil and danger in hunting wild beasts and find it a worrying business to keep them even when captured—for they frequently maul their owners—so it is with great pleasures: they prove to be a great misfortune and take their captor captive; the more and greater the pleasures are, the more inferior is that man the crowd calls happy, the greater is the number of masters he has to serve. I wish to dwell on this comparison for a moment longer. Just as the man who tracks down wild animals to their lairs and considers it a great delight

> With hunting noose to snare the beasts

and

> Round the spacious glades to cast a ring of hounds,*

so that he may pursue their tracks, leaves more important things and abandons many duties, so he who pursues pleasure puts off all business, and first of all takes no thought for his liberty, making this sacrifice to oblige his belly, and does not buy pleasures for himself but sells himself to pleasures.

15. 'But', comes the reply, 'what is to prevent virtue and pleasure blending into one, and the highest good being achieved in such a way that what is honourable and what is delightful may be the same thing?' I respond that what is honourable can have no part that is not honourable, and that the highest good will not preserve its state of purity if it discerns in itself something that differs from its better part. Not even the joy that springs from virtue, although it is a good, is still part of the absolute good, any more than are gladness and tranquillity, despite deriving from the noblest origins; for they may be goods, but they merely attend on the highest good, and do not bring it to perfection. But if a man forms an alliance between virtue and pleasure, and one that is not even equal, he dulls whatever strength the one good has by the weakness of the other, and sends under the yoke that freedom which stays invincible only so long as it finds nothing more valuable than itself. For it begins to need Fortune, and there is no greater servitude than this; there follows a life that is anxious, suspicious, and alarmed, that dreads misfortune and frets at the changes life brings. You are not giving virtue a solid and unshaken foundation but are inviting her to stand on a place that has no stability; but what is as unstable as waiting for Fortune to strike and the shifting

condition of the body and the things that affect the body? How can
a man like this obey God and accept with cheerful heart whatever
happens, not complaining about fate but interpreting in a genial spirit
his own misfortunes, if he is disconcerted by the tiny pinpricks of
pleasure and pain? But he is not even a good protector or champion
of his homeland, or a defender of his friends, if he inclines towards
pleasures. Accordingly, let the highest good ascend to a place from
which no power can drag it down, where there can be no access for pain
or hope or fear, or for anything which can diminish the authority of the
highest good; but only Virtue is able to make the ascent to that place.
It is her steps we must follow if that ascent is to be mastered; she will
stand bravely and endure whatever happens, not only with patience
but also with good cheer, knowing that every difficulty that time
brings proceeds from a law of Nature, and, like a good soldier,
she will bear her wounds, count her scars, and, as she dies, pierced
by weapons, she will love the one in whose service she falls, her
commander; she will keep in mind that old precept: follow God. But
whoever complains and weeps and groans, is compelled by force to
carry out commands, and, though unwilling, is hurried on regardless
to perform his bidden tasks. But what lunacy to prefer to be dragged
than to follow! This is tantamount, believe me, to the folly and ignorance of one's lot demonstrated when you grieve because you lack
something or have suffered a rather harsh experience, or, equally,
when you feel surprise or resentment at those things that happen
to good people as much as to bad, I mean illness and death and
infirmities, and all the other ills that strike at human life from unexpected quarters. Whatever we have to suffer as a result of the way the
universe is framed, let it be endured with great fortitude; this is the
solemn obligation to which we have sworn, that we will submit to our
mortal lot and not be confounded by those things it is not in our
power to avoid. We have been born under a monarchy:* obedience to
God is our liberty.

16. True happiness, therefore, resides in virtue. What counsel will
you be offered by this virtue? That you should not consider anything
either a good or an evil that will not proceed from either virtue or
vice; then that you should remain unmoved, whether you face evil
or enjoy good, so that, as far as is permitted, you may represent God
in your own person. What does she promise you in return for this
enterprise? Great blessings, equal to those the gods enjoy: no constraint

will bind you, nothing will you lack, freedom will be yours, together with safety and exemption from harm; no attempt you make will be in vain, no course of action will be barred to you; everything will befall you as you would wish, nothing hostile will happen, nothing contrary to your expectation and desire. 'Well, then, am I to take it that virtue is all one needs to live happily?'* As it is perfect and divine, why should it not be sufficient, indeed, abundantly so? For if a man has put himself beyond the reach of all desires, what can he lack? What need does he have of anything external, if he has concentrated all that he possesses in himself? But when a man is still journeying towards virtue, even if he has made considerable progress, he requires Fortune to show him some kindness as he continues his struggle in the net of human life, until he has untied that knot and all his mortal bonds. What, then, is the difference here?* In the fact that some are tightly bound, some manacled, some shackled in every limb: he who has advanced to higher regions and has ascended to a more exalted height drags a chain that is loose upon him, not yet a free man, but by this time virtually so.

17. If, therefore, one of those who bark against philosophy like dogs should put their usual question: 'Why, then, do you speak more bravely than you live? Why do you resort to submissive language before a superior and consider money a necessary accoutrement, why are you moved by a loss, shedding tears at the death of your wife or a friend, and why do you have regard for your reputation and let yourself be troubled by spiteful tongues? Why do you farm more extensively than your natural need requires? Why do you flout your own prescriptions when you have dinner? Why do you own furniture of some refinement? Why do you and your guests drink wine of greater years than yourself? Why is your tableware of gold? Why do you plant trees that will yield only shade? Why does your wife wear in her ears the income of a wealthy house? Why are your young servants dressed in expensive garments? Why is it a matter of art to wait at table in your house, why is the silverware not set out carelessly, just as you please, but served in expert fashion, and why is there a professional to carve your dishes?' Make, if you wish, the further point: 'Why do you own property overseas? Why more than you have set eyes on? Why, to your shame, are you so careless that you do not know your handful of slaves by sight, or so extravagant that you have a greater number than memory can recall to your knowledge?' I shall

add weight to your reproaches in due course and take myself to task more than you imagine, but for the present I give you this reply: I am not wise, and, to feed your spite, I shall never be so. And so demand of me, not that I should be equal to the best, but that I should be better than the wicked: I am satisfied if each day I make some reduction in the number of my vices and find fault with my mistakes. I have not arrived at perfect health, nor indeed shall I; my plan is to alleviate, not to banish, the gout that afflicts me,* and I am content if its visits are less frequent and its pains less severe: but when I see your feet, you cripples, I am an athlete by comparison. I do not say these things on my own behalf—for I am sunk in vices of every kind—but on behalf of the man who actually has some achievement to his credit.

18. 'You talk one way,' you say, 'but you live another.' You creatures full of spite, who loathe all men of quality, this was the criticism launched at Plato, yes, and at Epicurus, and at Zeno,* too; for they all described, not how they lived their own lives, but how they ought to live them. I speak of virtue, not of myself, and my abuse is directed at vices, especially at my own: when I can, I shall live as I should do. And that malice of yours, dyed deep with venom, will not discourage me from engaging with what is best; not even that poison you sprinkle on others, that poison with which you are killing yourselves, will hinder me from continuing to praise the life, not that I lead, but that I should lead, or from revering virtue and following her, though haltingly and at a great distance behind. After all, shall I expect anything to be sacrosanct in the eyes of malice, when it showed no reverence to Rutilius or Cato?* Should it worry anyone if he is thought too rich by men who thought Demetrius the Cynic* too poor? This man of enormous courage, who opposed all the desires of nature, who was poorer than all other Cynics, in that he not only banned himself from enjoying possessions but from desiring to have them, this man, they say, does not know true poverty. For you see: he has publicly declared a knowledge, not of virtue, but of poverty.

19. As for Diodorus, the Epicurean philosopher, who terminated his life by his own hand in the last few days, they say that in cutting his own throat he went against the teaching of Epicurus: some would have this action of his seen as madness, others as rashness. He, meanwhile, happy and filled with a good conscience, served as his own witness when he departed from life, and praised the peaceful nature

of the years he had spent anchored in a safe haven, speaking the words you have always been reluctant to hear, as if you also must do the same thing:

My life is o'er; Fortune's course I now have run.*

The life of one of these men and the death of the other are a theme of argument for you, and, on hearing the name of men who have attained greatness because of some outstanding merit, you bark, like little dogs that have encountered strangers; for you find it advantageous to you that no one should appear to be good, as if another man's virtue serves as a reproach to all your own faults. With a jealous eye you compare his glorious appearance with your own squalor, failing to understand how much harm you do yourselves by daring to do this. For if those men who pursue virtue are greedy, lustful, and ambitious, what are you yourselves, who hate the very name of virtue? You say that none of these men matches his words with actions or models his own life on the fine sentiments he utters: does this really surprise you, since their words are bold and grand, and survive all the storms that shake the lives of men? Try as they may to release themselves from their crosses—the very crosses each one of you nails himself to with his own hands—once driven to their execution there they hang, each man on his own gibbet: but these men who bring their own punishment on themselves are racked by as many desires as crosses. Yet they pour out their abuse, and are witty in hurling insults at others. I could well believe they had time for such things, if some of them did not spit at onlookers from their own cross.

20. 'Philosophers do not practise what they preach.' But they do practise much of what they preach, of what their honourable minds devise. How I wish their words were always matched by their actions: their happiness would then be supreme! Meanwhile there is no reason for you to be scornful of noble words and hearts filled with noble thoughts: it is praiseworthy to pursue wholesome studies even if they lead to no practical outcome. Is it so remarkable if those who attempt to scale the heights do not attain the summit? But if you are a man, look up with admiration at those who attempt great things, even if they fall. This is the sign of a noble heart—to aim at high things, measuring one's effort, not by one's own strength, but by the strength of one's nature, and to envisage enterprises beyond the accomplishment even of those equipped with heroic courage. The man who has

set before him such ideals as these: 'For my part, I shall look upon death with the same expression as when I hear of it. For my part, I shall undergo all hardships, however great they may be, supporting my body by means of my mind. For my part, I will hold riches in contempt, no less when they are mine to enjoy than when they are not, feeling no more dejected if they lie elsewhere, and no more emboldened if they shine around me. For my part, I will be indifferent to Fortune, whether she flows towards me or ebbs away. For my part, I shall view all lands as my own, and my own as belonging to others. For my part, I shall live as if I knew that I was born to benefit others, thanking Nature on this account: for in what way could my business prosper better? She has made a gift of me, the individual, to all men, and of all men to me, the individual. Whatever I possess, I shall not guard it in a miserly fashion, or squander it like a spendthrift; nothing shall seem to me to be truer possessions than those gifts I have made wisely. I shall not assess my benefactions by their number, or their weight, or by anything other than my estimation of the one who receives them; never shall what a worthy man receives count for much in my eyes. Nothing shall I do because of what others think, everything because of my conscience. Whatever I do with only myself as witness I shall regard as being done before the eyes of the people of Rome. The purpose of eating and drinking for me shall be to satisfy the desires of Nature, not to fill and empty my belly. I shall give pleasure to my friends, and treat my enemies with forbearance and indulgence. I shall be won over to mercy before it is asked of me, and be swift to accede to all decent appeals. I shall know that my homeland is the world, and that its rulers are the gods, and that they are the ones who stand above and around me, examining my acts and words with a severe eye. And whenever my breath of life is demanded back by Nature or released by my own reason, I shall take my leave, having shown to all that I have loved a good conscience and noble aspirations, and that by no action of mine has any man's freedom been impaired, least of all my own'—the man who shall resolve, shall wish, and shall attempt to do these things will be travelling the road that leads to the gods, yes, and such a man, even if he does not complete his journey,

Yet fails in no weak enterprise.*

Indeed you, with your hatred of virtue and the man who practises it, are doing nothing strange. For the sun strikes fear into sickly lights, and creatures of the night shun the brilliance of the day: awestruck from the moment dawn rises, they everywhere seek out their lairs and hide away in some hole they have found, fearful of the light. Whine away,* then, wag your wretched tongues in abuse of good men, open wide your mouths and bite hard: you will break your teeth far sooner than leaving any mark.

21. 'Why is that man so devoted to philosophy and yet lives a life of wealth?* Why does he say that riches should be despised and yet possesses them, why does he think that life should be despised and yet lives it, that health should be despised and yet guards it with the greatest care and prefers it to be excellent? And why does he regard exile as an empty name and say, "What evil is there in changing the country where you live?" and yet, if allowed, grows old in his home-land? And why does he judge there to be no difference between a long and a short span of life, and yet, if no circumstance prevents it, prolongs his years and flourishes peacefully in advanced old age?' He says such things should be despised, not to stop himself having them, but to avoid worry when he does have them; he does not drive them away, but accompanies them to the door, if they leave him, as an untroubled host. And where indeed will Fortune find a safer place to store wealth than with someone who will give it back without complaint when she asks for its return? When Marcus Cato was extolling Curius and Coruncanius* and that age when to have a few small silver coins* was an offence worthy of the censors' attention, he himself possessed four million sesterces, less undoubtedly than Crassus but more than Cato the Censor. Should they be compared, he had over-taken his great-grandfather by a greater margin than Crassus' lead over himself, and, had greater wealth come his way, he would not have despised it. For the wise man does not consider himself unworthy of any gifts from Fortune's hands: he does not love wealth but he would rather have it; he does not admit it into his heart but into his home, and what wealth is his he does not reject but keeps, wishing it to supply greater scope for him to practise his virtue.

22. What doubt can there be that the wise man has greater scope for displaying his powers if he is rich than if he is poor, since in the case of poverty only one kind of virtue exists—refusal to be bowed down and crushed—but wealth allows a spacious field to moderation, generosity, diligence, good organization, and magnanimity? The wise man will not despise himself, even if his stature is that of a dwarf, but

nonetheless he will want to be tall. And if he has a weak physique or only one eye, he will be strong but he will prefer to have a strong body, and this despite the fact that he knows he possesses something stronger than his body; he will endure bad health but will desire good health. For, though they may be small in relation to the whole, and can be removed without destroying the essential good, certain things do make a real contribution to the unending joy deriving from virtue: the influence of wealth on the wise man, the joy it brings him, is like a favourable wind that sweeps the sailor on his course, or a fine day and a sunny spot amid the chill of winter. Again, who among wise men—I speak of our own school of thinkers, who consider virtue to be the only good—denies that even the things we call 'indifferent' possess some inherent value, and that some are more to be prized than others? Some of these win from us a measure of honour, others a great deal; therefore, be under no illusion, wealth is one of the more valuable possessions. 'Why, then,' you say, 'do you mock me, since you give wealth the same status as I do?' Do you wish to know how differently we view it? In my case if wealth slips away, it will deprive me only of itself, but you will be struck dumb, you will think you have been deserted by your own self, if it leaves you; in my eyes wealth has a certain place, in yours it is centre-stage; to sum up, my wealth belongs to me, you belong to yours.

23. Enough, therefore, of your banning philosophers from possessing money: no one has condemned wisdom to poverty. The philosopher shall have considerable wealth, but it will not have been prised from any man's hands, and it will not be stained with another man's blood, but won without doing any man wrong or engaging in low profiteering, and there will be as much honour in its outlay as its acquisition; it will elicit groans only from the man of spite. Pile up that wealth of his as high as you please: it will have honour as long as, while including much that every man would wish to call his own, it includes nothing that any man is able to call his own. Now, of course, if Fortune is kind to him he will not shove her out of his way, and, should he gain an inheritance by honourable means, it will make him neither boastful nor ashamed. But he will have cause to boast if, on opening up his house and granting his fellow citizens access to his possessions, he can say: 'Any man may take away whatever he recognizes as his own.' What a great man he would be, how excellently rich, if after such an offer his wealth is in no way diminished! My meaning

is this: if at no risk and calmly he has allowed the people to make a thorough inspection, if nothing is discovered under his roof to which any man may lay claim, then he will be a rich man boldly and for all to see. The wise man will allow not a penny that enters dishonestly to cross his threshold; likewise he will not reject or refuse access to great wealth that is the gift of Fortune and the reward of virtue. For what reason has he for denying it decent quarters? Let it come, let it receive hospitality. He will neither display it ostentatiously nor hide it from men's eyes—the one is typical of a foolish mind, the other of a fearful and petty one that makes him keep a great blessing, so to speak, in his pocket—nor, as I have said, will he cast it out of his house. For what will he say? 'You have no use,' or 'I do not know how to use wealth'? Just as, even if he can complete a journey on foot, he will prefer to take a carriage, so, if he is able to be poor, he will wish to be rich. Therefore he will possess wealth but he will view it as capricious and liable to fly away, and he will not allow it to become burdensome to himself or to any other person. He will bestow it— why have you pricked up your ears, why do you make your pocket ready?—he will bestow it either on good men or on those he can make good, and, choosing with the most careful judgement the most deserving cases, he will bestow it as one who remembers that he must account for his expenses no less than his receipts; he will bestow it only for a proper and justifiable reason, for it counts as a shameful waste when the recipient is not worth the gift; he will have a pocket that is accessible but has no hole in it, one from which much may emerge but nothing drop.

24. Any man who thinks that the bestowing of money is an easy matter, is making a mistake: it is a most difficult business, provided that gifts are made sensibly, not scattered haphazardly and according to one's whim. To one man I do a service, to another I make a return; to another I offer help, to another pity; another I furnish with money because he does not deserve to be brought down by poverty or languish in its grip; to some I will deny my purse despite their need, because their need will not cease even if I should give it; to some I will offer assistance, in certain cases actually forcing them to accept. I cannot treat this matter carelessly; at no time do I register names more carefully than when making gifts. 'What's that?' you say. 'Do you give only to take back?' No, only to avoid waste; the giving of money should have this status: no return should be asked but a return can

be made. One should store away a benefit like a deeply buried treasure only to be dug up in time of necessity. Consider the very house of a wealthy man and how much opportunity it provides for conferring benefit! Who calls upon Roman citizens alone to enjoy his generosity? Nature prompts me to benefit all men. What difference does it make whether they are slaves or free men, freeborn or freedmen, owing their freedom to the laws or to a gift made in the presence of friends? Wherever there is a human being, there exists the opportunity for an act of kindness. One can, accordingly, be lavish with money even inside one's own house and find scope there for liberality, which is so called, not because it is owed to those who enjoy liberty, but because it proceeds from a mind at liberty. In the case of a wise man this is never thrown at undeserving men of low character and never makes the error of being so weary that it fails to flow from a full hand, as it were, whenever it finds a worthy candidate.

You are, therefore, unjustified in hearing wrongly the honourable, brave, and spirited utterances made by those who are devoted to wisdom. And take note above all of this point: it is one thing to be devoted to wisdom and another to have attained it already. A man in the first category will say to you: 'The words I utter are excellent but I still wallow in a host of vices. You are not justified in requiring that I live up to my own standard at the very time when I am creating and fashioning myself, attempting to raise myself to the height of a lofty ideal; if I succeed in reaching this great goal, then require that my actions correspond to my words.' But the man who has indeed reached the acme of human good will give you a different argument, and will say: 'In the first instance you have no justification for allowing yourself to pass judgement on your betters; I have already had the good fortune to earn the criticism of the wicked, which is a proof of my upright nature. But so that I may give you the explanation which I grudge to no man, hear what I profess and what value I put on each thing. I say that wealth is not a good; for if it was, it would make men good; as it is, since something that is found among wicked men cannot be called a good, I deny it this name. But that it is desirable, that is useful and confers great benefits on life, I do admit.

25. 'Since we both agree that it is a desirable thing, hear my reason for excluding it from the number of goods, and also the sense in which I differ from you in my attitude to it. Put me in the most sumptuous of mansions, put me in a place where gold and silver plate are used by one and all: I shall not think myself important because of those accoutrements which, though they are part of my house, are no part of me. Take me off to the Sublician Bridge* and throw me among the beggars there: I shall still not find any reason for despising myself because I sit among those who stretch out their hands for charity. For what difference does it make when a man is in need of a crust of bread if he does not lack the ability to die? My conclusion, then, you ask? I prefer that splendid mansion to the bridge. Surround me with expensive furnishings and luxurious fittings: I shall not believe myself to be a jot happier because I have a soft cloak or my guests recline on purple. Change my mattress: I shall not be in any way more wretched if my weary neck rests on a handful of hay, if I shall sleep on a circus cushion whose stuffing spills out from its patches of old cloth. And what is my point? I would rather display the state of my soul wearing a toga and shoes than having naked shoulders and cuts on my bare feet. Let every day pass as I would wish it to, let new congratulations join the old: I will not on this account give way to self-love. Alter this generosity of time to the opposite, let my soul be buffeted from this quarter and that by loss, by grief, by various misfortunes, let no hour lack some ground for complaint: I will not on this account call myself the most miserable of the miserable, I shall not on this account curse any one day; for I have seen to it that no one day shall be a black one for me. And what do I conclude? I would rather moderate my joys than suppress my sorrows.'

This is what you will be told by a Socrates:* 'Make me victorious over all the world's nations, let Bacchus' luxurious chariot bear me in triumph from the sunrise all the way to Thebes,* let monarchs seek laws from me; I shall especially consider myself a man in those moments when I am hailed on all sides as a god. Combine at once with such a lofty height a headlong plunge to altered fortune; let me be placed on a foreign litter* to grace the public procession of some proud and savage conqueror; I shall be just as humble when I am driven before another man's chariot as when I stood erect on my own. And what do I conclude? I still prefer to conquer rather than to become a captive. I will scorn the entire domain of Fortune, but I shall select the better part of it, if a choice be given me. Whatever happens to me shall become a good, but I would rather that my experience should be of things more agreeable and pleasant and less awkward to manage. For while there is no reason for you to suppose that any virtue is gained without effort, there are certain virtues that require the spur, certain ones the bridle. Just as the body must be held back on a downward slope, or forced up a steep one, so certain virtues are on a downward path, while certain others labour uphill. Can there be any doubt that patience, resolution, and perseverance, together with every other virtue that is opposed to hardship and masters Fortune, have to scale the heights and struggle and strive on the way? And what is my conclusion? Is it not equally clear that generosity, moderation, and kindness find themselves on a downward path? In their case we impose a check on the soul in case it should slip, but, where the others are concerned, we urge and spur it on like the most vigorous of horsemen. Accordingly, in the case of poverty we shall apply those more robust virtues that know how to fight, but in that of wealth those more circumspect ones that proceed on tiptoe and yet do not lose their balance. As this difference between them exists, my preference is to have recourse to the virtues that can be practised relatively peacefully rather than to those that draw blood and sweat from the man who engages in them. In consequence,' concludes our sage adviser, 'I do not live one way and speak another, but rather it is you who hear me in another way; the sound alone of my words reaches to your ears: the meaning of these words you do not enquire.'

26. 'What difference is there, accordingly, between me, the fool, and you, the wise man, if both of us wish to have wealth?' A very great one: for the wise man regards wealth as a slave, the fool as a master; the wise man accords no importance to wealth, but in your eyes wealth is everything; you make yourselves accustomed to it and cling to it, as though someone had promised that you would possess it for all time, but the wise man never gives more thought to poverty than when he finds himself surrounded by wealth. A commander never puts such trust in peace that he fails to prepare for a war that has been declared, even if it is not actually being waged: but you are made arrogant by a beautiful house, as though it cannot catch fire or collapse, you are reduced to astonishment by your riches, as though they have escaped all danger and have reached such proportions that Fortune has lost all power to destroy them. In your idleness you play with your wealth without foreseeing the danger it faces, in this respect resembling barbarians who, normally, when they are besieged, as they lack all knowledge of engines of war, stare with indifference at the toiling besiegers, not understanding the purpose of the artillery being erected

far off. The same thing is happening in your case: you take your ease amid your possessions without a thought for all the misfortunes that threaten them on every side, poised any moment now to carry off the valuable spoils. But in the case of the wise man, if anyone steals his wealth, he will still leave to him all that he truly possesses; for he lives happy in the present and untroubled by what the future holds.

'There is nothing', says a Socrates, or any other who has the same authority and the same capacity for dealing with human affairs, 'I am so determined on as my resolve not to let your views alter the course of my life. Pile the familiar criticisms from all sides on my head: I shall not think of you as heaping abuse on me but rather as wailing like the most wretched little babies.' These will be the words of the man who has discovered wisdom, whose soul, untarnished by any vice, prompts him to take other men to task, not out of hatred but so that he might bring them a cure. To these thoughts he will add the following: 'I am influenced by your opinion of me, not on my own account, but on yours, because to hate and assail virtue with your shouts is to abandon the hope of being good. You do no harm to me, but neither do these men do any harm to the gods when they overturn their altars. But a wicked intention and a wicked plan are plain to see even where they lack the power to do harm. In this way I tolerate your silly babblings, just as Jupiter Greatest and Best puts up with the foolish imaginings of poets, one of whom gives him wings,* another horns, while another has portrayed him as the great adulterer who stays up all hours; another, still, as cruel towards the gods, another as unjust towards men, another as the ravisher of freeborn youths and even of his relations, another as a father-killer and usurper of another's throne, his own father's as well: these men have achieved nothing more than to deprive men of a sense of shame at doing wrong, if they believe the gods are like this. But although such insults do me no harm, I nonetheless give you this advice for your own sake: admire virtue, believe those who have pursued her for a long time and who claim that they are themselves pursuing something which is great and which daily is seen to be greater, and revere her as you do the gods, and her exponents as you do their priests, and, whenever any mention is made of sacred writings, "show favour with your tongues". This expression derives not, as most people suppose, from "favour" as in "applause", but commands silence so that a sacred rite can be performed in the proper manner without being marred by the interruption of an

inauspicious word; but it is far more necessary that you subject yourselves to this command, so that, whenever some utterance proceeds
from that oracle, you may listen attentively and with hushed lips.
Whenever someone, brandishing the holy rattle,* affects to speak with
authority, whenever someone accomplished in slashing his own muscles with a light hand makes his arms and shoulders run with blood,
whenever some woman shrieks as she crawls along the road on her
knees, and some old man, wearing linen and carrying a laurel branch
and a lantern in front of him in broad daylight, cries out that a particular god is angry, you run together as a crowd and listen and, nurturing
one another's dumb astonishment, declare him to be divine.'

27. Hear now Socrates cry out from that prison* which he made
pure by entering it and made more honourable than any senate-house:
'What frenzy is this, what instinct for making war on gods and men
alike that leads you to disgrace the virtues and to profane by your
wicked talk things that are holy? If you are able, praise the good, if
not, speak not of them; but if it is your wish to give free rein to such
foul calumny, direct your attacks at one another. For when you rage
against heaven, I do not say, "You are committing sacrilege", but
"you are wasting your effort". I once provided Aristophanes with
subject-matter for his jokes,* the entire company of comic poets has
showered its barbs of poisoned wit upon me: the very means they
used to attack my virtue made it shine out the more; for it suits it to
be brought into the public eye and put to the test, and no men understand how great it is better than those who have come to know its
strength by assailing it: the hardness of flint no men know better than
those who strike it. I show myself like some desolate rock in shallow
seawaters that the waves never stop beating on, from whichever
quarter they have risen, but nonetheless they do not shake it from its
base or wear it away by their unending onslaught over many ages.
Leap upon me, make your attack: I will defeat you by endurance.
Whatever dashes against that which is steadfast and invincible uses
up its own power to its own detriment: therefore seek for some pliant
and yielding object in which to stick your weapons.

'But as for you, have you the leisure to examine other people's evils
and to pass judgement on anyone? "Why does this philosopher have so
extensive a house? Why does this man dine so elegantly?" Do you look
at other men's pimples when you are yourselves covered with a mass
of open sores? This is tantamount to a man who is being devoured

by a foul itch mocking moles or warts on very beautiful bodies. Criticize Plato* for seeking money, Aristotle for accepting it, Democritus for ignoring it, Epicurus for using it up; cast Alcibiades and Phaedrus in my own face as a reproach, though you will find yourselves at your happiest when you have the luck to be copying my vices. Why do you not take a look at your own sins that stab you on every side, some assailing you from outside, others raging in your very innards? Human affairs, even if you are not sufficiently aware of your own situation, are not yet in such a position that you may have such an abundance of leisure as to have the spare time to wag your tongue in vilifying your betters.

28. 'This is a point you fail to understand, and your faces wear an expression that hardly suits your condition, indeed, you are just like the numerous men who sit idly in the circus or a theatre, while their home is already a scene of mourning and they have not yet heard the terrible news. But I, gazing from on high, see the storms that threaten and in a short while from now will burst in torrents upon you, or, already near at hand, have advanced closer still, to sweep both you and yours away. Need I say more? Though you little realize it, are not your minds even now whirled round and spun about by some hurricane, as they flee and seek the same objects, at one moment raised up to highest heaven, at another dashed to the lowest abyss . . .'*

ON THE TRANQUILLITY OF THE MIND

TO SERENUS

1. SERENUS:* When I examined myself, Seneca, it appeared that certain of my vices are so plain to view that I can lay my hand on them, certain others are less visible and hide in a corner, while others, again, are not permanent but recur at intervals, and I should say that it is this last category which causes by far the greatest trouble, like an enemy that never stays still and leaps out at you as opportunity arises, allowing you neither to be ready as in war nor to drop your guard as in peace. However, the condition I find myself in predominantly (for why should I not confess the truth to you as I would to a doctor?),* is that in all honesty I have neither been set free from the things I feared and hated, nor, conversely, am I in their thrall; I find myself in a state that may not be the worst but is yet one of complaint and fretfulness: I am neither ill nor well. You need not point out that all the virtues are delicate at the outset but acquire firmness and strength in time; I am also fully aware that the virtues which strive for outward show, I mean for status and the great name of eloquence and whatever else comes under the judgement of others, do become stronger as time passes— both those that confer true strength and those that embellish the wearer with a sort of make-up to please the eye have to wait several years for length of time gradually to develop colour—but my particular fear is that habit, which brings stability to most things, will make this fault I have more deeply fixed in me: lengthy dealings with things evil, no less than good, cause us to love them.

The nature of this mental weakness which hovers between two alternatives, inclining strongly neither to the right nor to the wrong, I can better show you one part at a time than all at once; I will tell you my experience, you will find a name for my sickness. I am completely devoted, I admit, to frugality: I do not like a couch made up for show, or clothing produced from a chest or pressed by weights and a thousand mangles to make it shiny, but rather something homely and inexpensive that has not been kept specially or needs to be put on with anxious care; I like food that a household of slaves has not prepared, watching it with envy, that has not been ordered many days in advance or served up by many hands, but is easy to fetch and in ample supply; it has nothing outlandish or expensive about it, and will be readily available everywhere, it will not put a strain on one's purse or body, or return by the way it entered; I like for my servant a young house-bred slave without training or polish, for silverware my country-bred father's heavy plate that bears no maker's stamp, and for a table one that is not remarkable for the variety of its markings* or known to Rome for having passed through the hands of many stylish owners, but one that is there to be used, that makes no guest stare at it in endless pleasure or burning envy. Then, after finding perfect satisfaction in all such things, I find my mind is dazzled by the splendour of some training-school for pages, by the sight of slaves decked out in gold and more scrupulously dressed than bearers in a procession, and a whole troop of brilliant attendants; by the sight of a house where even the floor one treads is precious and riches are strewn in every corner, where the roofs themselves shine out, and the citizen body waits in attendance and dutifully accompanies an inheritance whose days are numbered; need I mention the waters, transparent to the bottom and flowing round the guests even as they dine, or the banquets that in no way disgrace their setting? Emerging from a long time of dedication to thrift, luxury has enveloped me in the riches of its splendour, filling my ears with all its sounds: my vision falters a little, for it is easier for me to raise my mind to it than my eyes; and so I come back, not a worse man, but a sadder one, I no longer walk with head so high among those worthless possessions of mine, and I feel the sharpness of a secret pain as the doubt arises whether that life is not the better one. None of these things alters me, but none fails to unsettle me.

It is my intention to follow the instructions of my teachers and to plunge into public life; it is my intention to attain public office and the consulship, not because I am attracted by the purple or the lictors' rods,* but so that I may be of greater service and usefulness to my friends and relatives and to all my fellow citizens, and then to all men. Readily I follow Zeno, Cleanthes, and Chrysippus,* though not one of them entered public life and not one failed to encourage others to do likewise. Whenever something disturbs my mind, that is unaccustomed to receiving shocks, whenever something happens that is either unworthy of me, as occurs often in the lives of all men, or that makes only sluggish progress, or when things not deserving serious consideration demand much of my time, I turn back to my leisure and quicken my pace towards home, as tired flocks will also do. It is my intention to restrict my life within its own walls: 'Let no one steal from me a single day, if he does not mean to make me a fitting return for such a loss; let my mind be rooted in itself, let it cultivate itself and involve itself in nothing external, nothing that requires an umpire; let it show love for the tranquillity that knows nothing of public or private concern.' But when my mind is roused by reading of high courage and goaded by examples of nobility, I want to dash into the forum, to lend my voice to one man and my support to another, a support that will attempt to benefit him, even if it will not actually do so, and to curb the pride of another whose head has become foolishly swollen by his successes.

In my studies I consider it definitely better to concentrate on the actual topic and to let this direct my speech,* while trusting the topic to provide the words so that spontaneous language may follow wherever it leads: 'What need is there to compose something that is going to last for centuries? Won't you stop trying to ensure that you will be talked of by future generations? Death is what you were born for, and a funeral without words is less irksome. Accordingly, to use up the time, write something in unaffected style, to suit your own purpose, not for publication: those who study for the day don't need to work so hard.' Again, when my mind has been uplifted by great thoughts, it is seized by ambition for words and a desire to make loftier expression match loftier aspirations, so that language emerges in keeping with the dignity of the topic; then I forget my rule and more restrictive judgement and soar to loftier heights, uttering words no longer my own.

Not to pursue details any longer, I am dogged in every sphere by this feebleness of good intention. I fear that little by little I am being eclipsed by it, or, which gives me more concern, that I am hanging on like a man in constant danger of falling, and that the situation is perhaps more serious than my own perception of it suggests; for we look kindly on our private concerns, and this bias constantly blocks our judgement. In my view many men would have attained to wisdom, had they not supposed they had already done so, had there not been certain inner failings they had pretended were not there, and certain ones they had passed by with their eyes shut. For you have no reason to judge that other people's flattery is more destructive to us than our own. Who ever dares to tell himself the truth? Who, though he stands in the midst of a herd of sycophants who sing his praises, is not despite all this his own greatest flatterer?

I ask you, therefore, if you possess any cure by which you can check this fluctuation of mine, to consider me worthy of being indebted to you for tranquillity. I am aware that these mental disturbances I suffer from are not dangerous and bring no threat of a storm; to express to you in a true analogy the source of my complaint, it is not a storm I labour under but seasickness: relieve me, then, of this malady, whatever it be, and hurry to aid one who struggles with land in his sight.

2. SENECA: For a long time now, Serenus, I assure you, I have been asking myself in silence to what I should liken this mental state of yours, and the closest parallel I can find is the condition of those who, having gained release from a lengthy and serious illness, are sometimes affected by feverish fits and minor disorders, and, despite being freed from the final traces of these, are still troubled by feelings of doubt and, now in full health, hold out their wrists to their doctors, complaining unfairly about any feeling of warmth in their body. With these people, Serenus, it is not that they are not quite well physically, but that they are not quite used to being well, just as even a tranquil sea will show a ripple or two, especially when it has subsided after a storm. Accordingly, you have no need of those harsher measures that we have already passed over, that of sometimes opposing yourself, of sometimes getting angry with yourself, of sometimes fiercely driving yourself on, but rather of the one that comes last, having confidence in yourself and believing that you are on the right path and have not been sidetracked by the footprints crossing over, left by many rushing in different directions, some of them wandering close to the path itself. But what you long for is a thing that is great, supreme, and very close to the state of being a god: to be unshaken. This constant state of mental composure the Greeks call *euthymia*, on which Democritus* has written an outstanding treatise; I call it tranquillity; for it is unnecessary to imitate and reproduce words in Greek lettering: the actual thing under discussion needs to be designated by some name which must have the force, not the form, of the Greek term. Our enquiry, then, is directed at how the mind should proceed always on a steady and favourable course, may have good intentions towards itself, and may take pleasure in regarding its state and have no interruption mar this joy, but remain in a peaceful condition, at no time raising itself up or casting itself down: this will be tranquillity. Let us seek universally how this can be attained: it will then be for you to choose from the universal solution whatever you wish. In the meantime it is necessary to drag the entire weakness into plain view, and everyone will then recognize what part of it ails him; at the same time you will understand how much less difficulty you have with self-criticism than those who, chained to some impressive declaration and struggling beneath some grand title, continue attached to the pretence they are making more by a sense of shame than by any desire.

Everyone is in the same predicament, both those who are tormented by inconstancy and boredom and an unending change of purpose, constantly taking more pleasure in what they have just abandoned, and those who idle away their time, yawning. Add to them those who twist and turn like insomniacs, trying all manner of positions until in their weariness they find repose: by altering the condition of their life repeatedly, they end up finally in the state that they are caught, not by dislike of change, but by old age that is reluctant to embrace anything new. Add also those who through the fault, not of determination but of idleness, are too constant in their ways, and live their lives not as they wish, but as they began. The sickness has countless characteristics but only one effect, dissatisfaction with oneself. This arises from a lack of mental balance and desires that are nervous or unfulfilled, when men's daring or attainment falls short of their desires and they depend entirely on hope; such are always lacking in stability and changeable, the inevitable consequence of living in a state of suspense. By every way they strive to realize their prayers, instructing and compelling themselves to do dishonourable and difficult things, and when their effort brings no reward, they feel the torment of the futile disgrace and are pained by the thought, not that their ambition was wrong, but that it was unproductive. That is when they feel regret at what they began and fear of beginning again, and there steals over them that agitation of a mind that can find no way out, because they can neither command nor obey their desires, together with the hesitancy of a life that cannot win freedom for itself and the torpor of a mind that lies sluggish amid abandoned prayers.

All these feelings are aggravated when disgust at the effort they have spent on becoming unsuccessful drives men to leisure, to solitary studies, which are unendurable for a mind intent on a public career, eager for employment, and by nature restless, since without doubt it possesses few enough resources for consolation; for this reason, once it has been deprived of those delights that business itself affords to active participants, the mind does not tolerate home, solitude, or the walls of a room, and does not enjoy seeing that it has been left to itself. This is the source of that boredom and dissatisfaction, of the wavering of a mind that finds no rest anywhere, and the sad and spiritless endurance of one's leisure; and particularly when one is ashamed to confess the reasons for these feelings, and diffidence drives its torments inwards, the desires, confined in a narrow space from which there is no escape, choke one-another; hence come grief and melancholy and the thousand fluctuations of an uncertain mind, held in suspense by early hopes and then reduced to sadness once they fail to materialize; this causes that feeling which makes men loathe their own leisure and complain that they themselves have nothing to keep them occupied, and also the bitterest feelings of jealousy of other men's successes. For envy is fostered by their unhappy inactivity, and they desire the ruin of everyone, as they have not been able to succeed themselves; then, as a result of this disgust at the progress of others and the feeling that no progress will ever be theirs, the mind of these men becomes angry at Fortune and complains about the times, withdrawing into corners and brooding over its sorry fate until it grows weary and irritated with itself. For by nature the mind of man is active and prone to movement. It welcomes all opportunities for excitement and diversion, and these are even more welcome to all those worst natures that enjoy wearing themselves out with whatever employs them; just as certain sores yearn for the hands that will harm them, delighting in their touch, and a foul itch of the body takes pleasure in whatever scratches it, in the same way, I would say, toil and trouble are a source of pleasure to these minds on which desires, like dangerous sores, have broken out. For there exist certain things that gratify our body also while bringing it a kind of pain, for example turning over and changing a side that is not yet tired and moving from one position to another in order to cool off: Homer's hero Achilles is like this,* now lying face-down, now on his back, adopting all manner of positions, and, like a man who is ill, tolerating nothing for any length of time and using change as a cure.

For this reason men undertake far-ranging travel abroad, wandering over shores, and their inconstancy, always at odds with the present, demonstrates itself now by sea, now by land. 'Let's make for

Campania* now.' But the life of luxury has already begun to pall: 'Let's see some wild country, let's go in search of the glens of Bruttium and Lucania.' But in that wilderness some beauty is found wanting, something to bring their pampered eyes relief from the unending desolation of the rugged landscape: 'Let's make for Tarentum, with its celebrated harbour and mild climate in the winter months, a region rich enough to have hundreds of inhabitants even in early days.' 'Oh, let's travel back to the city now:' for too long their ears have lacked the shouts and noise of the crowd, by now what they crave is even human blood. One journey after another they embark on, one spectacle they exchange for another. As Lucretius says,

> Thus each man ever flees himself.*

But what good does it do him if he does not escape from himself? He constantly follows himself and oppresses himself as his own most irksome companion. Accordingly, we ought to know that what makes us struggle is the fault, not of our locations, but of ourselves: we are weak when anything has to be endured, and unable to bear toil or pleasure or ourselves or anything for any length of time. This is what has driven certain men to death, because by frequently changing their intentions they were constantly brought back to the same things and had left themselves no scope for novelty: they began to grow sick of life and the world itself, and their self-indulgent ways that sapped their vigour gave rise to the thought: 'How long shall I put up with the same things?'

3. You ask what help in my opinion should be adopted to combat this feeling of boredom. The best course, as Athenodorus* says, would be to engage in practical matters, the administration of public business and the duties of a citizen. For as certain men spend the day in seeking out the sun and in the exercise and care of the body, and as it is most useful for athletes to spend the greater part of the day building up their muscles and stamina, to which alone they have dedicated themselves, so for men such as you, who are preparing the mind for the contests of public life, the finest course by far is to be engaged in a task; for since he has resolved to make himself useful to his fellow citizens and to mankind at large, he receives training and at the same time contributes if he has set himself right in the heart of public duties, serving both public and individual interests as best he can. 'But because,' he says, 'in this crazed world of ambition, with

so many people making false accusations and twisting right into wrong, there is little safety in honesty, which is always liable to meet with obstruction more than support, we should definitely withdraw from the forum and public life, but even in private life a great mind has scope for displaying itself freely; and the case of lions and other animals is different, for their energies are confined within their dens, but men's greatest achievements are the products of their seclusion. However, he should hide himself away on this condition, that, wherever the secret location of his leisure hours, he should make it his aim to benefit individual men and the world at large by means of his intellect, his voice, and his advice; for service to the state is not rendered solely by the man who brings forward candidates and defends the accused and gives his vote for peace and war, but also by the man who encourages young men, who in the great shortage of good teachers instils virtue into their minds, who lays hold of those who rush headlong in pursuit of money and luxury and pulls them back, and, if nothing else, at least checks their speed—this man is performing a public service, albeit in private life. Is a greater contribution made by that man who as praetor decides cases between citizens and foreigners or citizens and citizens, delivering to the parties a verdict his assistant has phrased, or by that man who teaches the nature of justice, of a sense of duty, of endurance, of courage, of contempt for death, of understanding the gods, of how free is the blessing of a good conscience? Accordingly, if you devote to studies the time you have stolen from public duties, you will neither have abandoned nor refused your office. For he is not the only kind of soldier who stands in the line of battle and defends the right wing or the left; there is also the one who guards the gates, occupying a post that is less dangerous but far from idle, who maintains a watch through the night and is in charge of the armoury; these tasks may not risk bloodshed, but they count as the service of a soldier. If you concentrate on studies, you will have escaped all your loathing of life, you will not long for nightfall through weariness of daylight, you will not be irksome to yourself or useless to others; you will win the friendship of many and those who collect at your side will be of the greatest merit. For virtue never goes undetected, however much obscured, but always indicates its presence: whoever is worthy will trace her whereabouts from her footprints. For if we dispense with all social intercourse and, turning our backs on the human race, we live turned in on ourselves alone, this solitary

state lacking in any interest will be followed by a lack of any projects
to be accomplished: we shall begin to build some buildings and to pull
down others, to push back the sea and to make waters flow despite the
difficulty of the terrain, and to regulate badly the time that Nature
has given us to use. Some of us are economical in using this, others
wasteful; some of us spend it in such a way that we are able to keep
an account, others in such a way that we have nothing left as balance,
which is the most shameful situation of all. Many a time an old man
well advanced in years has no other evidence to prove his length of
life than his age.'

4. It strikes me, my dearest Serenus, that Athenodorus has surren-
dered too readily to the times and beaten too hasty a retreat. I would
not myself ever deny that it is sometimes necessary to give ground,
but it should be a gradual withdrawal, and without prejudice to the
standards or to the honour of a soldier: men who come to terms keeping their weapons win greater respect from their foes and are less
likely to be harshly treated. This is what I consider should be done
by virtue and by its devotee: if Fortune triumphs and cuts off any
opportunity for action, let him not immediately turn round and,
casting away his weapons, flee in search of a place to hide, as though
there were any place where Fortune could not reach him, but rather
be more sparing in applying himself to his duties, and, exercising
choice, let him find some employment where he may be of service to
the state. Service in the army is denied him: let him seek public
office. He must live in a private capacity: let him plead cases. He is
condemned to observe silence: let him aid his fellow citizens by his
unvoiced support. It is dangerous for him even to enter the forum: in
private houses, at public entertainments, at dinner parties let him
show himself the good comrade, the loyal friend, the moderate
table companion. He has lost the duties of a citizen: let him practise
those of a man. This was our reason for showing magnanimity in not
confining ourselves within the walls of a single city, in journeying
forth to embrace contact with all the earth, in declaring the world to
be our homeland, namely that we might have a broader field for our
virtue. The tribunal has been closed to you and you are barred from
the speakers' platform or the hustings: look behind you at the number
of expansive countries that lie open, at the number of nations; never
shall you be blocked from a part so large that a larger one does not
remain at your disposal. But beware that this may be entirely your

own fault; you do not want to serve your country except as a consul or prytanis* or herald or sufes.* What if you were unwilling to serve in the army unless you were a general or a tribune? Even if others hold the front line and fate has placed you among the third row of soldiers, play your part from where you stand with your voice, your encouragement, your example, your spirit: even if his hands have been chopped off, a man finds something to do for his side in battle if he stands there nonetheless and shouts support. This is the sort of thing you should do: if Fortune has thrust you away from the first role in the state, you should still stand your ground and shout your support, and, if anyone blocks your throat, you should stand there nonetheless and support in silence. The service of a good citizen is never without some use: when he is heard or seen, by his expression, by a nod of the head, by his silent obduracy, by his very walk he confers benefit. As there are certain things conferring health that, without being tasted or touched, produce their effect by means of smell alone, so virtue sheds her benefit even from a distance and when hidden from our eyes. Whether she walks out of doors and employs herself of her own right, whether she appears in response to entreaty and is compelled to shorten sail, or is unemployed, without voice and narrowly confined, or is openly revealed; in whatever state she finds herself, she confers benefit. Why do you consider of little value the example of a man who makes honourable use of a life no longer active? It is, therefore, the best course by far to mix leisure with employment, whenever a life of activity is prevented by chance obstacles or the condition of the state; for never does a man find himself so barred from all pursuits that there is scope for no honourable activity.

5. Are you able to find any city in a more miserable condition than that of the Athenians when the Thirty Tyrants were dismembering it?* They had murdered thirteen-hundred of the city, all the best men, and were not ready to cease on that account, but rather their very savagery was sustained by its own energy. In that city where there was the Areopagus,* a most revered court, where there was a senate and an assembly of the people that resembled a senate, there used to meet every day a grim college of executioners, and the unhappy senate house was deprived of space to move by tyrants: could that city reach a state of peace when it contained as many tyrants as there might be hangers-on? Men's hearts could not be offered even any hope of regaining freedom, and there appeared to be no scope for any

remedy against the great power held by these wicked men; for where was the wretched city to look for enough men of Harmodius'* stamp? Socrates was, however, in their midst, offering comfort to the city fathers in their grief and encouragement to those who despaired of the state, and he castigated the rich citizens who were now dreading their own wealth for their late display of repentance of their dangerous greed, carrying round with him for those who wished to copy him an impressive example, as he walked a free man among thirty masters. Yet this was the man whom Athens itself put to death in prison, and liberty did not tolerate the liberty of the man who had with impunity mocked an entire troop of tyrants: you may learn from this both that a wise man has the opportunity even in a state in turmoil to make his mark, and that envy together with a thousand other craven vices reign in a city when it is flourishing and prosperous. Accordingly, we shall expand or contract our efforts depending on how the state accommodates to us and the scope we are given by Fortune, but in any case we shall continue to move and not become sluggish by letting fear make prisoners of us. No, the true man will be he who, when perils threaten on every side, and weapons and chains rattle around him, will neither bring his virtue into danger nor conceal it; for burying yourself is not saving yourself. It was truly said, in my view, by Curius Dentatus,* that he would rather be a dead man than a live one dead: it is the worst of evils to depart from the number of the living before you die. But your necessary course of action, should you coincide with a time when it is difficult to pursue a public career, will be to claim more time for leisure and literature, and, as if you were on a dangerous voyage, to make for harbour occasionally, and, without waiting for public affairs to set you free, to take the initiative in separating yourself from them.

6. But we shall be obliged to examine in the first place our own selves, then the business that we mean to undertake, then those people for whose sake or with whom we shall do this.

Before anything it is imperative that a man reaches an estimate of himself, because generally we suppose ourselves to be capable of more than we are: one man comes to grief by having confidence in his eloquence, another puts pressure on his ailing constitution by engaging in a laborious task. Certain men find that their modesty is not at all suited to civil matters, that require a bold front; certain ones have an inflexible nature that makes them unsuitable for the court; some do not have control over their anger and any kind of irritation prompts them to the use of rash words; some do not know how to control their humour and cannot stop indulging in dangerous witticisms: in the case of all such men retirement brings more advantage than business; a headstrong and intolerant nature should avoid all that might incite a freedom of speech that will do harm.

We must next evaluate what we propose to undertake, and compare our strength with the tasks we intend to attempt. For the person concerned in performing a task must always be stronger than the task: loads that are too heavy for their bearer must bring him to his knees. Besides, certain enterprises are not so much great as productive, and so lead to many more enterprises: you should shun those which will give rise to fresh business of many different kinds, and not approach any task from which you are not free to withdraw; you should take an active interest in those whose end you can achieve or, at least, expect to see, and leave alone those that expand more as you proceed and do not come to an end at the place you intended.

7. In our choice of men we must show particular care, considering whether they merit our devoting part of our life to them, or whether the loss of our time extends also to them; for some men actually hold us responsible for the services we render them. Athenodorus says that he would not accept even an invitation to dinner from a man who would not feel indebted to him for agreeing to come. I take it you understand that he would be much less inclined to dine with those who pay back the services of friends by their hospitality, who set out the different courses like cash donations, as though it made them extravagant to show honour to others: remove the witnesses and spectators from hosts like these and they will find little pleasure in eating without company.

You need to reflect whether your nature is more suited to participation in affairs or to leisurely study and contemplation, and you need to turn to that course to which the force of your natural ability shall guide you: Isocrates laid his hand on Ephorus' shoulder* and led him away from the forum, thinking he would be more of use in writing the records of history. Natural abilities do not respond well to compulsion; when Nature is in opposition, labour is fruitless.

Nothing, however, delights the mind as much as loving and loyal friendship. How great a blessing it is to have those whose hearts are ready to receive every secret in confidence, whose knowledge of you causes you less fear than your knowledge of yourself, whose conversation relieves your anxiety, whose opinion facilitates your decision, whose cheerfulness scatters your gloomy thoughts, whose very appearance makes you joyful! Our choice will naturally fall on those who, as far as possible, are free from personal desires; for vices move stealthily, and swiftly pass to all those nearest, spreading their contagion. Accordingly, just as in time of plague we must take care not to sit beside those bodies that have already been infected and burn with the disease, since we will attract danger and be at risk from their breath itself, so in selecting friends we shall pay attention to their characters so that we may enlist as few as possible who suffer from impurities: it is the beginning of disease to combine what is sick and what is healthy. But I would not instruct you to follow or to invite into your circle only a man of wisdom. For where will you discover that man whom we have been trying for so many centuries to find? As a substitute for the best man choose the least bad. You would scarcely have the chance to make a happier choice, if you were searching for good men among the Platos and Xenophons and all that great company of Socratic stock, or if you had at your command the age of Cato,* that produced very many men worthy of being born in Cato's time (just as it produced many of worse character than any other age had witnessed, and authors of the most heinous crimes; for both classes were required for a proper understanding of Cato to be achieved: he had to have both good men whose favour he might gain and bad ones on whom to test his powers): but these days, when good men are in such scant supply, you must be less scrupulous in making your choice. But you should avoid in particular those of a melancholy disposition who find cause for tears in everything and enjoy every opportunity for complaint. He may show you constant loyalty and goodwill, but a companion who is disturbed and laments everything is an enemy to tranquillity.

8. Let us turn now to inheritances, the greatest cause of human distress; for should you compare all the other ills that make us suffer — deaths, illnesses, fears, longings, endurance of pains and toils — with the evils that our money causes us, this portion will easily preponderate. We must therefore reflect how much easier to bear is the pain of not having money than that of losing it: and we will come to realize that the less opportunity for loss poverty provides, the less likely it is to torment us. For you are in error if you suppose that rich men put up

with losses more cheerfully: the largest bodies feel the pain of a wound no less than the smallest. It is a neat saying of Bion's* that bald men are just as irked by having their hairs plucked as those well-thatched. You may be sure that rich and poor men are in the same position, that their suffering is no different; for their money sticks fast to both groups, and cannot be torn away without their feeling it. But it is easier to endure, as I said, and less stressful not to acquire it than to lose it, and that is why you will see that those whom Fortune has never valued are happier than those she has abandoned. Diogenes* observed this, that man of mighty soul, and he saw to it that nothing could be snatched from him. You are free to call this state poverty, want, need, to give whatever shameful name you please to this composure: I shall regard him as not happy if you find me someone else who has nothing to lose. Either I delude myself or it is a kingly attribute to be the only man among all the misers, cheats, robbers, and plunderers who cannot be harmed. If anyone is in doubt about the happiness of Diogenes, he can likewise be in doubt about the state enjoyed by the immortal gods as well, whether their lives are not fortunate enough because they have no farms, no private parks, no valuable estates cultivated by a tenant overseas, no vast yield of interest in the forum. Do you not feel ashamed, all those of you who gape in admiration at riches? Come, direct your gaze at the heavens: you will see the gods going without, supplying everything, possessing nothing. Do you think this man who has stripped himself of all Fortune's trappings is poor or like the immortal gods? Do you call Demetrius, Pompey's freedman, who was not ashamed to be wealthier than Pompey, a happier man? This man, who would once have counted it wealth to have two under-slaves and a roomier hut, used to have the roll-call of his slaves reported to him each day as if he were the commander of an army. But Diogenes' only slave ran away and, when he was pointed out to him, he did not think it serious enough to bring him back. 'It would bring me little credit,' he said, 'if Manes can live without Diogenes but Diogenes cannot live without Manes.' I interpret his remark in this way: 'See to your own affairs, Fortune, Diogenes now has nothing of yours: my slave has run away—no, I have won my freedom, I have got away.' A household of servants requires clothing and feeding, so many stomachs of creatures with endless appetites must be catered for, clothing must be purchased for them and a close eye kept on their thieving hands, and we must employ the services of people who weep and curse: how much more fortunate is he who is indebted only to one whom he can most easily refuse, himself! But since we do not have so much strength of character, we should at least reduce the scale of our possessions, so that we may be less exposed to the injustices of Fortune. In war, better service is done by men whose bodies can be packed into their armour than by those whose bodies spill over, leaving their very bulk everywhere a target for wounds: where money is concerned, the ideal amount is one that does not fall into poverty and yet is not far removed from poverty.

9. On the other hand, we will be satisfied with this measure if we were satisfied previously by thrift, without which no quantity of wealth suffices, and no amount is insufficiently generous, particularly since the cure lies near at hand, and poverty of itself can transform itself into wealth by summoning the aid of thrift. Let us grow accustomed to distancing ourselves from mere show and to measuring the uses of things, not their outward attractions. Let food master hunger and drink thirst, let lust follow nature's course; let us learn to rely on our limbs, to make what we wear and eat conform, not to new fashions, but to the customs followed by our ancestors; let us learn to increase our moderation, to restrain our extravagance, to moderate our ambition, to quell our anger, to regard poverty without prejudice, to practise thrift, to apply to nature's wants cures that cost little, to keep in chains, so to speak, hopes that are wild and a mind always fixed on the future, and to make it our aim to seek riches, not from Fortune, but from ourselves.

All the many and diverse cruelties that chance inflicts can never be so repulsed that many storms will not swoop down on those who spread their canvas wide; we must restrict our actions to a narrow compass so that Fortune's arrows may fall on empty space, and this is why banishments and disasters have sometimes turned out to be remedies, and more serious misfortunes have been healed by less severe ones. When the mind defies instruction and cannot by gentler means be brought back to health, why should it not be to its advantage to be treated with a dose of poverty, disgrace, and reversal of fortune, matching evil with evil? Accordingly, let us grow accustomed to being able to take dinner without the people and to being the slave of fewer slaves, to getting clothes for the purpose they were intended for, and to living in less spacious quarters. Not only in the race and contests of the circus but in life's circuits we must keep to the inner circle.

Even in the case of studies, where expenditure is entirely honourable, one can justify it only as long as it observes moderation. What is the point of having books and libraries beyond number, if their owner can barely read through their titles in his whole lifetime? Such a vast collection does not instruct the learner but puts a burden on his back, and it is much better to give yourself up to a few authors than to wander through many. Forty thousand books were destroyed in flames at Alexandria;* let another praise this library as the finest memorial to royal wealth, as Titus Livius did, who described it as an outstanding achievement of the refinement and care shown by kings: that was not a case of 'refinement' or 'care' but of scholarly extravagance, no, not even 'scholarly', as they had acquired the books not for scholarship but for display, just as many who lack even a child's knowledge of literature use books not to further their studies but to decorate their dining-rooms. Accordingly, you should procure as many books as are sufficient, but none merely for show. 'There is more honour', you say, 'in lavishing money on this than on Corinthian bronzes and on pictures.' But all examples of excess become a fault. What reason do you have for excusing a man who seeks to own bookcases of citrus-wood and ivory, who collects the works of authors who are either unknown or discredited and yawns away, surrounded by so many thousands of volumes, who takes his greatest pleasure in the covers of his books and in their titles? It is, then, in the homes of the laziest men you will see a full collection of speeches and histories, and boxes for books piled as high as the roof; for by now, in addition to cold baths and hot baths, a library, too, is fitted out as a necessary embellishment of a great house. I would happily excuse such men, if their excessive enthusiasm for study was leading them astray: as it is, these acquisitions of the works of sacred genius, each with its own author's likeness, are purchased for display and to adorn their walls.

10. But perhaps you have fallen into some area of life that is difficult, and without your realizing it your public or private fortune has caught you in a noose which you can neither untie nor burst: reflect that prisoners at first find the weights and shackles on their legs hard to bear, but subsequently, once they have determined to endure them rather than chafe against them, necessity teaches them to bear them bravely, habit to bear them easily. In whatever sort of life you choose you will find there are delights and relaxations and pleasures, if you are willing to regard your evils as light rather than to make them

objects of hatred. In no respect has Nature done us a greater service, who, as she knew into what tribulations we were born, devised habit as a means of alleviating disasters, swiftly making us grow accustomed to the worst sufferings. No one would endure adversity if throughout its duration it retained the same force as when it first struck. We are all chained to Fortune: for some of us the chain is of gold and loose-fitting, for others, tight and of base metal, but what does it matter? All men are held fast in the same captivity, even those who have bound others have themselves been bound, unless you happen to think that a chain on the left-hand wrist is lighter. One man is held fast by public office, another by wealth; some are weighed down by their aristocratic birth, others by their humble origins; some are subject to another's supreme authority, others to their own; some are kept in one place by exile, others by a priesthood: all life is servitude. A man should therefore grow accustomed to his state and complain about it as little as possible, seizing upon whatever good it may have: no condition is so distressing that a balanced mind cannot find some comfort in it. Small spaces often reveal many different uses when a planner exercises his skill, and careful arrangement will make a place quite habitable, however small its dimensions. Apply reason to difficulties: what is hard can be softened, what is narrow can be expanded, and heavy loads can be less of a burden on the shoulders when borne skilfully. We should not, moreover, dispatch our desires on some distant quest but should grant them access to what is near at hand, since they cannot tolerate being confined altogether. Let us abandon those things that either cannot be done or can only be done with difficulty, and let us pursue what lies close to us and mocks our hope, but let us realize that all of them are equally unimportant, different to look at externally but inside equally futile. And let us not envy those who stand on a higher station: what appeared as heights are precipices.

Those, conversely, who have been put in a position of jeopardy by an unkind lot will be safer by curtailing their pride in things that are themselves proud, and by bringing their fortune down, as much as they can, to the ordinary level. Of course there are many who find it necessary to cling to their pinnacle, from which they cannot come down except by falling, but they may testify that this is the greatest burden they have, namely that they are compelled to be a burden to others, since they are not lifted, but nailed on high; by means of justice, of clemency, of gentleness, by generous and kindly giving let them prepare many defences against misfortunes to come, and, by placing their hope in these, let them bear their suspense in a less anxious frame of mind. Yet nothing can give us such effective release from these waverings of the mind as always to fix some limit on progress, and not leave it to Fortune to decide when it will cease, but to stop of our own volition far short of the limit; in this way there will be some desires to whet the mind but, as they have boundaries, they will not take it into unchartered regions where no certainty exists.

11. What I say above applies to those who are not yet fully formed, to the average and to the unsound, not to the wise man. He has no need to walk fearfully or step by step; so great is his self-confidence that he does not hesitate to confront Fortune and will never give ground to her. He has no grounds for fearing her, because he counts among transitory things not only his property and possessions and social standing but also his own body and his eyes and his hand and whatever else makes life particularly dear to a man, even his own self, and he lives as one who is on loan to himself and intends to return everything without complaint when the debt is recalled. He is not on this account worthless in his own eyes because he knows that he does not belong to himself, but he will do everything with all the care and scrupulousness that a devout and holy man is accustomed to show in looking after goods entrusted to his protection. But when the order comes for him to give them back, he will not remonstrate with Fortune, but will say: 'I thank you for what I have possessed and kept. It has brought me considerable reward to manage your property, but, as this is your command, I give it up, I surrender it with gratitude and pleasure. If you want me to have anything of yours even now, I will look after it; if you desire something else, I return to you my silver, both wrought and coined, my house, and my household.' If Nature should call back what she previously entrusted to us, to her also we shall say: 'Take back a soul that is better than the one you gave; I do not try to be evasive or to hang back; I am perfectly willing for you to have what you gave me before I had consciousness: take it away.' What is burdensome about returning to the place from which you came? The man who will not know how to die well will live badly. Accordingly, we must reduce the value we set on this, and count the breath of life among cheap things. As Cicero says,* if gladiators desire to save their life by every means, we view them with hostility; if they

display contempt for it, we favour them. You should realize that we are in the same situation; for often fear of dying is what causes a man to die. Dame Fortune, who uses us for her amusement, says: 'Why should I save your life, you low, cowardly creature? All the more will you be hacked and stabbed with wounds, as you do not know how to offer up your throat; no, you will both live longer and die more easily if you do not withdraw your neck or hold up your hands in defence but take the blow courageously.' The man who fears death will never do anything worthy of a man who is alive; but he who knows that these were the conditions drawn up for him when he was conceived will live according to this rule and at the same time, through the same strength of mind, he will ensure that none of what happens to him will come unexpectedly. For by looking ahead to all that may happen as though it were going to happen, he will soften the attacks of all ills, which bring nothing unforeseen to those who are prepared and expectant, but come as a serious blow to those who show no concern and expect only blessings. Sickness befalls a man, captivity, disaster, destruction by fire: none of these things, however, is unexpected; I knew in what rowdy company Nature had confined me. So many times in my neighbourhood has there been wailing raised for the dead; so many times have the funerals of those who died before their time passed by my front door, led by torch and taper; often at my side there sounds the crash of a building collapsing; often those bound to me by the forum, by the senate house, by conversation have been carried off by a single night that severs the bond of hands clasped in friendship: should it cause me wonder if dangers that have flitted around me constantly should have lighted eventually on me? A great many men on the point of taking to the sea give no thought to storms. I shall never be ashamed of quoting a bad author if the point he makes is good. Publilius,* who surpassed in vigour the writers of comedy and tragedy whenever he gave up foolish mimes and language aimed at pleasing the gallery, among many other lines more striking than anything served up in tragedy, to say nothing of comedy, also gave us this one:

> Whatever fate one man can strike can come to all of us alike.

If a man takes this truly to heart and remembers, when he views the evils of others, that are in vast supply every day, that they have free access to him also, he will arm himself against them long before their attack comes; too late does the mind equip itself to endure dangers once they have arrived. 'I did not think that this would happen' and 'Would you ever have believed that this would happen?' 'But why not?' is my reply. What wealth does not have following behind it poverty, hunger, and beggary? What position of importance exists whose robe of office and augur's wand and patrician bootlaces do not also have in their retinue rags and the rebuke of the censors' mark, a thousand stains and total disrepute? What kingdom is there for which there are not in store ruination and a trampling underfoot, the tyrant and the executioner? And the intervals that separate such events are not long, but between a man's occupying a throne and his bending at another's knees a mere hour can pass. Be aware, then, that every human condition is subject to change, and that whatever mishap can befall any man can also happen to you. You are wealthy: but are your riches greater than Pompey's? Yet he lacked even bread and water when Gaius, an old kinsman but a novel host, had opened to him Caesar's house so that he might close his own. He may have owned so many rivers whose places of rising and meeting the sea were all within his lands, but he still had to beg for drops of water; he died of hunger and thirst in the palace of his kinsman, and, as he starved, his heir was making arrangements to give him a public funeral. You have held the highest offices of state: were any of them as great or as unexpected or as all-embracing as those held by Sejanus?* On the day that he had the senate as his escort, the people tore him to pieces; of the man on whom men and gods had bestowed every honour that could be heaped on him, nothing survived for the executioner to drag to the Tiber. You are a king: Croesus* is not the monarch I will direct you to, who, while he still lived, witnessed his own funeral pyre being kindled and extinguished, and was made to survive, not just his kingdom, but his own death as well; nor will I direct you to Jugurtha,* whom the people of Rome viewed in chains in less than a year after he had filled them with terror: Ptolemy, king of Africa, and Mithridates,* king of Pontus, we have ourselves seen held prisoner by the guards of Gaius; the one was sent into exile, the other prayed to be sent there in better faith. Considering such great reversals of fortune, that veers now upwards, now downwards, unless you think that whatever can happen may well happen to you, you are delivering yourself into the power of adversity, which anyone can shatter if he sees it first.

12. Our next aim will be to avoid working either for pointless ends or pointlessly, that is, to avoid desiring what we cannot achieve, or what, once attained, will make us realize too late and after much sweat the emptiness of our desires. This means that neither should our effort be fruitless and produce no result, nor should the result be unworthy of our effort; for this generally is accompanied by sadness, if success eludes us or we are ashamed of succeeding. We must reduce the agitation displayed by a great many men when they wander through houses and theatres and forums: they involve themselves in the business affairs of others, always appearing to be engaged in a particular duty. If you ask one of them as he leaves the house, 'Where are you going? What do you have in mind?' he will reply, 'I really don't know; but I'm going to see some people, I have some business to carry out.' Without a plan they rove, searching for work to occupy them, and what they end up doing is not what they have intended to do but whatever they have bumped into; they scurry around without aim or purpose like ants crawling through bushes, that idly make their way to the top of some twig and then to the bottom: it is a life like this that most men lead, one that might justly be described as 'restless idleness'. When you see some of them running as though to some fire, you will feel pity for them: so much do they collide with those in their path, sending themselves and others flying, when all the time they have been running either to pay a call on someone who will not return the compliment, or to attend the funeral of a man they do not know, or the trial of someone who is hardly ever not bringing a suit, or the betrothal ceremony of some woman who frequently gets married, and, attaching themselves to some litter, have even in certain parts of the city carried it; then, as they make their way home, worn out to no purpose, they swear they do not know themselves what made them go out, or where they have been, but on the following day they will wander over the selfsame path they trod. Accordingly, let all your effort be directed towards a particular aim and keep a particular aim in sight. Men are not made restless by activity but driven to madness by false impressions of reality; for not even madmen become agitated unless some hope impels them: what excites them is the outward form of some object, whose falsity their afflicted mind fails to comprehend. In the same way every one of those men who leave home to swell the crowd is led round the city by vain and trivial reasons; and, though he has no business to conduct, daybreak drives him out of doors, and, when he has been crushed in the doorway of many men's houses, all for nothing, and has paid his respects to one nomenclator after another, and has been shut out by many, he discovers that, of them all, not one is harder to catch at home than himself. This evil is responsible for that most repellent vice of eavesdropping and prying into matters public and private, and acquiring knowledge of what is neither safe to tell of nor safe to listen to.

13. I think that this was in the mind of Democritus* when he began: 'If a man wishes to live in tranquillity, let him not engage in many activities either privately or publicly,' with reference, naturally, to superfluous business. For if necessity requires it, not only many but countless things should be done both privately and publicly; but in a case where we are not summoned by any religious duty, we should curtail our activities. For the man who busies himself in many things often gives Fortune power over him, and the safest course is to tempt her only rarely but always to keep her in one's thoughts, never placing any trust in her promises but saying instead: 'I will make the voyage unless something happens,' and 'I will become praetor unless something stands in my way,' and 'My business venture will succeed unless something interferes.' This is why we say that nothing happens to the wise man contrary to his expectation: we exempt him, not from the accidents, but the blunders that befall men, and everything turns out for him, not as he wished, but as he thought; but foremost in his thoughts was the possibility of something obstructing his plans. It is inevitable, furthermore, that the distress caused by the abandonment of a desire affects a man's mind less severely if you have not certainly promised him success.

14. We must also make ourselves flexible, to avoid becoming too devoted to the plans we have formed, and we should make the transition to the state that chance has brought us to without dreading a change either in our purpose or our condition, provided that we are not falling prey to fickleness, a vice entirely at odds with repose. For stubbornness, from which Fortune often forces some concession, must involve anxiety and wretchedness, and at the same time fickleness is much harder to bear when it fails to control itself in any situation. Both are hostile to tranquillity, both the inability to undergo any change and the inability to show endurance. Above all it is necessary for the mind to be withdrawn into itself, abjuring all external interests; let it have confidence in itself and take pleasure in itself, let it admire its

own possessions, withdraw as far as possible from those of others, let it not feel losses and put a kind interpretation even on adversities. When our master Zeno* received news of a shipwreck and heard that all his goods had been sunk, he said: 'This is Fortune's order to me to practise philosophy with less encumbrance.' A tyrant was threatening the philosopher Theodorus with death and even withholding burial: 'You have the right to please yourself,' he replied, 'and the power to take half a pint of my blood; for as far as burial is concerned, what a simpleton you are, if you think it matters to me whether I rot above or below ground!' Julius Canus, a man of greatness that few possess, whom not even the fact of his being born in our times prevents us from admiring, had been involved in a lengthy dispute with Gaius,* and, when he was taking his leave, that Phalaris* said to him, 'In case you happen to take comfort in a foolish hope, I have given orders for your execution.' 'Thank you, best of emperors,' said Canus in reply. I hesitate to say what he meant; for many possibilities occur to me. Did he wish to be insulting and to show how great his cruelty was when it made death a kindness? Or was it a reproach aimed at his daily display of madness?—for those whose children were murdered used to thank him, no less than those whose property was confiscated. Or did he accept death as a fortunate release from captivity? Whatever the explanation, it was a great-hearted response. Someone will say, 'It was possible after this that Gaius might order his life to be spared.' Canus had no fear of this; in such orders Gaius was known to be true to his word. Do you believe that Canus spent the ten days that intervened before his execution without the slightest anxiety? What that man said, what he did, how tranquil he was, strain all credulity. He was playing draughts when the centurion who was dragging off a troop of condemned men gave the order for him as well to be summoned. When he was called he counted the pieces and said to his companion, 'Mind you don't pretend you won after I'm dead;' then with a nod to the centurion he added, 'You will testify that I was one piece ahead.' Do you suppose that Canus played a game at that board? It was a game at the expense of death. His friends were sad at the prospect of losing such a man: 'Why are you sorrowful?' he said. 'You ask if souls are immortal: I will soon know.' And even at the end he did not cease to search for the truth and to make his own death a subject for examination. He was being accompanied by his own instructor in philosophy, and by this time they were not far from the hill on which a daily sacrifice was made to our god Caesar: this man said, 'What thoughts are in your head at this moment, Canus, or what is your state of mind?' He replied, 'I have determined to note whether the soul is aware that it is quitting the body when that swiftest of moments arrives,' and he promised that, if he did make some discovery, he would go round his friends and reveal to them what the condition of souls really is. Here is tranquillity in the midst of the storm, here is a mind worthy of immortality, one that calls upon its own fate to make proof of the truth, that, when poised to take that final step, questions the departing soul and learns, not only right up to the time of death, but wishes to learn something from death itself: no one has practised the philosopher's art any longer. So great a man shall not be abandoned hastily, we must speak his name with respectful lips: most glorious of souls, greatest of those slaughtered by Gaius, I will make you live in the minds of all to come.

15. But there is no benefit in having rid oneself of the causes of individual melancholy; for there are times when one is seized by a hatred of all the human race. When you reflect on how rare frankness is, how unknown innocence, and how honesty is virtually never found, except where it confers gain, and when you think of all the host of successful crimes, and of the profits and losses of lust, both equally loathsome, and of ambition, that is so far from containing itself within its own limits that it shines out through its own infamy, then the mind is plunged into night, and, as though the virtues, which it is now neither permitted to expect nor advantageous to possess, have been overthrown, darkness casts its pall over you. Accordingly, we must allow ourselves to be persuaded of the view that all the vices of the mob are not hateful, but ludicrous, and we should take Democritus as our model rather than Heraclitus.* For the latter, whenever he went out in public, used to weep, regarding all men's actions as misery, but the former would laugh, regarding them as folly. We must, therefore, take a less serious view of all things, tolerating them in a spirit of acceptance: it is more human to laugh at life than to weep tears over it. There is the further point that the human race is also more indebted to the man who laughs at it than to the one who mourns for it: the first leaves it some measure of optimism, while the second foolishly mourns for what he despairs of being remedied; and when he surveys the world, the man who does not hold back his laughter shows a greater mind than the one who does not hold back his tears, since he

gives vent to the gentlest of the emotions and thinks there is nothing important, nothing serious, or even miserable, in the whole great state of life. Let each man put before himself one by one the causes of our joy and sorrow and he will realize the truth of Bion's remark, that all the pursuits in which men engage are just like their beginnings, and that their life is no more sacred or serious than their conception, that they were born from nothingness and to nothingness they finally return. But it is preferable to accept calmly the behaviour of people at large and the vices of men, without succumbing either to laughter or to tears; for to be tormented by the sufferings of others is perpetual misery, while to be delighted by the sufferings of others is pleasure less than human, just as it is a useless display of a man's humanity to weep and assume a look of sorrow because someone is burying his son. Even where personal misfortunes are concerned, the right way to behave is to accord them as much grief as Nature, not custom, demands; for many men shed tears for show and have eyes that are dry whenever someone is not there to observe, as they judge it disgraceful to refrain from weeping when everyone is doing it: so deeply has it become implanted, this evil of depending on what others think, that even the most altruistic of emotions, grief, becomes an affectation.

16. There now follows a category which is accustomed with good reason to induce melancholy and cause us concern. When good men come to bad ends, when Socrates is forced to die in prison, Rutilius* to live in exile, Pompey and Cicero to present their throats for their own clients to slit, and great Cato, living embodiment of the virtues, by falling on his sword to pronounce the death-knell for himself and for the state at the same time, it is inevitable that we feel distress at Fortune paying her rewards so unjustly; and what hope would each of us then have for himself, when he sees the best men suffering the worst of ends? Where, then, does the answer lie? Observe the manner in which each of those men bore his fate, and, if they were brave, pray with your heart to have hearts like theirs, and, if they perished like women and as cowards, then nothing perished: either they deserve to have you admire their courage or they do not deserve to have you desire their cowardice. For what greater shame could there be, if the greatest men by dying bravely make others cowards? Let us repeatedly praise the man who deserves renown, saying, 'The braver a man is, the happier his fortune! You have escaped from all mishaps, from jealousy, from illness; you have left the bonds of imprisonment; it is not that the gods have judged you worthy of bad fortune, but rather unworthy of being any longer at the mercy of Fortune's power.' But there is no need to lay hands on those who draw back and even at death's door cast their eyes back on life. No one who is happy, no one who weeps, shall make me weep for him: the former has himself wiped away my tears, the latter by his own tears has forfeited the right to any more. Should I weep for Hercules because he is burned alive, or for Regulus* because he is fixed to the cross by so many nails, or for Cato because he inflicts so many wounds on himself? All these men, by a slight expenditure of time, discovered how to become immortal, and by dying reached immortality.

17. There is also this not inconsiderable cause of anxieties, namely, if you should worriedly assume a pose and not show yourself to any men frankly, like the many people whose lives are a sham, made up for display; for it is a torment to be watching oneself all the time, afraid of being detected outside one's usual role. And we are never released from care if we suppose that each time we are under observation we are under scrutiny; for many things happen that expose our true selves against our will, and, though such attention to oneself may succeed, life brings neither happiness nor peace of mind to those who live it constantly behind a mask. But what great pleasure lies in that frankness that is pure and in itself unadorned, veiling no part of its character! But even a life such as this is liable to be scorned, if all things lie open to all people; for there are those who turn up their noses at whatever has become too familiar. But virtue runs no risk of being undervalued when it is put right before our eyes, and it is better to be despised for being natural than to be tormented by constant pretence. Let us, however, show moderation in the matter: it makes a considerable difference whether you live naturally or carelessly.

Furthermore, we should often withdraw into ourselves; for mixing with persons of dissimilar natures throws into disorder our settled composure and wakens our passions anew, exacerbating whatever is weak in the mind and not properly healed. It is, however, necessary to combine the two things, solitude and the crowd, and to have recourse to them alternately: the former will make us long for people, the latter for ourselves, and the one will be a cure for the other: our distaste for the crowd will be cured by solitude, our boredom with solitude by the crowd.

And the mind should not be kept constantly at the same tension but should be turned aside to amusement. Socrates was not ashamed to play with small children, and Cato used to relax his mind with wine when cares of state had made it weary, and Scipio,* great soldier and winner of triumphs as he was, would dance to the sound of music, not gyrating voluptuously as is the custom nowadays, when even in walking men sway the hips more suggestively than women do, but adopting the manly style that was the normal practice of those men of old when they used to dance in times of entertainment and festivals without incurring any risk of losing dignity, even if they were being watched by their own enemies. We must allow our minds some relaxation: if rested, they will rise up the better and sharper to challenges. As one should not impose a strict regimen on rich fields— for, if their fertility is never granted remission, it will quickly exhaust them—so unremitting effort will shatter the mind's vigour, while it will regain strength if it is allowed a small release and relaxation; mental effort permanently sustained produces in the mind a certain sluggishness and lethargy. And men would not strive so eagerly to achieve this if there were not a certain natural pleasure to be found in merriment and jest; but regular use of these will rob the mind of all weight and all energy; for sleep also is essential for refreshment, but, should you prolong this day and night, it will be death. It makes a great difference, whether you ease or cancel a debt. Those who founded our laws established days of festival so that men would be compelled by the state to indulge in merriment, as they thought it was necessary to moderate their effort by some interruption of their toils; and certain great men, as I said, used to apportion fixed days to themselves each month as holidays, while some would divide every single day between work-time and leisure. I remember that one such man was Asinius Pollio,* the great orator, who never engaged in any business beyond the tenth hour;* after that hour he would not even read letters, in case some fresh matter needing his attention should arise, but rather in those two hours he would grant himself release from all the day's weariness. Some men take a break in the middle of the day and put off to the afternoon hours a task requiring less strenuous effort. Our ancestors also would not allow any new motion to be made in the senate after the tenth hour. The soldier divides his hours of watch from sunset to sunrise, and those who have returned from an expedition are excused any night-time duties. We should show kindness to the mind and from time to time grant it the leisure that serves it for sustenance and strength.

We should also take walks out of doors, so that our minds may be energized and refreshed by the open air and deep breathing; sometimes stimulus will be provided by a carriage journey and a change of place and convivial company and generous drinking. Occasionally we should reach the stage even of intoxication, allowing it, not to drown us, but to take over our senses; for it washes away our cares, and rouses the mind from its depths, acting as a cure for its melancholy as it does for certain maladies, and the Freedom-Giver* owes his name, not to the licence he gives the tongue, but to the fact that he frees the mind from bondage to anxieties, discharging it from slavery, granting it new life, and giving it greater boldness in every endeavour. But as in the case of freedom, so with wine, there is a healthy temperance. Solon and Arkesilaos* are believed to have enjoyed wine, while Cato has been charged with drunkenness: but the man who brings this charge will more easily make it honourable than he will make Cato infamous. However, this should be done only on few occasions, in case the mind develops a bad habit, and yet sometimes it should be diverted into rejoicing and liberty, and for a short while gloomy abstemiousness should be sent packing. For whether we share the Greek poet's belief that 'sometimes it is a pleasure even to be a madman,'* or Plato's that 'the man in control of his senses knocks in vain on poetry's door,' or Aristotle's that 'no great genius has ever existed without a dash of lunacy'*—whatever the truth, only the mind that is roused can utter something momentous that surpasses the thoughts of other men. When it has despised the vulgar and the ordinary, and, imbued with holy inspiration, has risen far on high, that is the moment when it utters a strain too magnificent for mortal lips. It cannot attain to any sublime and forbidding height as long as it is left to itself: it must quit the common path, it must be driven wild and bite its bit, whirling its rider away and carrying him off to a height it would have feared to scale by itself.

You now have the means, my dearest Serenus, for enabling you to preserve and to restore tranquillity, and for opposing the vices that creep up on it by stealth; but on this point be assured: not one of these is powerful enough to protect a thing so weak, unless we fortify the wavering mind with fervent and unremitting care.

ON THE SHORTNESS OF LIFE

TO PAULINUS

1. The greater part of mankind, Paulinus,* complains bitterly about the malice of Nature, in that we are born for a brief span of life, and even this allotted time rushes by so swiftly, so speedily, that with very few exceptions all find themselves abandoned by life just when they are preparing themselves to live. And this universal evil, as it is regarded, has not drawn tears of grief only from the common man, the foolish crowd: it has roused the voice of complaint also in men who have won distinction. This is what made the greatest of physicians exclaim, 'Life is short, but art long;'* this that prompted Aristotle,* when taking Nature to task, to file a complaint not at all becoming to a wise man, saying that 'in number of years she has shown such bias towards animals that they live out five or ten lifetimes, while a far shorter limit has been set for man, though he is born for so many great achievements.' It is not that we have a brief length of time to live, but that we squander a great deal of that time. Life is sufficiently long, and has been granted with enough generosity for us to accomplish the greatest things, provided that in its entirety it is well invested; but when it is dissipated in extravagance and carelessness, when it is spent on no good purpose, then, compelled at last by the final necessity, we realize it has passed away without our noticing its passing. So it stands: we do not receive a life that is short, but rather we make it so; we are not beggars in it, but spendthrifts. Just as great and princely wealth, when it falls into the hands of a bad owner, is squandered in a moment, while wealth that is by no means great, if it becomes the property of a good guardian, grows by use, so our span of life has ample measure for one who manages it properly.

2. Why do we complain about Nature? She has proved herself generous: life is long, if only you knew how to use it. But one man is held fast by a greed that knows no bounds, another by a tedious devotion to tasks that have no purpose; one man is besotted with wine, another paralysed by indolence; one man is exhausted by an ambition that constantly depends on the judgement of others, another is driven on by his greed as a trader and drawn over every land and

every sea by the hope of profit; some are tormented by their passion for soldiering, constantly either eager to bring danger to others or fearful in facing it themselves; some there are who are worn out by a self-inflicted slavery as they cultivate their superiors for little or no return; many are fully occupied in seeking to gain other men's wealth or in complaining about their own; many, having no fixed purpose, are plunged into ever-new schemes because, lacking direction or consistency, they are prey to vacillation that breeds dissatisfaction; some lack any belief by which to steer their course, and are caught by fate listless and half-asleep, so much so that I cannot doubt the truth of what we find in the greatest of poets,* delivered like an oracle: 'Small is the part of life we really live.' All that remains of our existence is not actually life but merely time. We are besieged by vices that encircle us, preventing us from rising up or lifting our eyes to contemplate the truth, and keeping us down once they have overwhelmed us, our attention fixed upon lust. Never are these prisoners allowed to return to their proper selves; if ever they chance to find some measure of release, like the deep sea whose waters continue to heave even after the wind has subsided, they toss and turn, and find no respite from their lusts. Do you suppose I am talking about those whose evils are admitted? Look at those whose prosperity men rush to view: they are suffocated by their own blessings. How many men find wealth a burden! How many pay in their own blood for their eloquence and daily effort to display their powers! How many are pale from unremitting pleasures! How many are left with no freedom by the crowd of clients that surges round them! Cast your eye over the whole range of these men, from the lowest to the highest: this one seeks a lawyer, that one answers the call, this one is on trial, that one defends him, that one judges his case, no one is his own champion, all waste their energies on others. Ask about those whose names are known by heart and you will see that these are the characteristics that set them apart: X cultivates Y, Y cultivates Z; no one is his own person. And then there is an indignation felt by certain men which borders on insanity: they complain about the scorn shown them by superiors in being too busy to see them when they wanted an audience! Does anyone dare to complain about the arrogance of someone else when he never has time to give to himself? Yet whoever you are, that dignitary has from time to time looked at you, even if his expression is an insolent one, he has bent to hear your words, he has given you a place at his side: but you at no time have deigned to look yourself in the eye, to listen to your own voice. Therefore there is no reason to consider anyone in your debt for such services, since, when you performed them, it was not that you were wishing for another man's company; it was that you could not settle for your own.

3. Even if all the brilliant minds of the ages focused their attention on this one subject, never could they sufficiently express their wonder at this blind spot in the human mind. Men do not allow anyone to take possession of their estates, and, if there is the slightest dispute about the limit of their property, they rush to pick up stones and weapons: but they allow others to make inroads into their life, even extending personal invitations to those who will one day possess it. No one is found who would be willing to divide up his own money: but when it comes to his life, each one of us gives others a share in it, and how many others! Men are tight-fisted in keeping control of their fortunes, but when it comes to the matter of wasting time, they are positively extravagant in the one area where there is honour in being miserly. Accordingly I would like to accost a member of the older fraternity and say to him, 'I see you have reached the final stage in a man's life, you are pressing on your hundredth year, or more; come now, recall your life and make a reckoning of it. Think of how much of your time was taken from you by a creditor, how much by a mistress, how much by a patron, how much by a client, how much by arguing with your wife, how much by punishing slaves, how much by running all over the city on business; add to this the illnesses that we have caused by our own behaviour, and the hours that have lain idle and unused: you will see that the years you have to your credit fall below the number you have counted. Recall the number of times when you had a fixed plan, how few days ended as you had intended, when you ever had time to spend on yourself, when your face ever kept its normal expression, when your mind did not succumb to fear, what work you have accomplished in so long a lifetime, how many people plundered your life without your realizing what you were losing, how much was taken from you by pointless sorrow, foolish happiness, greedy desire, the enticements of socializing, how little of what you had was left for you; you will understand that you are dying before your time.' So what is the reason for this? You live as though you were going to live for ever, at no time taking thought for your weakness, and you fail to note how much time has already passed by; you waste

hours as though you were drawing from a well that was full to overflowing, though all the while that very day you are giving to some person or thing is possibly your last. You fear everything as mortals but desire to have everything as gods. You will hear many men saying: 'After my fiftieth year I will retire from work, my sixtieth year will release me from official duties.' And tell me, please, what guarantee do you have that your life will be any longer? Who will allow this time to pass as you prescribe? Are you not ashamed to reserve for yourself just the remnants of life and to mark down for a healthy mindset only the time that cannot be used for any other purpose? How late it is to begin living only when one must stop! What foolish forgetfulness of mortality to put off well-considered plans to one's fiftieth and sixtieth year, and to want to begin life at a point that few have reached!

4. You will see that the most powerful men, the ones who have reached a position of eminence, make chance remarks in which they long for leisure and praise it, preferring it to all their blessings. At times their desire is to come down from that pinnacle they have achieved, provided this can be done without harm; for Fortune comes crashing down by its own weight, even if no external force attacks or shakes it. The deified Augustus, to whom the gods gave more blessings than to any other man, would constantly pray for rest and freedom from affairs of state; all his conversation repeatedly came back to this topic—his hope of leisure; this was the consolation, vain perhaps, but sweet nonetheless, he relied upon to cheer his labours, that the day would come when he would live for himself. In a letter sent to the senate,* in which he had promised that his rest would not be without dignity or inconsistent with his former renown, I find these words: 'but actions, not promises can illustrate these aims more worthily. However, since the reality of this happiness is not here yet, my desire for that time I so long for has prompted me to anticipate a measure of its pleasure by the delight of words.' So much did leisure mean to him that he forestalled it in thought because he could not enjoy it in reality. The man who saw everything depending on him alone, who administered Fortune to men and nations, reflected with the utmost joy on that day when he might put aside his greatness. He had learned how much sweat those blessings that shone throughout every land cost him, how much secret anxiety they concealed: compelled to wage war, first against his countrymen, then against his

colleagues, and lastly against his relatives, he shed blood by sea and land. Through Macedonia, Sicily, Egypt, Syria, Asia, and almost every land he moved from one battle to another, and when his armies were wearied with spilling the blood of Romans, he turned them to the task of foreign wars. While he was pacifying the region of the Alps and subjugating enemies who occupied the midst of a peaceful empire, while he was extending its boundaries beyond the Rhine, the Euphrates and the Danube, in Rome itself the swords of Murena, Caepio, Lepidus, Egnatius,* and others were being sharpened against him. He had not yet escaped the plotting of these men, when his failing years were alarmed by his daughter* and the many men of noble blood who were bound to her by adultery as if by an oath, not to mention Iullus and the second time there was reason to fear a woman in league with an Antony.* These ulcers he had cut away, together with the limbs themselves: others would grow underneath; just as a body with too great a mass of blood would always suffer a rupture somewhere. And so he longed for leisure, his labours were founded on the hope and thought of this, and this was the prayer of the man who could answer the prayers of others.

5. Marcus Cicero, buffeted in the company of men such as Catiline and Clodius and Pompey and Crassus,* some unambiguous enemies, others doubtful friends, while he was tossed on the waves along with the state and sought to keep the ship from foundering, only to be swept away at the end, incapable as he was of rest in prosperity or endurance in adversity, never ceases to curse that consulship of his which he had so praised without end, if not without reason. What tearful words he utters in a letter to Atticus* after the defeat of the elder Pompey, when that man's son was still trying to raise his father's tattered standard in Spain! 'You ask what I am doing here?' he writes. 'I am marking time in my villa at Tusculum, half a prisoner.' Then he makes some further remarks in which he mourns his former life and complains about his present one and despairs of his life to come. 'Half a prisoner', Cicero called himself: but, believe me, never will the wise man have recourse to so lowly a phrase, never will he be half a prisoner, possessing for ever, as he does, unqualified and unshakeable freedom, liberated, master of himself, and rising above other men. For what can be above the man who is above Fortune?

6. Or consider that man of spirit and energy, Livius Drusus.* Supported by a huge gathering of people from all Italy, he had proposed

new laws and the ruinous measures of the brothers Gracchus, and now that he could see no successful outcome for his policies, which he could neither enact nor leave abandoned when once begun, he is said to have cursed the unstable life he had led from infancy, saying that not even as a boy had he ever known a holiday. For, while he was still a ward and not yet wearing the clothes of manhood, he had the courage to plead for defendants before jurors and to make his influence felt in the lawcourts, to such good effect that in certain cases it is clear that he forced a favourable verdict. Could there be any limit to such premature ambition? One might have known that such precocious boldness would end in great disaster, both private and public. Too late, therefore, came those complaints of his that he had never known a holiday, when from boyhood he was troublesome and a pest in the forum. It is a matter of dispute whether he took his own life; for he collapsed from a sudden wound he received in the groin, causing some to doubt whether his death was premeditated but none whether it was timely. It would be otiose to mention more who, despite appearing very happy to others, gave true testimony against themselves from their own lips by declaring their loathing for every act of their years; but by means of these complaints they changed neither other people nor themselves; for when they have given vent to their feelings in this way, they slip back into their customary ways.

Lives such as yours—how true it is!—though they should exceed a thousand years, will contract into the smallest span: but those vices of yours will swallow up any amount of time. This length of time you have, that reason prolongs, however swift nature makes its sojourn, is bound to pass quickly through your fingers; for you do not grasp it, or seek to hold on to it, or try to delay the passing of the swiftest thing of all, but allow it to depart, as if it were something surplus to requirement and easily replaced.

7. But in the forefront I count also those men who find time only for wine and lust; for none are more shamefully engrossed. The others, even if they are imprisoned by the vain dream of glory, nonetheless err in a manner not unbecoming; you may read out to me the list of those who show greed or anger, or who pursue unjust hatreds or wars, yet all these have a manliness in their offences: there is nothing honourable in the stain that disfigures those who surrender themselves to the stomach and to lust. Examine all the hours of such as these, see how much time they spend on accounts, how much on making plots,

how much in fearing them, how much in paying respects, how much in receiving them, how much they are involved in giving or receiving bail, how much in dinner-parties, which are now themselves social duties: you will see how their activities, whether bad or good in your eyes, do not allow them to draw breath.

Finally, it is generally agreed that no activity can be properly undertaken by a man who is busy with many things—not eloquence, and not the liberal arts—since the mind, stretched in different directions, takes in nothing at any depth but spits out everything that has been, so to speak, crammed into it. Nothing concerns the busy man less than the business of living: nothing is so difficult to learn. In the case of other arts there are many men to be found everywhere who can teach them, indeed certain arts we have seen absorbed so thoroughly by boys that they could even give instruction themselves: one must spend an entire lifetime in learning how to live, and, which may surprise you more, an entire lifetime in learning how to die. So many great men, having dispensed with all hindrances and renounced wealth, business commitments, and pleasures, have concentrated on this one aim up to the very end of their lives, to know how to live; the majority even of these, however, depart from life admitting that the knowledge has still eluded them, and how much more this is true of those others.

Only a great man, believe me, and one whose excellence rises far above human failings, will not allow anything to be stolen from his own span of time, and his life is very long precisely because he has devoted to himself entirely any time that became available. None of it lay uncultivated and idle, none was under another man's control, for guarding it most jealously, he found nothing worth exchanging for his own precious time. It was, therefore, sufficient for him: but men whose life has been largely taken from them by the people have inevitably seen too little of it. And there is no reason for you to suppose that those men do not sometimes understand their loss: indeed you will hear many of those who suffer from great prosperity cry out sometimes in the midst of their swarms of clients, or when they are pleading in court, or engaged in the other miserable tasks that bring them honour, 'I am not being allowed to live!' Of course they are not! All those who summon you to their aid are taking you away from yourself. How many days has that man robbed you of, the one on trial? How many that candidate for office? How many that old woman worn out by attending the funerals of her heirs? How many that fellow pretending to be ill to stimulate the greed of legacy-hunters? How many that rather powerful friend who has you on the list, not of his friends, but of his retinue? Check off, I say, and total up the days of your life: you will see that very few have been left for you, and the dregs at that. That man who gained the fasces* he had prayed for now desires to lay them aside, and repeatedly says, 'When will this year end?' Another holds public games, having greatly prized the chance to do so, and says, 'When will I escape from these games?' Another, an advocate, is the toast of the whole forum, and fills the whole space with his large crowd of followers, further than his voice can carry: 'When will I be free from work?' is his cry. Everyone rushes his life on, and suffers from a yearning for the future and a boredom with the present. But that man who devotes every hour to his own needs, who plans every day as if it were his last, neither longs for nor fears tomorrow. For what new pleasure is there that any hour can now bring him? All are known, or have been tasted to the full. As to what remains, let Fortune make what distribution she will: his life is now beyond harm. Something can be added to it but nothing taken from it, and he will receive it as a man who is already satisfied and full takes some food which he does not desire, but can stomach. There is, therefore, no ground for thinking that, because of his white hairs or wrinkles, someone has lived too long: he has not lived a long time but existed a long time. It is as if you thought that a man had made a lengthy voyage if he had been caught by a terrible storm just after leaving port and, blown this way and that by different winds raging from every quarter, had been driven in a circle over the same waters. It was a lot of buffeting he had, not a lengthy voyage.

8. Many times I am surprised when I see some men seeking the time of others and those being asked most compliant; both parties are concentrating on why the request for time was made, neither on the time itself: it is as if nothing is being sought, nothing given. It is the most valuable commodity of all which is at stake; but it escapes their attention because it is a thing without bodily form, because it does not present itself to their sight, and that is why they value it so cheaply, or rather give it no value whatever. Pensions and monetary gifts people receive very gladly, hiring out their labour, service, effort for such things: no one puts a value on time; people use it indiscriminately,

as if it cost nothing. But you will see these same people, if the risk of death draws near, clasping their doctors' knees, and, if their fear is capital punishment, ready to spend all they have in order to live: such a conflict exists in their emotions. But if each of them could have placed before him the number of his future years, as could happen with his past years, how dismayed they would be who saw only a few remaining, how sparing in the way they use them! And yet it is an easy matter to dole out an amount that is fixed, however small it may be; you should guard a thing more carefully when you do not know when it will give out.

But there is no reason to suppose that those men do not know how valuable a thing time is: it is their habit to say to those they most dearly love that they are ready to give them some of their own years. They do give these, without realizing it; but their gift is such that they deprive themselves of years without adding to the total of their loved ones. But just this is what they do not know, whether they are depriving themselves; therefore they can endure the loss of something when they fail to notice its removal. No one will restore your years, no one will restore you once more to yourself. Your life will pursue the path it started on, and will no more check than reverse its course; it will create no uproar, give no warning of its speed: silently it will glide on its way. No further will it extend its course at the command of a king, or because of the people's approval; just as its path was set from your first day, so will it run, nowhere deviating, nowhere delaying. What will the outcome be? You have busied yourself, life hurries on: death meanwhile will arrive, and for it you must find time, whether you wish it or not.

9. Can anything be more thoughtless than the judgement of those men who boast of their forethought? They keep themselves inordinately busy with the task of how they may be able to live better, but they use up life in preparing themselves for life. They organize their thoughts with the distant future in mind; but the greatest waste of life consists in postponement: that is what takes away each day as it comes, that is what snatches away the present while promising something to follow. The greatest obstacle to living is expectation, which depends on tomorrow and wastes today. What lies in the hands of Fortune you deal with, what lies in your own hands you let slip. Where are you looking? Where are you bending your aim? All that is still to come lies in doubt: live here and now! Look how the greatest

of poets,* as if inspired with utterance from the gods, chants his beneficial verse:

> In wretched mortals' life the fairest day
> Is first to flee alway.

'Why do you linger?' he asks, 'Why do you do nothing? Unless you seize time, it runs away.' Even though you have seized it, it will still run away; and so in speed of using it you must match the swiftness of time and drink quickly, as though from a whirling torrent that is not always going to flow. The phrase was very well chosen to find fault with infinite delay when he said, not 'the fairest *age*', but 'the fairest *day*'. Why is it that, however much prompted by your greed, you stretch out before you the prospect of months and years in lengthy sequence, free from care and slow, though time passes so fast? The poet is talking to you about the day, about this very day that runs away. Can there, then, be any doubt that in the lives of wretched mortals, that is, of men engrossed, the fairest day is first to flee? Old age overtakes them while their minds are still those of children, and they come to it unprepared and unarmed. For they have shown no foresight in this: suddenly they tumble into it unexpectedly, without realizing it was advancing on them every day. Just as conversation or reading or some deep reflection deceives travellers, and they discover they have reached their goal before knowing they were approaching it, so it is with this unbroken and rapid journey of life, that we make at the same pace, whether awake or asleep: those who are busy with other things do not notice it until the end comes.

10. Should I wish to divide my thesis into sections with their separate proofs, no lack of arguments will occur to me by which I may prove that life for busy men is very short. Fabianus,* who was no academic philosopher of the modern sort but one of the genuine, old-fashioned school, was in the habit of saying that one should fight against the emotions with a frontal attack, not with cunning tactics, and that the enemy line should be turned, not by the delivery of slight wounds, but by a headlong assault; for they should be crushed, not nipped. However, in order that those men may have their particular faults censured, they should be taught, not just made the object of pity.

Life divides into three periods: that which has been, that which is, and that which is to be. Of these the time we spend is short, that we will spend doubtful, that we have spent fixed; for the last is the one

over which Fortune has lost control, which cannot be brought back
into any man's power. Men busy with other things lose this; for they
have not the time to review the past, and, if they had, the recollection of something they should regret gives no pleasure. And so they
are reluctant to think back to hours they spent badly, and men whose
vices become obvious if they consider the past anew, even the vices
disguised by some attraction of momentary pleasure, do not find the
courage to revisit those hours. No one who has not exposed all his
actions to the censure of his own conscience, which is never deceived,
is willing to direct his thoughts back to the past; the man who has
ambitiously longed to possess something, arrogantly shown contempt,
conquered without restraint, deceived through treachery, stolen out
of greed, squandered in excess, must fear remembering himself. And
yet this is the part of our time that is sacred and dedicated, that has
passed beyond all human accidents and is no longer subject to the
rule of Fortune, that is beyond the power of poverty, of fear, of attacks
of illness to disturb; this can neither be troubled nor snatched away: it
is a possession for all time, and need cause no alarm. The present offers
days that come only one at a time, and these moment by moment; but
all the days of the past will be present at your bidding, they will allow
you to look at them and keep them as you please, something for
which those who are busy have no time. An untroubled and calm
mind can visit all parts of its life: the minds of those who are busy
with other things, as if they are under the yoke, cannot turn around,
bend, and look back. Therefore their life disappears into an abyss, and
as there is no benefit in pouring in any amount of water, if a vessel
has no bottom to contain it, so it makes no difference how much time
is given, if there is no place for it to lodge, it passes out through the
cracks and chinks of the mind. Present time is very short, so short,
indeed, that some people think there is none; for it is constantly on
the move, like a rushing river; it ceases to exist before it has arrived,
and no more tolerates delay than the heavens or the stars, whose ever-
restless motion never lets them remain in the same track. Accordingly
those busy with other things concern themselves only with present
time, which is so short that it cannot be seized, and even this is stolen
from them, engrossed as they are in many different pursuits.

11. Do you want to know, finally, how it is they do not live long?
See how they desire to live long! Worn-out old men pray like street-
beggars for the addition of a few years; they pretend to be younger

than they are; they flatter themselves with lies and get as much pleasure from self-deception as if they were deceiving fate as well as themselves. When finally some weakness has reminded them of their mortality, how fearfully they meet death, as though they were not quitting life but being dragged away from it! They shout repeatedly that they have been fools, as they have not really lived, and, if only they escape from that illness, their lives will be devoted to leisure; that is when they reflect on how pointlessly they have toiled to gain what they did not enjoy, how all their effort has been utterly wasted. But for those whose life is spent far from all business, why should it not be generous in scope? None of it is assigned elsewhere, nothing scattered this way and that, nothing transferred from it to Fortune, nothing perishes from neglect, nothing is taken away by extravagance, nothing is excessive: all of it, so to speak, makes a profit. And so, however small it is, it is abundantly enough, and for that reason, whenever the final day comes, the wise man will not hesitate to approach death with a steady step.

12. Perhaps you ask which people I call 'busy with other things'. There is no reason for you to suppose I mean only those who are driven out of the lawcourts by the dogs that have finally been let in, or those you see being crushed impressively in their own crowd of clients or contemptuously in someone else's, or those whom social duties summon from their own houses to bump against the doorways of others, or whom the praetor's spear keeps busy in seeking profit that brings disgrace and will one day fester. With certain men their leisure is itself engrossed: in their villa or on their couch, in the midst of solitude, although they have withdrawn from everyone, they are a nuisance to themselves; their life should not be described as one of leisure but rather one of busy idleness. Do you call that man 'at leisure' who with anxious precision arranges his Corinthian bronzes, whose value is due to the mania of a few, and spends the greater part of his days on rusty bits of copper? Who sits in a wrestling-ground (for, and this is shameful! we suffer from vices that are not even Roman), supporting brawling youngsters? Who separates the gangs of his wrestlers into pairs according to age and colour? Who provides food for all the latest athletes? I ask you, do you call those men 'at leisure' who spend many hours with their barber, having any hairs that grew the previous night plucked, as a formal debate is held over each separate lock, as hair out of place is restored

to its proper position or thinning locks combed forward to the forehead from this side and that? How angry they become, if the barber has been a little careless, as though it were a real man he was shearing! How they flare up in rage, if anything is lopped off their mane, if any of it lies out of order, if every lock does not fall back into its proper ringlet! Which of these fellows would not rather have his country put in disorder than his hair? Who would not show more concern for his head being trim rather than safe? Who would not rather look smart than be a man of integrity? Do you call these 'at leisure' who busy themselves with a comb and mirror? What of those who occupy themselves with composing, hearing, and learning songs, while they stretch the voice, whose best and simplest course nature made uncomplicated, to accommodate the twists and turns of the silliest tune, whose fingers are constantly snapping as they beat out time to some song in their head, whom you can hear humming some ditty to themselves, when they have been asked to attend on matters that are serious and often even disquieting?

As for their banquets—heaven help us!—I couldn't give them a place among their unoccupied hours, since I see how anxiously they lay their silver plate, how carefully they tie up the tunics of their charming young slave-boys, how concerned they are at how stylishly the wild boar arrives from the hands of the cook, how swiftly at a given signal their smooth-cheeked servants run to carry out their various duties, how skilfully the birds are sliced into portions of just the right amount, how meticulously wretched little slaves wipe away the mess of drunken guests. These are the means by which they seek to win a name for elegance and stylishness, and to such an extent do their bad habits accompany them into all the backwaters of life that ostentation marks even their drinking and eating. And I would not number amongst the leisured those who are transported here and there by sedan-chair or litter, and are unfailingly punctual for their rides, as if they were not allowed to miss them, and are reminded by someone else when they must bathe, when they must swim, when they must have dinner; so enervated are they by the excessive listlessness of a pampered mind that they cannot determine for themselves if they are hungry! I hear that one of these pampered creatures—if 'pampering' is a sufficient term for forgetting all one has learned about the habits of human life—when he had been lifted by hands from the bath and placed in his sedan-chair, asked the question, *common conception of leisure as pampering*

'Am I seated now?' In your view, does this man, who does not know if he is sitting, know if he is alive or able to see, or if he is at leisure? I could not easily say whether I feel greater pity for him if he really did not know or if he pretended not to. There are many things these men genuinely forget, but many also they pretend to forget. Some vices give them pleasure as though furnishing proofs of their happiness; a man of the lowest birth, a figure of contempt, is capable of knowing what he is doing. Next you'll tell me that mimes show us a host of false impressions on stage, in order to mock extravagance! The fact is, they leave out more than they portray, and such a plethora of unimaginable vices has emerged in this generation, so talented in this respect alone, that we can now charge the mimes with neglect. To think that a man exists who is so lost in luxury that he depends on someone to tell him if he is seated! Well, this is not a man who is at leisure, you must find some other term for him: he is ill, or rather he is dead; that man is at leisure who actually perceives the leisure he has. But this other one who is half alive, who requires a man to tell him before he is aware of his own physical posture, how can he be master of any of his time?

13. It would be a lengthy business to mention all the different people who have spent their lives engaged in chess-playing or exercise with ball or the practice of roasting their bodies in the sun. They are not unoccupied when their pleasures form such busy occupation. No one will doubt that those men are energetic triflers who devote their hours to the study of useless literature, of whom there is now a considerable number even among the Romans. It was a foolish passion once confined to Greeks* to inquire into the number of oarsmen Ulysses had, whether the *Iliad* or *Odyssey* was written first, whether in addition both were by the same author, and other various questions of this type, that, should you keep them to yourself, in no way give pleasure to your secret heart, and, should you make them public, increase your reputation, not as a scholar, but as a bore. But it's a fact—this pointless interest in learning useless things has infiltrated the Romans as well. In recent days I heard a man describing who was the first Roman general to do this or that: the first to win a battle at sea was Duilius,* the first to have elephants in his triumphal procession was Curius Dentatus.* Even now these details, though they do not contribute to real glory, yet have their place in the roll-call of services to the state; no benefit will accrue from such knowledge, but

it serves to hold our attention through the attractiveness of facts that
have no importance. We should even be indulgent to those who pursue
the question who was first to persuade the Romans to board ships
(the man was Claudius, and it was for this reason he received the
surname Caudex, because our ancestors called a structure formed
by joining several planks together a *caudex*; this is also why the tables
of the laws are called *codices*, and why ships that follow the ancient
custom of carrying supplies up the Tiber are even today called
codicariae); no doubt the following may also have some relevance here,
the fact that Valerius Corvinus was the first conqueror of Messana,*
and the first member of the Valerii family to receive the surname
Messana after transferring to himself the name of the city he had
conquered; he was subsequently called Messala when the spelling
was gradually corrupted through popular usage; you will also, I am
sure, allow someone his interest in the fact that Lucius Sulla was the
first to exhibit lions without chains in the circus,* though at other
times they were presented restrained, and that spearsmen were sent
to finish them off by King Bocchus.* And this, too, would no doubt
be excused—but does it serve any useful purpose to know that
Pompey was the first to stage a fight in the circus involving eighteen
elephants, setting criminals against them in a sham battle. A leading
man of the state and, according to report, distinguished among the
foremost citizens of old for the kindness of his heart, he thought it
a noteworthy kind of spectacle to put men to death by a novel fashion.
Are they fighting to the death? It is not sufficient. Are they torn to
pieces? It is not sufficient: let them be crushed by creatures of enormous bulk! It would have been better for such things to be forgotten,
so that no man of power in the future should learn them and be jealous of an act so unworthy of a human being. O what darkness is cast
over our minds by great prosperity! At the time when he was throwing so many troops of wretched humans to wild beasts born under
a different sky, when he was forcing creatures so different to join
battle, when he was shedding so much blood before the eyes of the
Roman people, whom he would shortly compel to shed more from
their own veins, then he believed himself to be beyond the power of
Nature. But the same man subsequently was taken in by Alexandrian
treachery and offered himself to be stabbed by the lowest of slaves,*
only then understanding what an empty boast was contained in
his surname.

But to return to the point from which I digressed, and to show that some people busy themselves to no purpose on these same matters, the same man I spoke of related a story about Metellus: while celebrating his triumph after his conquest of the Carthaginians in Sicily, he was the only one of all the Romans to parade in front of his chariot one hundred and twenty captive elephants. He further said that Sulla was the last of the Romans to extend the pomerium,* which by custom from ancient times had only been extended after Italian territory had been acquired, never provincial. Is it more useful to know this than that, according to him, the Aventine Hill lies outside the pomerium for one of two reasons, either because it was the place chosen for their secession by the plebeians, or because the birds had not shown favour when Remus took the auspices in that place, or, in turn, to know countless other versions of events that are either untrue or strain veracity? For though you may grant that they say all these things in good faith and swear to the truth of what they write, will such accounts reduce the number of errors a man makes? Will they restrain a man's passions, or make him more brave, more just, more honourable? My friend Fabianus used to say he sometimes doubted whether it was not preferable to avoid studies altogether rather than to get entangled in these.

14. Of all men only those who find time for philosophy are at leisure, only they are truly alive; for it is not only their own lifetime they guard well; they add every age to their own; all the years that have passed before them they requisition for their store. Unless we have no gratitude at all, those glorious fashioners of sacred thoughts were born for us, for us they laid the foundations of life. By the efforts of other men we are led to contemplate things most lovely that have been unearthed from darkness and brought into light; no age has been denied to us, we are granted admission to all, and if we wish by greatness of mind to pass beyond the narrow confines of human weakness, there is a great tract of time for us to wander through. We may hold argument with Socrates, feel doubt with Carneades,* find tranquillity with Epicurus, conquer human nature with the Stoics, exceed it with the Cynics. Since nature permits us to have a share in every age, why should we not forsake this insignificant and fleeting span of time and devote ourselves with all our minds to the past, which is vast, which is eternal, which we share with better men? As for those who scurry to and fro performing social duties, giving no rest to others

or themselves, once they have given their madness full rein, crossing every man's doorstep each day and leaving no open door unentered, carrying their money-grubbing felicitations round houses that are widely apart, how few are the patrons they will be able to see out of a city so huge and racked by so many different desires! How many will there be who let sleep or self-indulgence or lack of kindness keep them outside their door! How many who rush past them, pretending to be in a hurry, after inflicting the torture of a lengthy wait! How many will decline to go out through a hall that is crammed with clients, preferring to make their escape by means of hidden doorways, as if it were not ruder to deceive visitors than to debar them! How many, half-asleep and nauseous from over-drinking the night before, will scarcely open their lips in the course of an insolent yawn to give the correct name, however many times it has been whispered, to those poor fellows who disturb their own slumber to wait on another man's! The ones you should regard as devoting time to the true duties of life are those who wish to have as their intimate friends every day Zeno, Pythagoras, Democritus, and all the other high-priests of good learning, and Aristotle and Theophrastus. None of these will be 'too busy', none will fail to send his visitor away a happier man or more devoted to his host, none will allow any man to leave him empty-handed; by night and by day all men on earth can enjoy their company.

15. None of these will compel you to die, yet all will teach you how to die; none of these will wear out your years but rather will make you a gift of his own; none will bring you danger by conversation with him, none death by his friendship, none expense by showing him regard. You will take from them whatever you wish; they will not be to blame if you fail to drink down as much as you can draw from the wine-bowl. What happiness, what an attractive old age awaits the man who has made these men his patrons! He will have men with whom to discuss matters great and small, whom he can consult each day about himself, from whom he can hear the truth without insult and praise without flattery, on whom he can model himself. We are accustomed to say it was not in our power to choose the parents we were allotted, that chance gave them to us: but we are allowed to be born from whatever parents we wish. The noblest intellects have their households; choose the one you wish to be enrolled in; you will inherit not their name alone, but even their property, which you will not have to guard in a mean or ungenerous spirit: it will increase in

size the more people you share it with. These men will set you on the
road to immortality, and raise you to that place from which no one is
cast down. This is the one way of prolonging mortality, or rather of
turning it into immortality. Honours, monuments, all that ambition
has commanded by decrees or raised in works of stone, are swift to
collapse, and all things are destroyed or displaced by the long march
of years; yet what philosophy has made sacred cannot suffer harm;
no age will destroy those works, no age diminish them; the age that
follows and each successive one will add to the awe they inspire,
since what is to hand attracts envy, while what is distant we admire
more unreservedly. Accordingly the life of the philosopher has wide
scope, and he is not confined by the same boundaries as the rest of men:
he alone is not shackled by the conditions of the human race, and all
ages are his servants as if he were a god. Should a period of time have
passed, he embraces it in his memory; if it is present, he makes use
of it; if it is to come, he anticipates it. By combining all times into one
he makes his life a long one.

   16. But those who forget the past, ignore the present, and fear for
the future have a life that is very brief and filled with anxiety: when
they come to face death, the wretches understand too late that for
such a long time they have busied themselves in doing nothing. And
you have no cause to think it any proof that they find life long
because from time to time they call for death to come: in their lack of
judgement they fall prey to shifting emotions that sweep them into
the very things they fear; it is because they fear death that they often
pray for it. Nor should you consider it any proof that life is lengthy
for them that often the day seems long to them, or that they complain
at the slow passage of the hours before the time set for dinner arrives;
for if ever their interests fail to occupy them, they toss and turn, left
with nothing to do, and have no idea how to manage this time or
draw it out. And so they strive to find something to occupy them, and
all the intervening time is tedious, very much as happens when the
day of a gladiatorial show has been announced, or when they are waiting for the fixed time of some other exhibition or pleasure, they want
to leap over the days in between. Anything that postpones what they
hope for seems long to them. Yet that time they love is short-lived
and swift, and it is their own fault that makes it much shorter; for
they rush from one pleasure to another and cannot remain absorbed
in a single passion. Days are not long in their eyes, but hateful; but,

on the other hand, how brief seem the nights they spend in the arms of prostitutes or in the tavern! This also lies behind the madness of poets in nurturing human error by their tales, representing Jupiter as doubling the night's length to satisfy his pleasure in a lover's embraces:* what else is it but inflaming our vices, to inscribe the gods as their sponsors and to give as an example to our own weakness their freedom to indulge themselves without complaint? Can the nights these men purchase so dearly fail to appear most brief to them? They lose the day in waiting for the night, and the night in dreading the day.

17. Their very pleasures are fearful and troubled by alarms of different kinds; at the very moment of rejoicing the anxious thought occurs to them: 'How long will this last?' This feeling has caused kings to weep over their own power; they have not experienced delight in the greatness of their Fortune but terror that it will some day come to an end. When the Persian king* in all his arrogance spread his army over the far-extending plains, unable to calculate their number but only their size, he shed tears because within a hundred years not one of that great host would still be living. But the very man who wept would bring them their doom and ruin, some on the sea, some on the land, some in battle, some in flight, and in the shortest of time he would destroy those he feared would not see their hundredth year. But why is it that even their pleasures are subject to fear? Because they are not based on stable causes, but are thrown into disarray for as little reason as they are born. What kind of times do you imagine they are that they themselves admit to be wretched, when even the pleasures that exalt them and raise them above mankind are far from unalloyed? All the greatest blessings are a source of worry, and it is never more foolish to trust Fortune than when it is best; to preserve prosperity one needs other prosperity, and to assist the prayers that have turned out well for us we must offer yet more prayers. For all that comes to us by chance lacks stability, and the higher it rises, the more likely it is to fall; no one, again, takes delight in what is destined to perish; therefore not only very brief but very miserable must be the life of those who labour hard to get what they must labour harder to keep. With great effort they acquire what they want, with anxiety they hold on to what they have acquired; all this while they take no account of the time that will never more come again: old pursuits give way to new ones, one hope gives rise to another, and so, too, with ambition. Instead of seeking an end to their miseries, they change the

reason for them. We have been tormented by our own public honours but those of others rob us of more time; we cease to exert ourselves as candidates for office and start to canvass for others; we give up the problems of bringing a prosecution and assume those of being a juror; a man stops being a juror and becomes president of a court; someone has grown old managing another's estate for a fee, and gets bogged down in administering his own property. Marius* has been released from the army, and takes on the strain of the consulship. Quintius* hastens to reach the end of his dictatorship, but he will be summoned back from the plough. Scipio will take the field against the Carthaginians before his years fit him for such a task; conqueror of Hannibal, conqueror of Antiochus, the glory of his own consulship and surety for his brother's, he will have his statue alongside Jupiter's, were it not for his own opposition: but discord among his fellow citizens will vex the man who gave them security, and, after scorning in his youth honours that rivalled the gods', he will be happy in old age with the ambition of stubborn exile. Never will there be a shortage of reasons for anxiety, whether born of happiness or misery; life will press on its way from one pursuit to another; leisure will never be enjoyed, though the prayer is constantly on our lips.

18. Therefore, my dearest Paulinus, tear yourself away from the mob, and, after enduring the buffeting of the sea more than your years deserve, find shelter at last in a peaceful harbour. Reflect on the number of waves you have met, the number of storms you have endured, some in private life, while others in public you have brought on your own head; you have now given sufficient proof of your virtue by labouring without respite for all to see: test what it can do in leisure. The greater part, certainly the better part of your life has been given to your country: take some of your time for yourself as well. I do not call you to a repose that is idle or inactive, or to drown all your personal energy in sleep and pleasures that delight the crowd: that is not to rest; you will discover in the release of your retirement tasks to keep you busy that outweigh all those you pursued with such energy before now. I know you manage the accounts of the world as honestly as you would any other man's, as scrupulously as your own, as faithfully as the state's; in an office in which it is difficult to avoid hatred you win love: but nevertheless, believe me, it is better for a man to know the accounts of his own life than those of the corn-market. You have a keen intelligence that is more than capable of dealing with

the greatest matters. Recall it from a service that certainly confers honour but is hardly conducive to a life of happiness, and reflect that in all your education in liberal studies from your earliest years your aim was not to have entrusted to your safe care many thousand pecks of corn: you inspired a hope of something more serious, more impressive. Rome will not lack men of financial probity and painstaking diligence: but slow pack-animals are much more suited to carrying loads than thoroughbred horses are, and who has ever curbed the speed of these aristocratic creatures by putting a heavy pack on their backs? Consider, further, all the anxiety you give yourself in taking on so great a task: it is the human stomach you have to deal with; when hungry, the people are deaf to reason, no appeal to fairness pacifies them, no appeal makes them waver. In very recent times, during those few days following the death of Gaius Caesar—still in great distress, if the dead have any feelings, that the Roman people were not yet dead and had enough food to last them certainly seven or eight days—while he was building his bridges with boats and playing with the empire's resources, we were afflicted by the worst evil men can suffer, even when under siege—lack of provisions; his imitation of a crazed foreign king in the grip of fatal pride nearly cost us destruction by famine and the wholesale revolution that accompanies famine. What must have been the feelings at that time of those charged with responsibility for the corn-market,* having to face stones, swords, firebrands, and Gaius? With the utmost pretence they sought to conceal the great evil lurking in the bowels of the state, no doubt acting with good reason; for certain illnesses must be treated without the patient's knowledge of them: many a man has died because he knew the disease that afflicted him.

19. Withdraw, then, to these more peaceful, safer, greater things! Do you think it is just the same whether you make sure that corn is poured into granaries, untainted by the dishonest or careless practices of those transporting it, that it does not become heated or spoiled by gathering moisture, that it tallies in measure and weight, or whether you enter upon these holy and lofty studies, in order to discover what substance, what will, what manner of existence, what shape God has; what fate is waiting for your soul; where nature gives us rest once we have been released from our bodies; what it is that supports all the heaviest matter in the centre of this world, keeps light things poised on high, carries fire to the highest point, summons the stars to the

changes they undergo—and all the other matters in turn, full of great wonders? Come, leave the ground behind and direct your mind's gaze on those things! Now, while the blood is warm, we must step out vigorously on the path to better things. Many things worth knowing wait for you in this manner of life—the love and exercise of the virtues, the ability to forget the passions, the knowledge of living and of dying, a state of deep repose.

The condition of all men who are busy with other things is wretched, but most wretched is that of men who busy themselves energetically in pursuits that are not even their own, who sleep to suit another's sleeping pattern, who walk to suit another's pace, who feel love and hatred—the freest of all emotions—at another's bidding. If these men want to know how brief their life is, let them consider how small a part of it belongs to them.

So when you see a man regularly wearing the robe of a magistrate, when you see one whose name is well known in the forum, do not feel envy: these things are bought by sacrificing one's life. In order to have a single year reckoned by their name, they will squander all their years. Life has abandoned some men during their early struggles, before they could toil to the top of ambition's ladder; some, who have crawled up through a thousand indignities to the highest dignity of all, have been struck by the unhappy thought that all their efforts have won them an inscription on a tombstone; others, who have reached advanced old age, while they adjust to new hopes, as if they were still young men, fail out of weakness in the course of their great and brazen endeavours. How shameful it is for a man to expire in court when, advanced in age and still trying to win the approval of an ignorant crowd, he is pleading the case of some utterly obscure litigant! How disgraceful for a man to collapse in the midst of his duties when his way of life has drained him of energy sooner than his efforts! Disgraceful, too, when a man dies in the act of receiving payments on account, to the amusement of the heir he has kept waiting for so long! I cannot omit an example that has occurred to me: Sextus Turannius was an old man, punctilious to a fault, who was released from his duties of office after reaching the age of ninety by the order of Gaius Caesar himself. His reaction was to order that he be laid out on his bed and mourned by his household standing around him, as though he were dead. All the house lamented the enforced leisure of its old master and did not cease from grief until the work he loved was restored to him. Is it really such a source of pleasure to die engaged in one's work? A great many people do hold this view: their desire for work lasts longer than their capacity for it; they fight against the body's weakness, and judge old age to be irksome solely on the grounds that it relegates them to a position of unimportance. The law does not enrol a soldier after his fiftieth year, or summon a senator to office after his sixtieth: men find it more difficult to obtain leisure from themselves than from the law. In the meantime, while they rob others and are robbed in turn, while one man disturbs another's peace, while they bring misery on one-another, their life is without benefit, without pleasure, without any advancement of the mind: no one keeps death in his sight, no one abstains from entertaining ambitious hopes, and some men even make arrangements for matters lying beyond life, tombs of massive size, dedications of public works, gifts to be made at their funeral pyres and extravagant funerals. But believe me, torches and tapers of wax should accompany the funerals of men like this, as if they had lived for the shortest of times.

CONSOLATION TO HELVIA

1. Many times before now, my best of mothers,* I have felt inclined to offer you consolation, and many times I have checked the impulse. There were numerous reasons that prompted me to such boldness: first, I imagined that I would rid myself of all my troubles, when, even if I could not stop you shedding tears, I had in the meantime at least wiped them away; secondly, I had no doubt that I would have more power to lift your spirits, if I had first lifted my own; I was, moreover, troubled by the fear that Fortune, though defeated by me, might defeat someone I held dear. Therefore I was trying as best I could to creep up to bind your wounds, having put a hand over the gash I had suffered myself. On the other hand, as regards this resolve of mine, certain factors existed to cause me delay: I knew it was wrong to intrude on your grief while its intensity was fresh, in case my very attempts at consolation should provoke and kindle it to flame—for in physical ailments, too, nothing does more harm than medicine applied too early; and so I was waiting for your grief to master its violence by natural means and to tolerate being touched and treated, once an interval of time had made it more amenable to submitting to remedies. Besides, when I opened up all the works written by the most celebrated minds for the purpose of curbing and moderating feelings of sorrow, I discovered no instance of a man who had consoled his loved ones when he was himself the object of their grief; accordingly, finding myself in a novel position, I entertained some doubts and misgivings in case my efforts should aggravate rather than console. Again, when a man was lifting his head from the very bier to comfort his loved ones, he would certainly need to find words that were fresh-minted and not drawn from the currency of ordinary, everyday speech! But the greatness of every grief that exceeds limits will inevitably snatch from one the power to choose one's words, as not infrequently it stifles the voice itself. I will make the attempt as best I can, not trusting to my own powers of speech, but to the belief that, by offering consolation in my own person, I can represent the most effective form of consolation. As one who could deny me nothing, I hope you will surely not deny me this request, however persistent all sorrow may be, that you consent to my imposing some limit on your grief.

2. Observe what a great gift I have promised myself from your indulgence: I have no doubt that I shall wield more power over you than your grief, though there is nothing that exercises more power over the wretched. Therefore, to avoid joining battle with it immediately, I shall first sustain it and not be sparing in applying the means to promote it; every wound that has by now closed over I shall expose and tear open. Someone will say: 'What form of consolation is this, to call back suffering that has been consigned to oblivion and to set the mind, when it can scarcely endure one tribulation, in full view of all its tribulations?' But let that man consider that, whenever illnesses become so life-threatening that their virulence grows despite treatment, a cure is often effected by opposite methods. Accordingly, I will display to the afflicted mind all its sorrows, all its garments of mourning: this will be no gentle path to working a remedy, but that of cautery and the knife. What shall I gain? I shall cause a heart that has triumphed over so many afflictions to feel shame at lamenting a single wound on a body marked by so many scars. Let us, then, have endless tears and groans from those whose pampered minds have been unmanned by long happiness, let them collapse in a faint if menaced by the slightest injury: but let those whose years have all been spent in disasters bear even the harshest blows of Fortune with a strong resolution that nothing can shake. There is one blessing conferred by constant misfortune, that it finally brings strength to those it always plagues.

Fortune has denied you any respite whatever from the heaviest sorrows, not even making an exception of the day you were born: you lost your mother at the moment of your birth, or rather while you were being born, and on entering life you became, in a sense, an outcast. You grew up under a stepmother,* compelling her to become a mother by showing her every form of obedience and devotion, no less than can be observed in a true daughter; no child, however, has failed to pay a heavy price for a stepmother, even a good one. My most affectionate uncle, an excellent man of great bravery, was lost to you when you were awaiting his arrival; and, so that Fortune should not make her cruelty easier to bear by dividing it, within thirty days you buried your dearest husband, who had made you the mother of three children. This grievous blow was announced to you when you were already grieving, and at a time when you lacked the company of all your children, as though your miseries had deliberately been concentrated on that period of time when your sorrow would have no source of comfort. I say nothing of all the dangers, all the fears you endured as they assailed you unceasingly: only recently, into the very same lap from which you had let go three grandchildren, you took back the bones of three grandchildren; less than twenty days after you had committed my son to the grave, who died in your arms receiving your kisses, you heard that I had been snatched from you: this was a sorrow you had hitherto been spared, to mourn the living.

3. The wound you have recently sustained has been the most serious, I admit, of all those your body has ever received; it did not merely break the surface of your skin but pierced the heart and very vitals. But just as recruits to the army cry out when lightly wounded and dread the hands of surgeons more than the sword, while tried soldiers, though badly injured, patiently and without groaning allow their suppurating wounds to be cleansed, as if it were another's body and not their own, so it is your duty now to offer yourself bravely to treatment. Have done with lamentations and cries of sorrow and other means by which women generally express their noisy grief; for you have not understood the lesson of so much suffering, if you have not yet learned how to be wretched. Do you think I have shown enough directness in dealing with you? I have concealed not one of your misfortunes from you, but have set them all down before you in a pile.

4. I have done this in a spirit of boldness; for I have determined to conquer your grief, not to confine it. And I shall conquer it, I think, if, first, I show that there is nothing in my state to justify my being described as wretched, far less to cause wretchedness in any of those to whom I am related; and secondly, if I turn to you and demonstrate that not even your fortune, which depends entirely on mine, is cause for distress.

I shall first attempt to prove what your love as a mother longs to hear, that I am not suffering any ill. If I am able, I shall make clear that the very circumstances which you imagine oppress me are quite capable of being endured; but if this proves beyond your credence, I, at any rate, shall please myself the more, if I prove I am happy in a situation that usually causes others to be miserable. You have no reason to believe what others report about me: to spare you any distress at hearing views of doubtful authenticity, I reveal to you myself that I am not wretched. I will add, to spare you any further concerns, that it is not even possible for me to become wretched.

5. The conditions under which we are born would be favourable if only we did not abandon them. Nature's intention was that we should need no great equipment for living in happiness: every one of us is capable of making himself happy. Little importance is to be attached to external things, and they cannot possess great influence in either direction: the wise man is neither raised up by prosperity nor cast down by adversity; for always he has striven to rely predominantly on himself, and to derive all joy from himself. What, then? Am I saying that I am a wise man? Not at all; for if I were able to make that claim, not only would I say that I am not wretched, I would also declare that I am the most blessed of all men and had been brought into the presence of God: as it is, adopting what suffices to relieve all sorrows, I have entrusted myself to wise men and, not yet having the strength to help myself, I have sought refuge in the camp of others, of men who evidently find it no great task to protect themselves and their followers. They have ordered me to hold my position continually, like a soldier placed on guard, and to anticipate all the attempts, all the attacks of Fortune long before she launches them. Her blows are heavy for those she catches unprepared: the man who constantly expects her meets her attack with ease. For the enemy's arrival also overthrows only those whom it catches off guard: but those who have prepared themselves for the ensuing war before the war, in good order and ready for action, meet with ease the first onslaught, which is always the most violent. Never have I put my trust in Fortune, even when she appeared to be offering peace; all those gifts she bestowed on me in her kindness—money, position, influence—I stored where she would be able to reclaim them with no disturbance to me. I have kept a broad space between them and me; and so she has taken them away, not wrested them, from me. No man is crushed by misfortune unless he has first been deceived by prosperity. Those who love her gifts as if they are theirs to enjoy for ever, who wish to be highly regarded because of them, lie prostrate in mourning whenever these false and fickle delights abandon their vacuous, childish minds that know nothing of any lasting pleasure: but the man who has not become puffed up by happy fortune does not collapse when there is a reversal. In the face of either state he keeps his mind unconquered, for his strength of purpose has long been put to the test; even in prosperity he makes trial of his strength to face adversity. Therefore in those things that all men pray for I have always held there exists no true good, rather I have found in them empty things, painted over with garish and misleading colours and possessing nothing inside that matches their outward looks; even now, among these so-called evils I find nothing so frightening and harsh as the fancy of the mob threatened would ensue. The very name of exile, thanks to a form of persuasion and general agreement, now falls more harshly on the ear, striking the hearer as something dismal and accursed: for this is how the people have decreed; but decrees of the people are for the most part annulled by wise men.

6. Dispensing, then, with the verdict of most people, who are swept away by the first appearance of things, whatever their ground for trust is, let us see what exile is. Of course it is a change of place. I do not wish to narrow the force of this and remove the worst it holds, so I admit that disadvantages do accompany this changing of place, such as poverty, loss of reputation, and scorn. I shall combat these points subsequently: in the meantime the question I wish to examine first is what disagreeable state is brought about by the mere changing of place.

'To be deprived of one's country is beyond endurance.' But come now, consider this throng of people, for whom the houses of our vast city scarcely are enough: most of this number are deprived of their country. They have flocked here from their townships and colonies, in short, from every part of the world: some have been drawn by ambition, some by the obligation of a public service, some by the office of envoy entrusted to them, some by luxury seeking a suitable and rich field for vice, some by desire for higher studies, some by public shows; some have been attracted by friendship, some by an appetite for work, seeing the generous scope for displaying energy; some have brought their looks for sale, some their eloquence. There is no class of person that has not swarmed into the city with its high prizes set for virtue and vice alike. Have them all summoned to answer their name and ask each one of them, 'Where do you call home?': you will see that more than half of them have quit their own homes and come to this city, which is indeed of great size and beauty, but not their own. Then leave this city, which can be described, in a sense, as belonging to all, and travel from one city to another: every one of them contains a large number of inhabitants from foreign parts. Move on from those cities whose beauty of location and advantageous position entice great numbers and let your eye survey desert regions and barren islands, Sciathus and Seriphus, Gyara and Cossura:* not one place of exile will you find where someone does not linger of his own volition. What can be found as barren, as sheer on all sides, as this rock?* What more impoverished, if its resources be examined? What more uncivilized in terms of humans? What more forbidding in terms of the actual topography of the site? What more intemperate with regard to the nature of its climate? Yet its population contains more foreigners than natives.

The mere changing of places is, therefore, so far from being a hardship that even this place has drawn some from their native land. I find some people who say that a certain restlessness dwells naturally in the hearts of men, prompting them to change their dwelling-places and find new homes; for man has been given an inconstant and restless mind that lingers nowhere, but travels far and wide, dispatching its thoughts to all places known and unknown, roving, intolerant of rest, and delighting in new environments. This will cause you no surprise, if you consider the source from which it originates: it was not formed from earthly and heavy matter but came down from that spirit in the heavens; but things of heavenly nature are in constant motion, they speed on their way and the swiftest course drives them on. Look at the planets that give light to the world: not one of them keeps its place. The sun glides on constantly, moving from one place to another, and though it revolves with the universe, nonetheless it moves in a direction opposite to that of the world itself, speeding through all the signs of the zodiac and never coming to rest; incessant in its onward course it changes from one location to another. All the planets revolve constantly and pass on; as Nature's inviolable law has prescribed, they are carried from one place to another; when they have completed their orbits over fixed periods of years, they will once more resume the pathways by which they came: how foolish, then, to suppose that the mind of man, formed from the same elements as these heavenly bodies, is resentful of journeying and changing its home, when God's nature finds delight, or, should I say, its preservation in constant and swiftest change of location.

7. Come now, leave divine matters and direct your mind to the affairs of men: you will see that entire tribes and peoples have changed their place of habitation. What purpose do Greek cities have in the very heart of barbarian lands? What purpose the Macedonian tongue among Indians and Persians? Scythia* and all that region inhabited

by wild beasts and untamed tribes display Greek cities established on the shores of Pontus: neither the savagery of unending winter nor the character of the inhabitants, as forbidding as their climate, have deterred men from moving their homes there. A great number of Athenians live in Asia; to all parts Miletus* has sent out in streams enough citizens to fill seventy-five cities; the entire coast of Italy that was washed by the Lower Sea became a greater Greece.* Asia claims the Etruscans as her own;* the people of Tyre inhabit Africa,* those of Carthage Spain; Greeks occupied Gaul* and Gauls Greece;* the Pyrenees did not prevent the Germans from crossing over*—through regions trackless and unknown the restlessness of man has forged a path. Children, wives, parents bowed with age they trailed in their wake. Some, after enduring the buffets of lengthy wandering, have not chosen a site through judgement but seized the nearest one in their fatigue, others by the sword have won rights for themselves in foreign lands; some tribes, while making for unknown regions, were swallowed up by the sea, others settled where a lack of all provisions left them stranded.

Not all had the same reason for leaving and seeking a homeland: some, escaping the destruction of their own cities, have been driven into strange lands when deprived of their own; others have been displaced by civil strife; others have been sent out to relieve the pressure of overcrowding caused by a surplus of citizens; others have been cast out by plague or a succession of earthquakes or certain failings of an infertile soil that were past endurance; some have been seduced by the reputation of a productive coastline that won excessive praise. Different reasons have prompted different people to leave their homes: this at least is clear, none has remained in the place that gave it birth. The human race rushes to and fro without cease; every day some change occurs in so vast a world: foundations for new cities are laid, the names of new peoples emerge, as former ones pass into oblivion or change when annexed by a stronger. But what are all these transmigrations of peoples except the banishment of communities?

Why should I drag you through the long circle of examples? What need is there to cite Antenor, founder of Padua, and Evander, who established his kingdom of Arcadians on Tiber's bank? Why speak of Diomedes* and the others, victors as well as vanquished, scattered by the Trojan War throughout strange lands? Indeed, the very empire of Rome looks back for its founder to an exile, a refugee when his native city was captured, whom destiny brought to Italy, bringing with him his few remaining people and forced by fear of the conqueror to seek a distant country. But how many colonies has this people, in turn, dispatched to every province? Everywhere the Roman has been victorious, he makes a home. In order to effect this change of abode men would willingly give in their names, and, leaving his altars behind, the old fellow would accompany the settlers across the seas. The matter has no need of my citing further instances; but I will add one which demands our attention: this very island has many times changed its inhabitants before now. To pass over older examples shrouded by antiquity, the Greeks who now inhabit Marseilles, having left Phocis,* first settled in this island, and there is no certainty as to what drove them from it, whether it was the inclemency of the climate, or the sight of so powerful a neighbour as Italy, or the fact that nature had denied their coastline any harbours; we can be sure the reason was not the fierce nature of the inhabitants, since they had established themselves among men who were at that time the most savage and barbarous peoples of Gaul. Subsequently Ligurians crossed over into the island, as did Spaniards, as is shown by the similarity of customs; for the inhabitants have the same headgear and the same form of footwear as the Cantabrians, and share with them certain words; for through conversing with Greeks and Ligurians their language as a whole has forfeited its native character. After this two colonies of Roman citizens were transported there, one by Marius, the other by Sulla: so frequently has the population of this barren, thistle-grown rock undergone change! In short you will scarcely find any land which retains a native population to this day; the inhabitants everywhere are of mixed race and foreign stock. One people has succeeded another: what one rejected with scorn, another was eager to possess; one that drove out another from its land, has itself been compelled to go. This is the decree of fate, that nothing should stand for ever in the same degree of fortune.

8. The most learned of the Romans, Varro,* considers that, discounting all the other inconveniences of exile, adequate compensation for the mere changing of place is provided by the fact that, wherever we come, we must encounter there the same order of nature; Marcus Brutus* thinks that this is enough, the fact that those who go into exile are permitted to take their own virtues with them.

Even if someone judges that neither of these beliefs is sufficient in itself to console the exile, he will grant that the two of them in combination are all-powerful. For what a trivial amount it is that we are losing! Two most beautiful things will follow us wherever we go, universal Nature and our own virtue. This, believe me, was the will of the great creator of the universe, whoever he was, whether a god with power over all, or incorporeal reason, the designer of mighty works, or a divine spirit permeating all things great and small with equal energy, or fate and an unchangeable sequence of causes that cling one to another; this, I say, was his will, in order that only the most trivial of our possessions should fall under the control of another. All that is of the greatest worth for a man lies outside the power of his fellow men, and can neither be given nor taken away. This universe, the greatest and most splendidly furnished of Nature's creations, and the most magnificent part of it, the mind of man, that surveys and marvels at the universe, are our own possessions in perpetuity, and will remain with us as long as we ourselves remain. And so, eagerly, with heads high and unfaltering steps, let us hasten wherever circumstances take us, let us traverse each and every land: no place of exile can be found within the universe, for nothing within the universe is foreign to man. Wherever you lift your gaze from the earth to the heavens, a distance that nothing can alter separates man's realm from the gods'. Accordingly, provided my eyes are not deprived of that sight of which they never have their fill; provided I may look upon the sun and moon, and let my gaze be fixed upon the other planets, as I trace their risings and settings, their relative distances and the causes of their movements, be they swift or slow; provided I may observe the host of stars that twinkle through the night, some of them not moving, others not entering upon a great circuit but orbiting within their own field, certain ones suddenly bursting forth, while others by scattering their fire dazzle the eyesight, as if they were falling, or flying past with a long trail of brilliant light; provided I may share the company of these and mingle with heavenly creations, as far as a man may be permitted to; provided I may always keep my mind directed upon the sight of kindred phenomena on high, what difference does it make to me what soil lies beneath my feet?

9. 'But this land does not yield fruit-bearing or pleasant trees; no great or navigable river-channels water it; it produces nothing to attract

the interest of other tribes, and its fertility barely extends to meet the needs of its own inhabitants; no precious stones are mined here, no veins of gold and silver extracted from the soil.' But it is a narrow mind that takes delight in earthly things: it should be directed rather to things above that everywhere appear the same and everywhere have the same splendour. One should reflect on this point as well, that true blessings are obscured from us by these earthly things owing to values that are misguided and wrongly held. The longer a man extends his colonnades, the higher he raises his towers, the more widely he stretches out his mansions, the deeper he digs caverns for summer apartments, the vaster appear the roofs for banqueting halls he builds, the more there will be to hide the sky from his view. Accident has cast you into a part of the world where the most elegant place of shelter is a cottage: what an impoverished spirit you show, how meanly you console yourself, if your reason for enduring this bravely is that you know the cottage of Romulus. Say this, rather: 'So this humble hovel grants access to the virtues, does it? Soon it will have a greater beauty than any temple, when one sees under its roof justice and temperance, wisdom and righteousness, an understanding of the proper distribution of all duties and knowledge of things human and divine. No place is narrow that contains as great a number of virtues as impressive as these; no exile is hard to bear when one is allowed to embark on it with companions such as these.'

In the book that he wrote on virtue, Brutus says that he saw Marcellus* in exile at Mytilene, living most happily, as far as the limitations of human nature allowed, and at no other time in his life displaying such an appetite for liberal studies. Therefore he adds that, as he was about to return to Rome, he felt he was going into exile himself rather than leaving his friend in exile. Fortune certainly smiled more on Marcellus at that time when, as an exile, he won Brutus' approval than when, as a consul, he won the senate's. Only a man of true greatness could have made someone think of himself as an exile because he was taking leave of an exile. Only a man of true greatness could have won the admiration of a person whom Cato, his kinsman, felt impelled to admire. Brutus says also that Gaius Caesar sailed past Mytilene because he could not bear to see a great man brought low. Indeed the senate by appealing to the people did succeed in obtaining his recall, showing such sadness and concern that they seemed that day to share the feelings of Brutus and to be pleading, not for Marcellus, but for themselves, to avoid the fate of exile through being deprived of his company; but he gained far more on that day when Brutus was not able to leave him, and Caesar to see him, in exile. For it was his good fortune to have testimony from both men: Brutus felt sorrow at returning without him and Caesar felt shame. Surely you do not doubt that a man as great as Marcellus often gave himself such encouragement as this to bear exile with a calm mind: 'The loss of your homeland is not unhappiness: you have so early accustomed yourself to studies as to know that for the wise man every place is his homeland. And, besides, did not the very man who caused your exile spend ten successive years absent from his homeland? It is quite true that the reason for this was his extension of the empire, but he was still absent from his homeland. Now, look, he is drawn towards Africa, which teems with threats of resurgent war, drawn also towards Spain, which nurtures to fresh life forces once broken and shattered, drawn towards traitorous Egypt, in short towards the whole world, which looks eagerly for the opportunity to attack our stricken empire; with which danger shall he engage first? What area shall he first combat? He will be driven through every land by his own victory. Let him be revered and worshipped by nations: you should live happy to be admired by Brutus.'

10. Nobly, therefore, did Marcellus endure his exile, and nothing in his mind was changed by his change of place, although poverty accompanied it; but that this involves no disaster, is known to all men who have not yet succumbed to the madness of greed and luxury, which overturn everything. For how trifling a sum is necessary to provide a man's care? And who can fail to have this trifle, if he possesses a modicum of virtue? As far as I myself am concerned, I know that it is not wealth I have lost but my occupations. The body's wants are of little significance: it desires the removal of cold, and the satisfying of hunger and thirst by food and drink; if there is anything we crave beyond these, the effort we expend is for our vices, not our needs. It is not necessary to ransack the depths of every sea or to load our bellies with the meat of slaughtered creatures or to extract shellfish from unknown shores of the furthest sea: the curses of gods and goddesses land on the heads of those whose luxury exceeds the limits of an empire already the object of too much envy! They want game that is caught beyond the Phasis* to stock their immodest kitchens, and are not embarrassed to get birds from the Parthians,

when we haven't yet got our revenge from them.* From the world
over they gather together every known delicacy to satisfy a critical
palate; from the furthest ocean is delivered the food that their stomachs,
ruined by indulgence, can scarcely retain; they vomit in order to eat,
they eat in order to vomit, and do not see fit even to digest the
banquets for which they scour the whole world. If a man holds such
things in contempt, what harm can poverty inflict on him? If a man
craves them, poverty actually becomes beneficial for him; for he recov-
ers health in spite of himself and, if even under duress he will not
take his medicine, for a while at least, while he cannot attain them, he
is like someone who does not want them. Gaius Caesar,* whom
Nature produced, in my view, to demonstrate what supreme vice
allied to supreme power was capable of, had dinner one day at a cost
of ten million sesterces; and despite all the guests providing their
ingenuity to assist him, he still could hardly devise how to make
a single dinner cost the tribute from three provinces. How wretched
they are, those men whose appetite is only stirred at the sight of
expensive foods! And the reason for the expense is not their exqui-
site taste or a particular delight they bring to the palate but their
rarity and the difficulty of acquiring them. Otherwise, should men
want to return to a healthy state of mind, what need is there of so
many arts that serve the belly? What need of commerce? What need
of laying waste to forests? What need of plundering the deep? All
around us lie the foods that Nature has placed in all locations; but as
though lacking the power of sight, men pass these by and traverse
every region, crossing seas, and stimulating their hunger at considerable cost, when at small expense they might appease it. It is tempt-
ing to say: 'Why do you launch ships? Why do you arm your bands
against both men and beasts? Why do you scurry here and there in
such great confusion? Why do you pile wealth upon wealth? Are you
reluctant to reflect on the small size of your own bodies? Surely it is
madness, indeed the wildest lunacy, when you can hold so little, to
desire so much. You may, therefore, increase your revenues and
extend your boundaries, but never will you enlarge the bodies you
have been given. Your business transactions may flourish, you may
derive great profit from warfare, you may gather for your table foods
hunted down from every quarter, but you will have no place to store
these splendid acquisitions you own. Why do you seek so many things?
No doubt our ancestors were unhappy fellows, those men whose virtue

even today sustains our vices—they won their food by their own hands and used the earth as their bed, the roofs of their homes as yet lacked gold to make them glitter and their temples precious stones to dazzle the eye; in those days, then, oaths were solemnly made with gods of clay as witnesses: men who had sworn by such gods would return to their enemy rather than prove false,* though it meant their death. And then there is our dictator, the man who gave audience to the Samnites' envoys* while he stood at his hearth, cooking the cheapest sort of food with his own hand, that hand that had by then so often struck down our enemies and placed on the lap of Jupiter on the Capitoline a wreath of laurel—no doubt he enjoyed a less happy life than Apicius* did in our own memory, the man who in that city which philosophers were once ordered to leave as "corruptors of youth" polluted his contemporaries with his teaching, as a professor of the noble art of the cookshop.' It is worth while being informed of the man's end. After squandering a hundred million sesterces on his kitchen, after drinking up at each one of his riotous dinners as much as the emperors distributed in largess and the vast income of the Capitol, he foundered under his debts and only then was forced to examine his accounts: he worked out that he would have ten million sesterces left over and ended his life by taking poison, on the basis that it would be a life of extreme starvation if supported only by ten million. How luxurious a life he had if he regarded ten million as poverty! Now go and take the view that quantity of money is what matters, not quality of mind. One man dreaded ten million sesterces, and a sum that other men seek in their prayers he shunned by taking poison! In the case of a man so corrupted in mind, that final drink brought him nothing but health: the time when he ate and drank poisons was when he not only delighted in but boasted of gigantic banquets, when he paraded his vices, when he drew the attention of all Rome to his extravagances, when he seduced the young into imitating him, who even when they lack bad examples make ready students without encouragement. This is the fate of those who measure riches not by reason, whose boundaries are fixed, but by the viciousness we have made habitual in our lives, though its powers are beyond measurement and scope. Greed is satisfied by nothing, but nature finds satisfaction even in scant measure. The poverty of an exile is, therefore, no disadvantage to him; for no place of exile is so lacking in resources that it does not prove richly fertile for supplying a man's needs.

11. 'But the exile is going to miss his clothes and his house.' Will he miss these also simply to the extent of his need? Then he will not go without either shelter or covering; for equally little is required to cover the body as to give it nourishment; Nature has made nothing difficult for a man which she also made necessary for him. But if he desires purple cloth steeped in rich dye, threaded with gold and tricked out with patterns and colours of different kinds, then it is his own fault, not Nature's, if he is poor. Even if you restore to him what he has lost, your effort will be wasted; for once restored, he will lack more of whatever he desires than he lacked of all his former possessions when he was an exile. But suppose he desires furniture that gleams with gold vessels and silverware distinguished by the names of ancient artists, bronze whose high value depends on the mad impulse of a few, and a crowd of servants that would make even a vast mansion seem cramped, pack-animals with bodies crammed and forced to grow fat, and marbles from every part of the world—though he should pile up all of these, never will they satisfy his insatiable mind, any more than any quantity of water will be enough to satisfy a man whose desire springs, not from need, but from the fire that burns in his innards; for this is not thirst, but a sickness. And it is not merely money or food that leads to this result; the same nature is to be found in every desire that derives, not from need, but from vice: all that you pile up to satisfy it will not terminate but advance desire. Accordingly, the man who keeps himself within the bounds of nature will not feel poverty; the man who trespasses beyond them will be pursued by poverty even if he possesses the greatest wealth. Things that are necessary even places of exile will supply, those that are superfluous not even kingdoms. It is the mind that makes us rich; this is what accompanies us into exile, and in the most forbidding wilderness it discovers all that our bodies require for sustenance and then itself overflows in the enjoyment of its own advantages: money has no relevance to the mind, no more than it has to the immortal gods. All those things that men's untutored thoughts admire, enslaved as they are to their bodies—precious stones, gold, silver, polished tables, round and vast in size—all these are earthly dross that cannot be loved by the pure spirit, mindful of its own nature, as it is itself light and lacks encumbrance, and is destined to soar to the heights once released from the confines of the body; meanwhile, restricted by mortal limbs and the heavy load of enveloping flesh, it does its best

to survey heavenly matter by means of swift and winged thought. This is the reason why it can never suffer exile, being free and kindred to the gods, undismayed by any world or any age; for its thought traverses all of heaven, and projects itself into all time, past and yet to come. But this feeble body of ours, the spirit's gaol and fetters, is tossed in all directions, and bears the brunt of punishments, robberies, and diseases alike; but the spirit itself is sacred and everlasting, and no hand can be laid upon it.

12. In case you think that I am using only the teachings of philosophers to make light of the ills of poverty, something felt to be disagreeable only by those who think it so, consider, first, how many more poor people there are, and yet you will notice that in no way do they suffer more from unhappiness and anxiety than the rich: indeed I am inclined to think they are happier, because they have fewer things to vex their minds. Let us turn our attention to those who possess wealth: how many occasions there are when they resemble the poor! When they travel abroad, they have to cut down their luggage, and whenever the pressure of the journey compels them to hurry, they dismiss their host of attendants. If they are on campaign, what fraction of their possessions do they have with them, since all luxury is banned by the discipline of the camp! It is not only requirements imposed by certain times and places that put them on a level with the poor in terms of want: they choose certain days when boredom with wealth overcomes them to have dinner on the ground and use earthenware vessels, dispensing with their gold and silver plate. Madmen! They sometimes crave the state that keeps them in perpetual dread. Oh, what darkness of mind, what ignorance of truth hampers them, as they feign poverty for the sake of pleasure!

For myself, whenever I consider the great examples of early days, I am ashamed to seek consolations for poverty, since the luxury of our times has reached such a pitch that the allowance now granted to an exile exceeds the sum inherited in those days by prominent men. It is generally agreed that Homer had only one slave, Plato three, and Zeno, who founded the strict and manly Stoic school of thinkers, none: will anyone, then, say that those men lived wretched lives without making everyone regard him as completely wretched himself for saying this? Menenius Agrippa,* whose mediation between senate and people achieved harmony in the state, had a funeral that was financed by public subscription. Atilius Regulus,* while he was busy routing the Carthaginians in Africa, wrote to the senate that his hired-hand had run off and left his farm abandoned; the senate decreed that Regulus' farm should be maintained at public expense while he was away: was it not worth his while to go without a servant's services so that the Roman people might become his labourer? The daughters of Scipio* received their dowry from the public treasury because their father had left them nothing: undoubtedly it was only fair that the Roman people should pay tribute to Scipio on one occasion as he was constantly exacting it from Carthage. How fortunate those maidens' husbands were to have the Roman people as a father-in-law! Who do you suppose are the happier, those whose daughters dance upon the stage and marry with a dowry of a million sesterces, or Scipio, whose children enjoyed the guardianship of the senate and received for their dowry a weight of copper? Can any man scorn poverty, when it boasts such exalted ancestors? Can a man in exile resent the lack of any commodity when Scipio lacked a dowry, Regulus a hired-hand, and Menenius a funeral, when what all those men needed was provided to their greater honour precisely because they had had the need? With such helpers as these, therefore, poverty enjoys not only security but desirability as well.

13. The reply may be made: 'Why do you cleverly distinguish things that can be tolerated, if taken separately, but cannot be, if combined? Change of place can be tolerated, if it is only the place you change; poverty can be tolerated if it does not involve a loss of reputation, which even on its own is accustomed to crush men's spirits.' In answer to this man, who is intent on frightening me with a plethora of woes, I shall have to use the following words: 'If you possess enough strength to combat any one part of Fortune, you will have enough to meet all. Once virtue has hardened the mind, it renders you invulnerable from every quarter. If greed, the worst vice that plagues the human race, relaxes its hold, ambition will not detain you; if you regard your last day, not as a punishment, but as, so to speak, a law of nature, then you will have cast out from your breast the fear of death and the fear of nothing else will dare to enter there; if you consider that sexual desire was given to man, not for the sake of pleasure, but in order to continue the human race, then, once this secret and deadly impulse implanted in our very vitals has failed to work its poison on you, every other desire will pass you by untainted.

Reason overthrows vices, not one by one, but all together: once for all is the victory gained.' Do you suppose that loss of reputation can influence any wise man, who is entirely self-sufficient and has distanced himself from the views of the common folk? More serious even than loss of reputation is a shameful death: but Socrates showed the same expression on his face on entering prison as he had when once, single-handed, he put the Thirty Tyrants* in their place, and so he was able to remove any disgrace even from that place; for no place that contained Socrates could possibly appear to be a prison. Who has become so blind to perceiving the truth that he regards Marcus Cato's two failures to be elected praetor and consul as bringing disgrace on him? That disgrace fell on the praetorship and consulship, to which Cato was bringing honour. No one is the object of another man's contempt, unless he is first the object of his own. A submissive and abject mind exposes itself to such insult; but the man who rises up to face the cruellest blows of Fortune and overthrows those troubles that overwhelm others wears these very sorrows as a badge of reverence, since our instinct makes nothing compel our profound admiration as much as a man who shows courage in adversity. At Athens, when Aristides* was being led to execution, every man who crossed his path lowered his gaze and uttered a groan, thinking that it was not merely a just man who was suffering punishment but justice itself; but one man was found who spat in his face. This might have stirred him to anger, since he knew that no one with clean lips would have dared such an act; but he merely wiped his face and said with a smile to the magistrate accompanying him, 'Remind that fellow to avoid opening his mouth so offensively in future.' This was crowning his insult with insult. I am aware that certain people say that nothing is harder to bear than contempt, that death itself is preferable in their eyes. To them I will reply that even exile is often free from any form of contempt: if a great man falls, he remains great though he is prostrate, and men no more despise him, I say, than they trample on the fallen walls of a temple, that attract from the devout as much reverence as when they were standing.

14. Since you have no reason, dearest mother, to be driven to endless weeping on my account, it follows that reasons of your own are vexing you. Now, there are two possibilities; either you are affected by the thought that you have lost some protection, or you are not able to bear the actual longing you feel for me.

The first of these I must touch upon only lightly; for I know that your heart loves nothing in your dear ones other than themselves. Let that be the concern of those mothers who, with a woman's lack of self-control, make use of a son's power, who, because women are prevented from holding office, pursue their ambitions through their sons, who both drain their sons' inheritances and plan to become their heirs, who wear out their eloquence in bestowing it on others: but in the case of your own children's blessings, you have always taken the greatest pleasure in them, while making the least use of them; you have always set limits to our generosity without setting any to your own; although you were still subject to your father's authority, you voluntarily made presents to your wealthy sons; you showed such care in managing our inheritances that you exerted yourself as if they were your own and showed such scruple that they might have belonged to a stranger; you made so little use of our influence that you might have been dealing with the property of a stranger, and all that accrued to you when we were elected to office was the pleasure and the expense it caused you. At no time did your care for us look to your own advantage; accordingly, in the loss of a son you cannot miss what you never regarded as your concern while he was free from harm.

15. I must concentrate all my effort at consolation on the latter point, the true source of the force that informs a mother's grief: 'Well then, I am denied the embrace of my beloved son; I am not able to enjoy the pleasure of seeing him, the pleasure of his conversation. Where is he, the one who by his very sight took the wrinkles from my troubled brow, to whom I gave the burden of all my anxious thoughts? Where are the talks we shared, of which I could never have my fill? Where are the studies that I shared with more than a woman's delight, with more than a mother's friendship? Where those meetings we had? Where the boyish merriment every time you saw your mother?' To these you add the actual places that witnessed the joyous exchanges between us, and the things that remind you of our recent association, inevitably the most potent source of distress to the mind. For Fortune has been cruel in engineering even this blow against you, that she decreed that you should take your leave of me only two days before exile struck, at a time when you were free from anxieties and had no fear of any such disaster. It is a blessing that we had been separated before by a great distance, a blessing that my absence of

several years had prepared you for this misfortune: in returning to Rome you denied yourself the pleasure of seeing your son and forfeited the habit of bearing his absence. Had you been absent a long time earlier, you would have endured my fate with greater fortitude, as separation itself diminishes our sense of loss; if you had not gone away, you would at least have achieved the final pleasure of seeing your son two days longer: as it is, fate in its cruelty arranged that you should not be with me when misfortune struck, and should not have grown accustomed to my absence. But the harder these trials are, the more bravery you must summon, and the more fiercely you must engage with an enemy you know and have often before now defeated. This body of yours from which the blood now flows is not without wounds: you have been struck in the very scars they left.

16. It is not open to you to use the excuse of being a woman, who has virtually been granted the right to excessive, though not boundless, tears; and this is why our ancestors prescribed a period of ten months for women to mourn their husbands, in order to curb the obduracy of a woman's grief by means of a public ordinance. They did not prevent, but set a limit to, their mourning; for when you have lost one who is most dear, it is stupid indulgence to grieve endlessly, but inhuman hardness not to grieve at all: the mean between conjugal affection and reason is best, feeling the loss and yet mastering it. Nor is there any cause for you to look to certain women, whose mourning, once assumed, ended only with their deaths (some you know who donned the garb of mourning on losing their sons and never took it off): life, that was more exacting from the start, demands more of you; the excuse of being a woman cannot apply to one who has always been free from all the female weaknesses. The greatest evil of our age, betrayal of a husband's bed, has not enrolled you with the majority of women; your head has not been turned by jewels or pearls; the gleam of wealth has not seemed to your eyes the greatest blessing of the human race; you have not been seduced by the imitation of worse women that proves dangerous even to the virtuous, raised as you were soundly in an ancient and strict household; never were you ashamed of the number of your children, as if it cast aspersions on your years, never as other women, whose recommendation lies solely in their beauty, have you attempted to conceal your pregnancy as though it were a burden that brought you dishonour, or ever crushed the hopes of the children conceived within your womb; you have not defiled

your features with paints and cosmetics; never have you been drawn to the sort of dress that exposes no more flesh once taken off: you present to the eye that unequalled ornament, that fairest beauty that time cannot wither, that supreme distinction of womanly virtue. Accordingly, it is not open to you to claim your female sex as an excuse for persistent grief, as your own excellent qualities make you a stranger to this; you should be as far removed from the tears, as from the vices, of women. Not even women will permit you to pine away from your wound, but will tell you to make a swift end of necessary grief before rising with a lighter heart, if only you are prepared to contemplate those women whose evident courage has won them a place in the ranks of great men.

Cornelia* gave birth to twelve children, but Fortune had reduced these to two: if you wished to count Cornelia's losses, she had lost ten, but if you wished to evaluate them, she had lost the Gracchi. Yet when mourners gathered around her, cursing her fate, she forbade them to put the blame on Fortune, as Fortune had given her the Gracchi as sons. It was right that this should be the woman to have given birth to the man who exclaimed in the popular assembly: 'Have you the presumption to speak ill of the mother who gave me birth?' But in my view far more spirit is to be found in his mother's utterance: the son valued highly the birthdays of the Gracchi, but the mother their funerals as well. Rutilia accompanied her son Cotta* into exile and was so bound up with her love for him that she chose to suffer exile rather than longing, and only returned to her homeland when her son did. But when he had been restored and had achieved prominence in the state, he was lost to her: in this she displayed as much courage as when she had followed him into exile, and no one ever observed her weeping after the funeral of her son. In the case of his banishment she showed bravery, in that of his death, wisdom; for just as nothing deterred her from the love she owed a son, so nothing made her linger in sorrow that was superfluous and foolish. These are the women I would have you numbered with; theirs are the lives you have always taken as your pattern, and, in restraining and suppressing your grief, theirs is the example you will best follow.

17. I am aware that this matter does not lie in our power, and that no emotion is submissive, particularly if it originates in grief; for it is ungoverned and stubbornly opposes every attempt at cure. Sometimes we want to crush it and to swallow down our groans; we wear a false

expression of calm on our faces, but still the tears pour down our cheeks. Sometimes we resort to the games or gladiatorial displays to occupy the mind; but even during the diversion of the very spectacles we watch, it is undermined by some trivial detail that awakes our sense of longing. For this reason it is better to conquer our sadness than to deceive it; for once it has departed, seduced by pleasures or engrossing pursuits, it rises up again and gathers fresh momentum for its fury from its very rest; but any grief that has yielded to reason is laid to rest for ever. Accordingly, I do not propose to point out to you the methods that I know many have resorted to, such as distracting or delighting your mind by foreign travel, whether to distant or charming places, or spending considerable time in the careful scrutiny of your accounts and the management of your property, or constantly involving yourself in some new piece of business: all such things are only of short-lived benefit and do not cure sorrow but merely hinder it; but my preference is for it to be brought to an end, not beguiled. Therefore I am guiding you to the place where all who seek to escape from Fortune must seek refuge, philosophical studies: they will heal your wound, they will pluck from your memory every rooted sorrow. Even if you had not made them your constant companion before, you would need to make use of them now; but within the scope afforded you by my father's old-fashioned strictness, while you may not have grasped fully all the liberal arts, yet you have formed some acquaintance with them. If only my father, that best of men, had been willing to relax his devotion to the practice of his forefathers and consented to your being given a thorough grounding in the teachings of philosophy rather than a mere smattering! In that case you would now not have to seek help against Fortune but only to display your own defence against her. Because of those women who do not use learning as a means to wisdom but furnish themselves with it for display, he did not permit you to continue your studies. However, thanks to your mind's capacity for acquiring knowledge, you imbibed more than might have been expected in the time you were given; the foundations for all areas of study have been laid: return to these studies now; they will bring you safety. They will console you, they will delight you, and if they enter your mind in earnest, never more shall grief find access there, never more anxiety, never more the pointless distress of unnecessary misery. To none of these will your heart be exposed; for it has long been closed to all other weaknesses.

These studies are your surest protection and alone are able to rescue you from Fortune.

18. But since there are certain props on which you need to lean before reaching that harbour promised to you by philosophy, I wish meanwhile to reveal to you the consolations you still possess. Consider my brothers;* while they continue to live, it would be a sin to complain of Fortune. In each of them, for all the difference of their merits, you have cause for delight: the one by his energy has won the distinction of public office, the other with his wisdom has treated it with contempt. Take comfort in the high standing of the one son, in the seclusion of the other, in the filial love of both. I am acquainted with my brothers' secret motives: the one burnishes his prestige in order that it may bring honour to you, the other has withdrawn to a life of peaceful repose in order to have time to devote to you. Fortune has been gracious in so arranging the lives of your sons that they confer upon you both assistance and delight: you are able to find protection in the prestige of one and enjoyment in the leisure of the other. They will compete in their services to you, and the devotion of two will make up for the longing you feel for one. I can with complete confidence make you this assurance: you will lack nothing except their full number.

From them now turn your gaze on your grandchildren as well: on Marcus, a most charming lad, the mere sight of whom is enough to banish any sad thoughts; no one's heart can be tormented by a grief so great or so fresh that an embrace from him will not soothe the pain. Whose tears would not be suppressed by his cheerfulness? Whose mind fettered by anxiety would not be set free by his witty remarks? Who will not be roused to joking by that carefree mood of his? What man intent on his own thoughts will he not draw to himself and divert by means of that talkativeness of which no one will ever tire? I pray the gods that he may outlive us! May all the cruelty of fate stop, exhausted, at me; whatever sorrow you must endure as a mother, whatever as a grandmother, may it all be transferred to me! May all the rest of my troop have the blessing of keeping their present fortune intact: I shall make no complaint about my lack of children, none about my present fortune, provided I may be a scapegoat for my family and know it will be spared any further grief.

Clasp to your bosom Novatilla, who so soon will present you with great-grandchildren; I had so transferred her to myself, had so adopted her as my own, that she may well think herself an orphan in losing me, though her father still lives; love her for my sake also! Fortune lately stole her mother from her: through your devotion you can cause her merely to grieve, not really to know, the loss of her mother. Now is the time to regulate her character, now the time to give it shape: instruction goes deeper when its imprint is made on minds not yet hardened by time. Let her become accustomed to your conversation, let her be fashioned according to your taste: you will give her much, even if all you give is your example. A duty as sacred as this will serve as a cure for your ills; for only philosophy or an occupation that brings honour can deflect from its distress the heart that mourns out of devotion.

I would number among your considerable consolations your father as well, if he were not away at present. But, as it is, let the love you bear for him make you reflect on the love he bears for you: you will understand how much more just it is for you to be preserved for him than sacrificed for me. Whenever grief afflicts you with excessive force and bids you follow, consider your father. Admittedly, by giving him so many grandchildren and great-grandchildren, you have given him no cause to regard you as his only joy; yet on you depends the crowning happiness of a life he has led with good fortune. While he lives, it would be wrong of you to complain of having lived.

19. I have so far said nothing of your greatest source of comfort, your sister,* that heart so full of loyalty to you, into which you pour all your cares unreservedly, that lady who feels as a mother towards us all. With her you have shed tears in common, in her comforting arms you first learned to breathe anew. She shares all your feelings, it is true, but, where I am concerned, her grief is expressed not only for you. In her arms I was carried to the city, hers was the devoted and maternal nursing that enabled me to recover health after a lengthy period of illness; she it was who furnished kindly support when I stood for the quaestorship, and for my sake mastered her shyness through her love, when she lacked the confidence even for conversation or a loud greeting. Neither her secluded manner of life, nor her old-fashioned modesty at a time when so many women lack all modesty, nor her quiet ways, nor her customary seclusion and love of leisure, none of these, I say, prevented her from becoming even ambitious in order to further my cause. This woman, dearest mother, is the comfort to give you fresh heart: attach yourself to her with all your strength,

clasp her to you in the tightest of embraces. It is the habit of mourners to shun what most they love and to seek freedom for the display of their grief: but you must seek out her company whatever thoughts occur to you; whether you wish to maintain your mood or to be free of it, you will find in her one who will either end or share your sorrow. But if I know the good sense of this paragon among women, she will not allow you to be worn away by a grief that will bring no profit, and she will tell you the story of an experience of her own, which I also witnessed in person.

In the very midst of a voyage she lost her beloved husband, my uncle, whom she had married as a young woman; but she showed endurance, resisting at the same time both grief and fear, and, conquering the storm, she brought his body safe to shore despite shipwreck. Ah, how many are the women whose noble acts lie in obscurity! If she had been fortunate enough to live in days of old when men showed open admiration for deeds of heroism, how vigorously would poets compete in extolling the wife who, forgetful of her own weakness, forgetful of the sea, that even the bravest hearts must fear, exposed her own life to dangers so that another might receive burial, and, in planning her husband's funeral, had no fears for her own! All poets celebrate in their verse the woman who gave herself to death in place of her husband:* but it is a nobler act for a woman to seek burial for her husband by endangering her own life; it is a greater love that wins smaller recompense for a danger equally shared.

After this it would surprise no one that throughout the sixteen years of her husband's governorship of Egypt she was never seen in public, never granted a native of that country access to her home, never made a request of her husband or allowed him to make one of her. Accordingly, that province so given to gossip, so adept at inventing insults for its rulers, where even those who avoided blame did not escape a bad reputation, looked up to her as a unique instance of a virtuous nature and suppressed every tendency to talk too freely about her, no easy task for a people that enjoys even dangerous witticisms, and to this day lives in the constant hope, though hardly expectation, of seeing another like her. It would be a great achievement if over sixteen years she had gained the approval of that province: it was greater still that she escaped its notice. I do not mention these things in order to enumerate her praiseworthy qualities, for to catalogue them so inadequately is to do them scant justice, but so that you may understand the nobility of mind of a woman who has not yielded to the desire for power or to the desire for wealth, those companions and curses of all authority, who, when her ship had now lost its rigging and her own shipwreck was in sight, was not deterred by the fear of death from clinging to her lifeless husband and searching for a means, not to escape from the vessel, but to bring him with her. You are obliged to display a bravery that matches hers, to summon your mind back from sorrow, and to behave in such a way that no one thinks you regret your motherhood.

20. But since, although you have taken every precaution, it is inevitable that your thoughts return occasionally to me, and that of all your children none under present circumstances occupies your mind more frequently—not that they are less dear to you but that it is natural to lay one's hand more often on the part that causes pain—let me tell you how you should regard me: as one no less happy or cheerful than when his fortunes were best. And they are indeed now best, as my mind, free from all other occupation, has leisure for its own tasks, sometimes delighting in less serious studies, sometimes, in its passion for the truth, rising to the contemplation of its own nature and that of the universe. It strives to know, first, the lands of the earth and where they lie, then the laws which govern the surrounding sea with its recurring motions of ebb and flow; then it examines all that, filled with terrors, lies between heaven and earth, this expanse disturbed by thunder, lightning, blasts of winds, and the rain and snow and hail that fall upon our heads; then, once it has ranged over the lower spaces, it bursts through to the heights, and enjoys the beautiful spectacle of divine things, and, remembering its own immortality, it proceeds to all that has been and will come into being throughout all time's ages.

ON MERCY

BOOK I

TO THE EMPEROR NERO

1. I have assumed the task, Nero Caesar, of writing about mercy, so that in some sense I might fulfil the purpose of a mirror and reveal you to yourself as one who is destined to gain the greatest of all pleasures. For, although the real profit of noble actions lies in their performance, and there is no worthy reward for virtuous acts apart from themselves, it still gives pleasure to make a tour of inspection of a good conscience, then to let one's eye take in this numberless mass of people, contentious, turbulent, headstrong, ready, if it breaks this yoke, to run riot for the destruction of itself and others alike, and then to reason with oneself as follows: 'Have I of all mortals been chosen, have I found favour with the gods so that I should serve as their representative on earth? I am the judge of life and death for nations; in my hands rests what kind of lot and condition each man enjoys; from my lips Fortune declares what gift she wishes to be given to each of mankind; from my pronouncement peoples and cities form their reasons for happiness; no part of the wide world prospers without my consent and favour; all these thousands of swords held in check by my peace will be drawn at the nod of my head; which nations should be utterly destroyed, which banished, which granted freedom's gift, which deprived of it, which kings should become slaves and which should have their heads crowned with regal honour, which cities shall tumble and which shall rise, this is for me to decree. Having all this within my power, I have not been driven to inflict unjust punishments by anger, or by a young man's impulse, or by the rashness and stubbornness of men which have frequently wrested tolerance from even the most placid souls, or even by that pride in status that uses terror to display authority, a dreadful but not infrequent characteristic of those who rule great empires. In my case the sword is concealed, no, buried in its sheath, and with the greatest reluctance would I spill even the meanest blood; no one is deprived of favour from me, though he lacks everything but the name of man. Sternness I keep concealed, but mercy always in readiness; such guard

do I keep over myself as though I am going to render an account to the laws that I have called forth from the darkness of decay into daylight. One man's youthful years moves me, another's advanced age; one I have pardoned for his high standing, another for his low; whenever I discovered no excuse for pity, I spared the man for my own sake. Today I am prepared to give the immortal gods a full tally of the human race, should they require a reckoning from me.'

This is a declaration, Caesar, you can boldly make, that everything which has passed into your trust and protection, is kept safe still, and that through you no loss is suffered by the state, either by force or by fraud. It is the rarest of praises, and one not hitherto granted to any emperor, that you have set your heart on winning—a blameless soul. The effort has not been made in vain, nor has that goodness of yours, which knows no equal, found men ungrateful or mean in bestowing their appreciation. You are the recipient of thanks; no human being has ever been so loved by another as you are by the people of Rome, its considerable and permanent blessing. But you have set upon your shoulders a burden that is vast; no man these days talks of the deified Augustus or of the early years of Tiberius Caesar, or looks for a model that he would have you copy other than yourself; your principate is tested and found to be worthy of reverence. This would have been hard to achieve, were it not that your goodness springs from your own nature and has not been assumed to meet the occasion. For no one can wear a mask for long; falsity swiftly lapses back into its true nature; whatever has the truth as its basis, and, as it were, rises up from firm soil, grows through the mere passing of time into something greater and better.

No small risk was facing the Roman people as long as it was uncertain what direction that noble disposition of yours would take; now the nation's prayers are assured; for no danger exists that you may suddenly forget yourself. Excessive prosperity does indeed create greed in men, and never are desires so well controlled that they vanish once satisfied; men's steps pass from great to greater heights, and they embrace the most reckless hopes once they have attained what they did not hope for; yet all your subjects today are to a man forced to admit that they are fortunate and, furthermore, that all that can be added to their present blessings is that they may never cease. Many circumstances compel them to this admission, one which more than any other a man is reluctant to make: a deep and swelling sense of peace, and justice set above all injustice; before their gaze is the fairest prospect of a state that is only denied the most complete freedom by its own liberty to destroy itself. Most strikingly, however, your mercy wins the admiration of the most eminent and most lowly citizens alike; for, whereas in the case of other blessings each man experiences or expects the share commensurate with his status, from mercy all hope to receive the same measure; and no man exists who is so satisfied with his own innocence as not to feel glad that mercy stands in sight, ready to respond to human errors.

2. I am, however, aware that there are certain people who hold that mercy sustains the worst type of men, since it has no purpose unless a crime has been committed and is the only virtue that finds no employment among those who are guiltless. But first of all, just as medicine is used by those who are ill but also honoured by those who are well, so mercy, although appealed for by those deserving punishment, is held in respect also by innocent men. Again, even in the case of the innocent this virtue may come into play, for sometimes fortune takes the place of guilt; it is not only innocence that mercy can rescue but often virtue as well, since undoubtedly the state of the times can give rise to certain actions which, though praised, may yet earn punishment. There is the further point that a great many people are capable of returning to virtue's path if punishment is waived. But pardon should not be exercised in an unthinking way; for once the distinction between bad men and good is removed, what follows is confusion and the outbreak of vice; accordingly a wise restraint should be shown, such as is capable of distinguishing between curable characters and ones past hope. The mercy we exercise ought not to be indiscriminate and for all and sundry but it should not be withheld completely; for pardoning all involves no less cruelty than pardoning none. We must preserve a mean; but because equilibrium is not easily achieved, whatever is likely to tilt the balance should incline the scale in the more benign direction.

3. But these matters will be treated more fittingly in their appropriate place. For the moment I intend to divide this subject as a whole into three sections. The first will deal with the remission of punishment; the second will attempt to show the nature and appearance of mercy: for since there are certain vices that simulate virtues, they cannot be distinguished without the stamp of marks that enable you to tell them apart; in the third place I shall look into the question

of how the mind is led to adopt this virtue, how it establishes it and through use makes it its own.

Since no virtue is more human, it must be generally accepted that no other is more appropriate for man, a belief to be held not just by those of us who regard man as a social creature, born for the good of all, but also by those who consign man to pleasure, whose words and actions all look to their own advantage; for if repose and quiet are what a man seeks, then he finds this virtue, which loves peace and holds back the hand, consonant with his own nature. But of all men mercy becomes none so well as a king or an emperor. For great power bestows grace and glory only when its potency is for benefit; it is undoubtedly a deadly force whose power can only work harm. That man alone possesses greatness that is secure and of firm foundation who is known by all men as their friend no less than their superior, whose concern for the welfare of each and every citizen they daily find to be vigilant, whose approach does not cause them to scatter, as though some monster or dangerous beast has leapt forth from its lair, but rather to vie with one another in rushing up to him, as though towards a brilliant and benevolent star. They are quite ready, in his defence, to expose themselves to assassins' sword-points, and to lay down their own bodies, if he must forge a path to safety through slaughtered men; they protect his sleep with nightly vigils and guard his person with an encircling barrier, meeting the assault of dangers like a wall.

It is not without reason that cities and peoples with such unanimity show such loving protection to their kings, and fling themselves and all that is theirs at whatever danger the ruler's safety requires; and it is not because they hold their lives cheap or have lost their wits that so many thousands meet the sword for a single man's sake, and with many deaths ransom the one life of one who is sometimes old and feeble. A comparison: the whole body is the mind's slave, and though the former is so much larger and more attractive to the eye, while, in its insubstantial state, the mind remains unseen, ignorant of where its secret dwelling lies, yet the hands, the feet, the eyes do its bidding; this skin is its protection, according to its orders we lie idle or run around without rest; when it gives the command, if it is a greedy master, we ransack the ocean for profit; if one eager for fame, before now we have thrust our right hands into flames or of our own volition plunged into the earth's bowels; it is the same with this vast throng that surrounds the life of one man: it is ruled by his spirit and guided by his reason, and would crush and smash itself with its own strength, if it were not sustained by his good counsel.

4. It is, accordingly, their own safety that men love when for one man's sake they lead ten legions at a time to battle, when they dash to the front line and brave wounds with their chests, so that their emperor's standards may not turn in defeat. For he is the bond that unites the state, he is the breath of life drawn by all these thousands, who would in their own strength constitute nothing but a burden to themselves and a prey to others, should that mind of empire be withdrawn.

> If safe their king, all have one mind;
> If lost, they leave all loyalty behind.*

Such a disaster will be the destruction of the Roman peace, such a disaster will bring the fortune of so mighty a nation crashing down; such a danger will not threaten this people only as long as it shall know how to yield to the rein, but if ever it breaks free from the rein, or refuses to accept the bit once more in its mouth, should some mishap shake it loose, this unity and this fabric of an empire most mighty will fly into many parts, and the end of this city's exercise of power will be one with the end of her obedience. This is why it is unsurprising that emperors and kings and those who safeguard the commonwealth, under whatever other title, inspire greater love than even those to whom we are bound by private ties of affection; for if right-minded people regard public interests as more important than private, it follows that the man to whom the whole state turns for guidance will also be held more dear. For at an earlier date a Caesar so dressed himself in the powers of state that the one could not be separated from the other without both being destroyed; for when a Caesar has need of power, then the state, too, has need of a head.

5. My speech seems to have departed some distance from its purpose, but, be assured, it touches closely upon the real issue. For if, as it means this far to establish, you are the soul of the state and the state your body, you see, I imagine, how necessary mercy is; for you are sparing yourself when it seems you are sparing another. Accordingly, even blameworthy citizens should be spared inasmuch as they are the weak parts of the body, and if ever blood has to be shed, the hand must be kept in control to prevent it from cutting deeper than may

be necessary. It is, therefore, as I was saying, in accordance with nature for all men to show mercy, but it lends a particular grace to rulers, since in their case it has a greater scope and has more generous opportunities for revealing itself. For how insignificant is the harm that a private citizen can inflict! When emperors are moved to fury, war ensues. But although virtues exist in mutual harmony and no one is better or more honourable than another, yet a certain virtue is more suited to certain characters. Greatness of soul befits every kind of human, even the man so reduced in circumstance that he has no further to fall; for what is greater or braver than to beat down the swords of misfortune? However, this greatness of soul is less restricted in scope when a man enjoys good fortune, and makes a better display on the judge's bench than on the courtroom floor.

Whatever house Mercy enters she will make happy and peaceful, but in a palace she will excite the greater wonder, as her visits are rarer. For what is more remarkable than that the man whose anger overpowers all resistance, whose verdict, however harsh, wins acceptance even from the victims, whom no man will interrupt, no, not even venture to contradict, if his temper grows particularly heated—that this man should lay a hand upon himself and use his power to better, less violent ends, reasoning thus with himself: 'Taking a man's life contrary to the law is within any man's power, but only I have the power to save it.' A great spirit befits great fortune, but if it does rise to the level of its fortune and stand above it, then that fortune, too, is dragged down to the ground; again, it is characteristic of a great spirit to be calm and at peace, and to show a lofty indifference to wrongs and vexations. It is for a woman to rage in anger, for wild beasts, indeed, and yet not even the noblest of these, to bite and worry their prey once brought to ground. Elephants and lions pass by what they have struck down; it is the beast lacking in nobility that does not let its victim be. Savage and relentless anger is unbecoming in a king, for in this he does not rise much above the other man but puts himself on the same level by displaying anger; but if he grants life, if he grants positions to those who deserve to lose them, having put them at risk, he is doing what only one who is a sovereign may; for although one can take life even from a superior, it can never be granted to any but an inferior. To save life is the special privilege of the loftiest rank, which never has greater claim on admiration than when it has the good fortune to have the same power as the gods, by whose kindness all of us, good and bad alike, are brought forth into the light. Accordingly, let an emperor appropriate to himself the spirit of the gods and take pleasure in the sight of some of his citizens because they are good and useful, while leaving others to make up the number; let him rejoice that some live, and others let him tolerate.

6. Turn your thoughts to this city, in which the crowd that flows endlessly through the widest streets is crushed utterly whenever anything gets in the way to impede its course as it sweeps along like a rushing torrent, this city in which the seating-space of three theatres is required at the same time, in which the produce of the plough from the world over is consumed—how desolate and lonely a place do you think it would be, if all that was left were those acquitted by a strict judge?

How few men there are presiding in criminal trials who would not be convicted under the very law they cite in such trials? How few prosecutors are free from blame? And I should not be surprised if the greatest reluctance to grant pardon is shown by the one who again and again has had reason to ask for it. We have all done wrong, some in serious things, some in trifling, some out of deliberate intention, some by chance impulse or because another's wickedness carried us away; some of us have not stood strongly enough by good intentions, and against our will have lost our innocence, still trying to hold on to it; and not only have we done wrong but we shall continue to do so, right to the end of our days. Even if a man exists who has so completely cleansed his mind now that nothing can confound or betray him any more, it is still through doing wrong that he has reached his state of blamelessness.

7. Since I have mentioned the gods, it will be best for me to lay down this as the pattern on which an emperor should seek to model himself—that he should wish to treat his people as he would wish the gods to treat him. Is it, then, of benefit to have deities that refuse to show mercy to our crimes and mistakes? Is it of benefit to have them hostile to the extent of our utter ruin? And which king will escape the danger of having his shattered limbs gathered up by soothsayers? But if the gods in their mercy and justice do not at once punish with lightning-bolts the crimes of the great, how much more justice is there in a man who has been set over other men exercising his power with a forgiving heart and reflecting on which condition of the world is more pleasing to the eye and more beautiful—when the

day is radiant and cloudless, or when all nature shakes with frequent thunderclaps, and forks of lightning-flash, now here in the sky, now there? And yet the appearance of a peaceful, ordered empire is not dissimilar to that of a cloudless, shining sky. A cruel reign is stormy and shrouded in gloom, and while men shudder and are filled with dread by the sudden clamour, not even the one who causes all the alarm fails to shake. It is an easier thing to pardon private citizens if they persist stubbornly in seeking revenge; for they can be injured and their resentment has its source in a feeling of injustice; in addition they are afraid of earning contempt, and it seems weakness, not mercy, not to return the compliment when one has suffered injury; but the man who can take vengeance with ease wins undisputed praise for clemency if he forfeits the opportunity. Men of lowly position have more freedom to resort to force, to seek legal redress, to rush into a brawl, and to indulge their anger; when opponents are evenly matched the blows are not heavy; but in a king, even loud speech and unrestrained language ill accord with his majesty.

8. You regard it as a serious matter to deprive kings of their right to speak freely, which even the humblest men may do. 'That,' you say, 'is slavery, not sovereignty.' What? Does it escape you that we are the sovereign, and you the slave? Very different is the position of those who remain hidden in a crowd that they do not rise above, whose virtues have a long struggle in order to be seen, whose vices are wrapped in darkness; but the deeds and words of men such as you are taken up by rumour, so that those who, irrespective of what reputation they may merit, are bound to have a great one, should show more concern than all others for the character of their reputation. How many are the things denied to you which your kindness allows us to enjoy! I am able without fear to walk alone in any part of the city I choose, although I am attended by no companion, and have no sword in my home or at my side; you are obliged to live armed amid the peace you have created. Escape from your lot is not within your power; it lays siege to you and pursues you with great ceremony whenever you come down from the heights. In this lies the slavery inherent in supreme greatness: it is unable to become less great; but you share with the gods this inescapable condition. For even they are held prisoner by heaven, and it is no more granted to them to forsake the heights than it is safe for you; you are nailed to your pinnacle. The movements we make attract the attention of few, we may come

forth and go back and change our clothing without everyone noticing; you are no more at liberty to shun men's eyes than the sun is. You are enveloped in a wealth of light to which all men's eyes are directed. Do you imagine you are coming forth? You are rising. You are unable to speak without your words being heard by every nation in the world; you cannot become angry without everything trembling as a result, since you cannot strike down anyone without all that surrounds him being shaken. As strokes of lightning bring danger to few but fear to all, so the punishment that great power inflicts induces more widespread fear than harm, and not without reason; for when a man's power has no limit, it is not the scale of his actions performed that occupies men's thoughts but that of the actions he is liable to perform. Take into account also that, while private men by submitting to wrongs they have received become more liable to receiving other ones, kings by showing mercy consolidate yet further their own peace of mind, as few men's hatred is crushed by repeated punishment, but every man's hatred is stirred by it. The desire to vent one's anger should not exceed the cause of that anger; otherwise, just as trees that have been trimmed put forth numerous branches in reply, and many kinds of plants are pruned to cause them to grow thicker, so a king's cruelty, by doing away with his enemies, causes their number to increase; for the parents and children of those who have been killed, as well as their relatives and friends, take the place of each single victim.

9. I wish to remind you of how true this is by an example taken from your own family. The deified Augustus was a lenient emperor, should one attempt to judge him from the period of his rule; but when he shared political power with others, he wielded the sword. When he was the same age as you are now, having passed his eighteenth year, he had already buried daggers in the bosom of friends, he had already by stealthy means aimed to strike the consul, Mark Antony, in the side, and had already been a partner in proscription. But when he had passed his fortieth year and was spending time in Gaul, information was brought to him that Lucius Cinna,* a man of little intelligence, was plotting against him; the place, the time, and the manner of the intended attack were made known to him; it was one of the accomplices who supplied the information. Augustus decided to take his revenge on the man and gave the order for a council of his friends to be convened. He spent a troubled night, as he reflected that the one to be condemned was a youth of good family, the grandson of

Gnaeus Pompey, with no stain on his character apart from this business; he could not bring himself to end the life of one man, though over dinner together Mark Antony had dictated to him the edict of proscription. He groaned, and from time to time uttered words that were impulsive and contradictory: 'Oh, what am I to do? Should I let my assassin walk at large, untroubled, while I am prey to fears? When my life has been sought without success in so many civil wars and saved from harm in so many battles of fleets and infantry, after peace has been won by land and sea, shall punishment be withheld from a man who is planning, not my murder, but my sacrifice?' (For the intention had been to attack him as he was making sacrifice.) Again, after an interval of silence, in a louder voice he would express far greater anger at himself than at Cinna: 'Why do you go on living if it matters to so many that you should die? When shall the punishments and bloodshed come to an end? It is my life that has become the obvious target for young men of noble family, for them to sharpen their swords against; my life is not worth the price, if so many must die in order that I may not.' Finally his wife, Livia, broke in and said: 'Will you listen to a woman's counsel? Follow the practice of doctors, who adopt the opposite treatments when the normal ones fail. You have achieved nothing so far from an unrelenting approach; Salvidienus was followed by Lepidus, Lepidus by Murena, Murena by Caepio, Caepio by Egnatius,* not to mention the others whose frightful daring makes one ashamed. Now try how mercy works for you; pardon Lucius Cinna. He has been arrested; he can no longer harm you but he can benefit your reputation.' Delighted to have found a supporter, he thanked his wife and, issuing immediate instructions that his request to his friends to confer with him be countermanded, he summoned Cinna alone to his presence. When he had sent everyone away from his room, he ordered that a second chair to be placed for Cinna and said: 'My first request to you is that you do not interrupt me as I am speaking or raise any protest in the course of my words; you will be given free opportunity to speak. Although I discovered you, Cinna, in the camp of the foe, not made but born my bitter enemy, I saved you, I gave you permission to keep all that your father had bequeathed to you. Today you are a man of such wealth, such good fortune, that in defeat you are envied by those who defeated you. When you asked to be made a priest, I gave you this office, passing over several men whose fathers had fought at my side; despite receiving such kindness at my hands you decided to take my life.' When Cinna protested at these words that he was far from acting with such madness, Augustus replied: 'You are not keeping to your word, Cinna; we had agreed that you would not interrupt. You are planning, I say, to end my life;' he gave further details of the location, the confederates, the day, the plan of the plot, the man whose job it was to wield the dagger. And when he saw that Cinna's eyes were lowered and that he was now silent, not because of their agreement, but from guilt, he said: 'What is your intention in this action? Is it to become emperor yourself? What a poor lookout for the Roman people, believe me, if I am all that stands between you and the purple. You cannot guard your own home, losing in a private suit only the other day through the influence of a former slave; it is clearly mere child's play for you to take action against Caesar. Tell me, if I alone am frustrating your hopes, will Paulus and Fabius Maximus put up with you, will the Cossi and the Servilii, and all that line of noble Romans, men who do not represent names of no consequence, but themselves lend distinction to their worthy ancestors?'

I do not wish to fill a great part of my book by quoting his speech in its entirety (for he is agreed to have spoken for more than two hours, prolonging this punishment which alone was going to satisfy him). At last he said: 'I grant you life a second time, Cinna, though earlier you were an enemy but now you are a plotter and parricide. From this day onwards let friendship commence between us; let us see which of us acts in better faith—I in giving you your life or you in owing it to me.' After this, without being asked, he conferred the consulship on him, taking him to task for not having the courage to make the request. He received from Cinna the strongest friendship and loyalty, and became his only heir. There were no further cases of anyone plotting against him.

10. Your great-great-grandfather pardoned those he had defeated; for if he had not done so, who would have been his subjects? From the camp of his enemies he won over Sallustius and a Cocceius and a Deillius, and all the troop that formed his inner circle; and now his own mercifulness had won him men like Domitius, Messala, Asinius, Cicero, and all the elite of the state. What a long time he allowed even Lepidus to die! For many a year he permitted him to keep the insignia of a ruler, and only after that man's death would he have the office of chief priest transferred to himself; for he preferred that it be called an honour rather than a victor's trophy. This merciful attitude led him to safety and security; it won him the affection and favour of the Roman people, though their necks had not yet learned to bow when he put his hand on them; and today it is this that preserves for him a good name that emperors can scarcely enjoy even in their lifetimes. We believe him to be divine, but not because we are commanded to; we admit that he was a good emperor, that the name of father became him well, quite simply because he would not avenge with cruelty even personal insults, which emperors usually resent more bitterly than wrongs; because he was amused when people were rude about him; because, when he was punishing a man, he seemed to share his pain; because not only did he spare the lives of those men he convicted of committing adultery with his daughter but banished them for their greater safety, supplying them with their credentials. When you know there will be many to express anger on your behalf and to gratify you by spilling another man's blood, then not only to grant safety but to guarantee it—this is true forgiveness.

11. This was how Augustus behaved in old age, or when he was on the verge of old age; in his young days he was fiery and blazed up with anger, doing many things he was ashamed to recall. No one will dare to compare the leniency of the deified Augustus with your own, even if he brings an old age that was more than mature into competition with the years of youth. He may well have displayed moderation and mercy, but this was after the sea at Actium had been stained with Roman blood, after his own fleet and an enemy's had been wrecked off Sicily, after the sacrifices conducted at Perusia and the proscriptions. I certainly do not give the name of mercy to weariness of cruelty; this mercy that you exhibit, Caesar, is true mercy, that does not spring from a regret for savage treatment, that has no stain upon it, and has never shed the blood of one's own countrymen; when one exercises supreme power this is self-control in the truest sense and a love that embraces all one's fellow men as oneself—not to be corrupted by any earthly desire, or by rashness of nature, or by precedents set by former emperors into putting to the test how much licence one may enjoy over fellow citizens, but rather to blunt the edge of supreme power. You, Caesar, have made us the gift of a state unspotted by blood, and with pride you have boasted that throughout the whole world you have not spilled a drop of human blood; this is all the more impressive and surprising as no one had ever been entrusted so early in his life with a sword.

Mercy, therefore, makes rulers not only more honourable but more secure from harm, and is at the same time an adornment to, and the surest protection of, sovereign power. For why is it that kings have reached old age and passed on their thrones to their children and grandchildren, while the power of tyrants is accursed and short-lived? What difference is there between a tyrant and a king (for they are alike in the mere aspect of their fortune and freedom to act), except that tyrants vent their rage to serve their own whims, kings only for a reason and out of necessity?

12. 'Well, then,' you say, 'is it not also common for kings to kill?' Yes, but only when they are convinced that the public good requires this course; with tyrants cruelty is a source of pleasure. But a tyrant differs from a king by his actions, not by name; for, as the elder Dionysius* can rightly and justly be regarded as superior to many kings, so there is no reason why we should not give the name of tyrant to Lucius Sulla,* who only ceased from killing when he had no more enemies to despatch. He may have resigned from his office of dictator and returned to the life of a private citizen, but which tyrant ever displayed such a keen thirst for human blood as that man, who ordered seven thousand Roman citizens to be butchered at one time, and, on hearing the cry of so many thousands groaning beneath the sword from his seat nearby at the temple of Bellona, said to the terror-stricken senate, 'Let us turn to our business, gentlemen of the senate; a handful of insurgents are being killed on my orders'? He told no lie here; to Sulla they seemed a few. But concerning Sulla we shall have more to say presently, when we ask the question how anger is to be directed at enemies, especially if they are fellow citizens who have broken from the body politic and passed into the category of enemies; meanwhile, as I was saying, mercy is what causes the great difference between king and tyrant, though both are equally sustained by the protection of weapons; but the one uses weapons to fortify peace, the other to suppress great hatred by great fear, and yet he cannot view without concern those very hands to which he has entrusted himself. Opposite courses drive him to opposite ends; for, as the hatred he arouses in men stems from their fear, he wants to be feared because he is hated, and, not realizing the terrible madness induced by hatred that has grown too great, he falls back on that accursed verse that has sent many a man to his ruin:

Let them hate, if only they fear.*

For fear in moderation controls men's passions, but fear that is persistent and intense and causes desperation makes men without spirit bold, and prompts them to try anything. Similarly, wild animals may be kept imprisoned by a line of feathers, but once a rider comes at them from behind with his spears, they will try to escape through what had made them flee, trampling their panic underfoot. Courage has its sharpest edge when forged by utter desperation. Fear ought to leave some degree of security, and show the promise of hope much more than of danger; otherwise, when someone who presents no risk is made to fear the same danger as other men, he is more than happy to rush into danger and end his life, as if it were another's.

13. A peaceful and merciful king puts trust in his guards, as he uses them for everyone's safety, and the soldier, with pride in his heart (for he sees his service is given to the security of the state) happily endures all toil as the protector of his country's father; but that ruler who is harsh and bloodthirsty can only earn the ill-will of his henchmen. No man can count on loyalty or goodwill in servants if he employs them as instruments of torture and death, like the rack and the axe, throwing men to them as if to wild beasts; he is more wretched and troubled than any criminal on trial, since he fears men and gods, the witnesses and avengers of crimes, and has reached the point where he is incapable of changing his ways. For among all its other woes this is perhaps the greatest curse of cruelty—a man must persist in it, and has no prospect of returning to a better course; for it is crime that must safeguard crime. But what creature can be more wretched than the man who now has no escape from the path of wickedness? What a pitiable soul he is, at least to himself! For it would offend the gods that others should pity him, a man who has used his power to commit murder and pillage, who has roused suspicion in all his actions, whether abroad or at home, who seeks the help of the sword because the sword is his fear, who trusts neither the loyalty of friends nor the affection owed by his children; who, when he has examined what he has done and what he intends to do, and has laid bare his conscience weighed down by acts of crime and torture, often fears death but more often prays for it, hating himself more than his servants do. On the contrary, the man who cares for all, who guards some things more diligently, some less, but fosters every single part of the state as though it were part of himself, who inclines to the more forgiving course even where it is to his advantage to punish, showing how reluctant he is to turn his hand to severe treatment; whose mind lacks

all hostility, all savagery, who uses his power mildly and for people's benefit, desiring his countrymen's approval for his acts as a ruler, who thinks his cup of happiness overflows if he makes his subjects share his own good fortune, who is genial in conversation, easy of approach and access, lovable in his features, which most of all wins the hearts of the masses, kindly disposed to just petitions and avoiding harshness even when they are unjust—a man like this wins from the entire state love, protection, and deep respect. People say the same things about him in secret as they do in the street. They are eager to raise children, and the ban on having offspring, once imposed in time of public malaise, is now lifted; no one doubts that his children will be in his debt for introducing them to such an age. An emperor of this stamp, protected by his own good actions, has no need of a bodyguard; the weapons he wears are merely an adornment.

14. What, then, constitutes his duty? It is that of good parents, who are accustomed to scold their children, sometimes gently, sometimes with threats, and at times to enforce correction even with a beating. Surely no father in his right mind disinherits his son for a first offence! Only when his patience has been undermined by persistent and serious misdemeanours, only when what he fears is greater than what he admonishes, does he resort to the decisive pen; but before this he makes many attempts to recall a character that inclines to the worse side but is still wavering in the balance; when hope is gone, he adopts extreme measures. No one reaches the point of punishing without using up all means of cure. This is the action to be expected not just of a father but also of an emperor, whom no mere empty flattery has prompted us to call 'Father of his Country'.* Other surnames have been awarded by way of honour; some we have hailed as 'the Great', as 'the Fortunate', as 'the August', and have heaped on their ambitious claims to power all the titles we could as a tribute to them; but in bestowing the title 'Father of his Country' we wish him to know that he has been given the power of a father, which shows the greatest toleration in looking to the welfare of his children and places his own interests behind theirs. No father would rush to cut off his own limbs, and, having done so, would certainly long to restore them, and as he wielded the knife he would groan aloud, hesitating often and long; for if a man is swift to condemn, he comes close to enjoying it, and if he does it too often, he may well be unjust.

15. In my own memory the people in the forum used their writing implements to stab a Roman knight, Tricho, who had flogged his own son to death; the authority of Augustus Caesar barely rescued him from the hostile hands of fathers no less than sons. But Tarius, when he had discovered his son in a plot to kill his father and found him guilty after examining the case, gained the admiration of everyone because he contented himself with the penalty of exile, and a luxurious one at that, and kept the parricide at Marseilles, providing him with the same healthy allowance he had been accustomed to give him before his crime; the result of this generosity was that, in a community where no villain need go without a defender, no one doubted that the accused had been rightly condemned, since the father who could not hate him had been able to condemn him.

I will use this very case to show you an example of a good emperor whom you may compare with the good father. When Tarius was about to hold the investigation on his son, he invited Augustus Caesar to assist him as an adviser; Augustus entered the house of a private citizen, sat down beside him, and participated in an investigation that concerned another family. He did not say, 'No, I prefer that he come to my own house'; had this happened, it would have been Caesar's investigation, not the father's.

When he had heard the case and the evidence had been sifted— what the young man had said in his own defence and what was advanced to prove him guilty—Caesar asked that each man should write down his verdict to prevent everyone from falling into agreement with his own; then, before the tablets might be opened, he declared solemnly that he would not accept a bequest from Tarius, who was a man of some wealth. Someone will say: 'It was weak-minded of him to fear that, if he found the son guilty, people might think he was seeking to clear the field for his own prospects.' I take a different view; any one of us might well have had enough confidence in his own good conscience to combat waspish criticism, but emperors are obliged to take serious notice of their reputation with the people. He declared solemnly that he would not accept a bequest. It is true that on one and the same day Tarius lost a second heir, but Caesar ensured that the integrity of his vote would not be tainted; and after he had made it clear that his severe decision was made without bias, a point always to be observed by an emperor, he said that the son should be banished to wherever his father saw fit. He did not sentence

him to the sack* or to snakes or to prison, for his thoughts were not
on the man being judged but on the man who had sought his counsel;
he said that the father should content himself with the mildest form
of punishment, as his son was only a youth who had been prompted
to commit that crime, but in undertaking it had acted half-heartedly,
which is tantamount to innocence; he should be banished from the
city and from his father's sight.

16. How deserving he was of being asked by parents to assist their
deliberations! How deserving of being enrolled as co-heir to children
who had committed no crime! This is the quality of mercy that lends
grace to an emperor; wherever he comes, he should make everything
more tranquil.

No man should count for so little in the eyes of a king that his death
passes unnoticed, however small a part of the realm he occupies. Let
us seek a parallel for great power from examples of less impressive
authority. There is more than one form of wielding power: an emperor
holds power over his subjects, a father over his children, a teacher
over his pupils, a tribune or centurion over his soldiers. Will we not
have the lowest opinion of that father who uses constant beatings to
keep his children in check for even the most trivial misdemeanours?
And which teacher more worthily represents liberal studies—the one
who flays his pupils' backs if their memory fails, or if the eye is not
quick and falters in reading, or the one who prefers to use gentle criticism and a sense of shame to impart correction and instruction? Give
me a tribune or a centurion who is brutal: he will create deserters, who
still deserve pardon. It is surely in no way fair that a man should be
ruled more severely and harshly than a dumb beast! And yet when a
skilful breaker of horses is at work he does not subject the creature to
the terror of frequent beatings; for it will become timorous and obsti-
nate, if you do not soothe it with caressing hand. The same practice is
seen in the hunter, whether he is training young hounds to follow the
trail, or using those already trained to raise or chase game: he neither
resorts to constant threats (for he will break their spirit, and all their
natural qualities will be diminished in a fearfulness that betrays their
breed), nor allows them the freedom of wandering and roving in all
directions. You may add to this list the drivers even of less active pack-
animals: these creatures may be born for abusive treatment and misery,
but undue cruelty may drive them to refuse the yoke.

17. No creature is more fretful, or to be treated with greater skill, than
man, and none should be treated with greater forbearance. For what is

more foolish than to feel shame at venting one's anger on pack-animals and dogs, but to let one man subject another to the worst of treatment? Illnesses prompt us to attempt a cure, not to become angry with them; and yet we have here too an illness, but of the mind; it requires gentle treatment and a doctor who is himself entirely sympathetic to his patient. It is the mark of a bad doctor to despair of finding a cure; in the case of those whose minds have become afflicted, the same procedure will be the duty of the man to whom has been entrusted the general welfare of his subjects, not to abandon hope too quickly or to declare the symptoms fatal; he should wrestle with their difficulties and seek to stem their advance, taking some to task over their illness and taking in others by means of a placebo in order to effect a speedier and sounder cure through misleading remedies; the emperor should aim not only to produce health but also to leave no shameful scar. Cruel punishment brings no renown to a king (everyone recognizes his capacity for this behaviour), but on the other hand if he restrains his own power, if he rescues many from the anger of others and exposes no one to his own, the greatest renown is his.

18. Moderate use of one's power over slaves is praiseworthy. Even where a humble slave is concerned one should consider, not how much punishment he can be made to endure without retaliation, but how much scope is allowed you by the principles of justice and right, which require that you show mercy even to prisoners of war and slaves you have purchased. How much more justice appears in their requirement that free, free-born, and honourable men should not be treated as mere vassals but as those who, though your inferiors in rank, have been entrusted to you to be their guardians, not their masters? Slaves are permitted to seek refuge at a god's statue; it may be legal to do anything to a slave, but the right shared by all living creatures sets a particular limit on what a human being may suffer. Who did not feel greater loathing of Vedius Pollio* than his own slaves did, because he fattened his lampreys on human blood and ordered that those who had offended him in some way be thrown into his fishpond, or should I say his snakepit? That creature deserved a thousand deaths, whether he threw his slaves as food to lampreys he intended to eat, or whether his sole purpose in keeping lampreys was to treat them to such a diet.

Just as cruel masters are pointed out all over the city and hated and loathed, so it is with kings: their unjust actions have wider scope, and the notoriety and hatred they incur is handed down from age to age; how much better for them not to have been born than to be numbered among those born to plague the state!

19. No one will be able to conceive of a quality more becoming in a ruler than that of mercy, no matter how or by what right he has been set above all others. We shall, of course, grant that this quality is the more lovely and splendid, the greater the power under which it is shown, which need not be harmful if it conforms to the law of Nature. For it is Nature who has devised the notion of a king, which we may recognize from other creatures but in particular from bees; their king has the most spacious chamber, located in the central, safest spot; moreover, he does not work himself but oversees the work of others, and when they lose their king they all scatter, never allowing more than one to rule at any time and using battle to select the best; besides, their king is outstanding in appearance and distinguished from the others both in size and lustre. But what marks him off especially is this: bees are extremely prone to anger and, considering their physical size, excellent fighters, leaving their sting behind when they inflict a wound; but the king himself has no sting; Nature, not wanting him to be savage or to seek a revenge that would cost so dear, removed his weapon and left his anger unarmed.

Here lies a powerful example for great kings to follow; for it is a habit of Nature to exercise herself in small things and to scatter the smallest proofs of mighty principles. It would be shameful not to draw lessons from the tiniest creatures, since the human mind should exercise restraint in proportion to its far greater capacity for doing harm.

Ah, if only a man was bound by the same law and his anger broken off at the same time as his weapon, and he was not allowed to inflict harm any more than once or to vent his anger by using the strength of others! For he would weary of his rage soon enough if he himself was the only means of expressing it, and if he risked death by giving his violence free rein! But even as matters stand, no safe course is open to him; for he must feel as much fear as he wishes men to feel, and watch the hands of everyone, thinking he is under attack even when no one has designs on him, and not having a single moment free from fear. Does any man endure to live such a life as this when, doing no harm to others and so free from worry, he may exercise his beneficent privilege of power to everyone's happiness? For that man is mistaken who thinks that a king is safe in circumstances where nothing is safe from the king; for security is bought by an interchange of security. There is no need for him to build up to the skies his lofty castles, or to fortify steep hills against ascent, or to cut away the sides of mountains, or to fence himself in with layers of walls and towers: mercy will guarantee a king's safety though he stands in an open field. The one fortification he has that will defy all attacks is the love of his people.

What is more splendid than to live a life that all men wish to continue, voicing their prayers for this with none to watch them? To stir fear, not hope, in men's hearts, if one's health falters a little? That no possession should be so dear to a subject that he is not happy to give it in exchange for his leader's health? Ah, surely one so fortunate would owe it even to himself to remain alive; to this end he has demonstrated by regular proofs of his goodness that the state does not belong to him but he to the state. Who would dare to plan any danger for such a man? Who would not wish, if he could, to protect him even from misfortune, a ruler under whom justice, peace, regard for morals, security, and honour flourish, under whom the common-wealth enjoys wealth and teems with a store of all blessings? Indeed, they gaze upon their ruler with the kind of emotion that we should feel in gazing upon the immortal gods—one of reverence and worship—should they grant us the power to see them. Is it not so? That man who conducts himself as would the gods, who is charitable and generous and uses his power for the better end, does he not occupy a place second only to the gods? This is the model it is fitting that you should aspire to, this the one you should seek to emulate: to be thought the greatest man, only if at the same time you are thought to be the best.

20. An emperor is accustomed to inflict punishment for one of two reasons, either to avenge himself or to avenge another man. I shall start by discussing the situation which affects him personally; for it is more difficult to show moderation when personal resentment rather than discipline determines the act of vengeance. It is superfluous at this point to warn him to be reluctant to believe, to sift out the truth, to look with favour on innocence and to be aware that it is as much the business of the judge as of the defendant that innocence should be proved; for this is a matter, not of mercy, but of justice. I now urge him to keep his emotions under control, however manifest the injury he has suffered, and to remit the punishment, if he can do so without risk; if he cannot, he should reduce it and show far more willingness

to be forgiving of wrongs done to him than of those done to others. For just as a man's magnanimity consists, not in being generous with what is another man's, but in depriving himself of what he bestows on another, so I shall not give the name 'merciful' to someone who is calm when another man feels the sting of injustice, but rather to the one who does not leap forward when he is personally galled, who understands that magnanimity lies in tolerating wrongs when one has supreme power, and that nothing is more splendid than an emperor who has been wronged yet has taken no vengeance.

21. Vengeance normally achieves one of two ends: it either brings compensation to the injured party or peace of mind for the future. An emperor's fortune is too great for him to be in need of compensation, and his power too obvious for him to court a reputation for strength by injuring another. What I speak of here fits the situation where he has been attacked and outraged by men of lower rank; for if it is a case of men whom he at one time counted his equals, his vengeance is satisfied if he sees them brought beneath his heel. A king's life may be ended by a slave, by a snake, by an arrow; but every man who saves another's life is greater than the man he saved. The man, therefore, who has the power of conferring and taking away life must use so great a gift from the gods in a spirit of nobility. If he achieves this supremacy over those who, as he knows, at one time occupied a lofty position equal to his own, then on them especially he has already satisfied his revenge and realized all that true punishment demanded; for the man who owes his life to another has lost it, and any one who has been cast down from on high to his enemy's feet, and waited for another's judgement on his life and throne, lives on to the renown of his saviour, and does more credit to that man's name by being saved than if he had been removed from men's sight. For he is a lasting example to the eyes of men of another's excellence; in a triumph he would have swiftly passed from sight. But if it has proved possible for even his throne to be left in his possession without harm ensuing, and for him to be restored to the position from which he fell, then with increasing greatness swells the praise of that man who defeated a king but was content to take from him only his renown. This is to triumph over his own victory itself, and to demonstrate that he found nothing worthy of the conqueror among the conquered.

He should deal more moderately with his fellow citizens and with men of obscure or low rank, as it is of less consequence to him to bring them down. Some men you should spare gladly, while some you should think it beneath you to be avenged on, withdrawing from them as from tiny insects that soil the hand that crushes them; but where those men are concerned who will attract talk in the state, whether they are spared or punished, the opportunity for a remarkable display of mercy is to be used.

22. Let us pass to the question of wrongs done to others, in punishing which these three aims, which the law has pursued, should be pursued also by an emperor: either to improve the man who is punished, or through his punishment to make the rest better, or by removing the bad ones to enable the rest to live less fearful lives. The guilty themselves you will reform by the lighter type of punishment; for a man lives with more circumspection if he has something left to lose. No one shows regard for a reputation he has lost; when he no longer has any room for punishment, a man enjoys a kind of immunity from it. In the case of the state, however, a sparing hand in applying punishments is more successful in improving morals; for the large number of offenders makes offending habitual, and there is less opprobrium in the censors' mark if the sheer number of those condemned weakens its force, while severity, which is the most effective cure, loses its authority if it is constantly applied. Good morals are implanted in a state and vices wiped out if an emperor shows tolerance of vice, not as though he approved of it, but as though he resorted to punishing it unwillingly and with considerable pain. A ruler's mercy of itself makes men embarrassed to offend; there is thought to be far greater severity in a punishment that a forbearing man decrees.

23. Moreover, you will see that the offences regularly punished are the ones regularly committed. Your father caused more men to be sewn up in the sack over five years than we are told were sewn up in all our history. Children were far less ready to perpetrate the ultimate in wickedness as long as the crime did not fall within the scope of the law. They showed the greatest wisdom, those men of lofty distinction and profound understanding of nature's ways, in electing to disregard the crime as exceeding belief and audacity rather than to punish it and so show the possibility of its being committed; accordingly, the act of killing a parent began with the law condemning it, and children were shown the way to the deed by its punishment; loving duty to a parent was indeed in its sorriest state when sacks were more often to be seen than crosses. A sympathetic attitude to

integrity is formed in that state where men are seldom punished, and the virtue receives encouragement as if it were a public good. Let a state think of itself as free from criminal tendencies, and it shall be; it will show more anger towards those not subscribing to the general avoidance of excess if it sees they are few. It is a dangerous thing, believe me, to reveal to a state how much wicked men are in the majority.

24. The proposal was made once by the senate that slaves should be distinguished by their clothing from free men; it then appeared how great the imminent danger would be if our slaves should begin to count our number. Let me assure you, we would have no less a danger to fear if we spared no man punishment; it will quickly become clear how much heavier in the scales is the worse element in the state. Many executions bring as much disgrace to an emperor as many deaths to a doctor; the more lenient the ruler, the better he is obeyed. The human spirit is by nature unyielding; it struggles against opposition and difficulty, and is more inclined to follow than to be led; and, as horses of good breeding and spirit are better controlled by a loose rein, so through its own impulse a spontaneous desire to do right is consequent upon mercy, which in its own interest the state considers a quality worthy of being preserved. Accordingly, more good is achieved by this course.

25. Cruelty is an evil in no way appropriate for a man, and is unworthy of his spirit that is so gentle; it is the madness of a wild beast to delight in blood and wounds, and, shedding the mantle of humanity, to change into a creature of the woodland. For what difference does it make, Alexander, I ask you, whether you throw Lysimachus* to a lion or tear him apart yourself with your own teeth? That great mouth is your own, as is that savagery. Oh, how you would have wished those claws to be yours, and yours those gaping jaws wide enough to devour men! We do not demand of you that that hand of yours, so unhesitating a destroyer of close friends, should spare the life of any man, or that your headstrong spirit, the insatiable curse of nations, should stop short of bloody slaughter in seeking satisfaction; it is now described as mercy if the executioner is chosen to kill a friend from among humans. The reason why brutality should arouse perhaps our strongest loathing is this: it exceeds first all normal, then all human limits, it seeks out novel forms of torture, summons ingenuity to devise instruments that will enable pain to be varied and

prolonged, and takes delight in the sufferings of men; the moment when that man's terrible disease of the mind has reached the furthest stage of madness is when cruelty becomes transformed into pleasure, and it is now a source of delight to put a man to death. Hot on such a man's heels come disgust, hatred, poison, and the sword; for each of the many men whose life he threatens there is a corresponding danger that assails him, and he is besieged sometimes by plots of individuals, sometimes, indeed, by an insurrection of the people. For entire cities are not stirred into action by the unimportant destruction of individual citizens; but every dagger is drawn against something that begins to rage indiscriminately, making every man its target. Very small snakes escape notice and are not hunted down by everyone; but when one exceeds normal size and has grown into a monster, when it infects springs with its venom, scorching and wasting them with its breath, then, wherever it makes its way, it comes under attack from engines of war. Insignificant ills may be able to foil us and escape, but we go out to confront great ones. In the same way the illness of one person does not cause alarm even in his own household; but when many deaths make it clear that there is a plague, all the members of the community raise a clamour and seek to escape, raising their hands in anger at the very gods. Should a fire appear under one particular roof, the household and neighbours throw water on it; but an extensive conflagration that has already consumed many houses is extinguished only by part of the city.

26. The cruelty even of private citizens has been avenged by the hands of slaves, despite the certain danger of their facing the cross; in the case of tyrants' cruelty, nations and peoples, both those suffering from it and those labouring under its threat, have made it their task to root it out. Sometimes the tyrants' own guards have risen up against them, practising on their masters the treachery and disloyalty and savagery and everything else they had learned from them. For what can anyone expect from someone he has trained in wickedness? A villainous heart does not show obedience for long, and the scale of its crimes does not depend on the orders it is given.

But suppose that a cruel ruler can enjoy security—what is the nature of his kingdom? Nothing but the outline of captured cities and the looks of terror on all his subjects' faces. All is sorrow, panic, and tumult; pleasures themselves are the cause of fear; men are anxious when they go to another man's house for dinner, for even the drunkard there must guard his tongue with care, anxious, too, when they attend public shows, where the opportunity is sought to incriminate and ruin them. These may be staged at vast expense, with royal magnificence, and with artists of the finest reputation, but what man would find pleasure in games from a prison cell? Heavens above, what monstrous thing is this—to kill, to rage, to be delighted by the clank of chains, to cut off the heads of fellow citizens, to shed streams of blood wherever one goes, and to cause men to flee in terror whenever one appears? Would life be any different if lions and bears were our rulers, if snakes and all the most dangerous creatures had power over us? These, lacking in reason and condemned to death by us on the charge of being savage, yet show mercy to their own kind, and even among wild beasts to be like another creature is to be safe from it; but not even kinship makes tyrants control their rage, and they treat alike both strangers and friends, displaying the more violence, the more they resort to fury. Then from the killing of one man, then of another, this fury creeps on to the destruction of nations, thinking it an indication of power to put houses to the torch and drive the plough over ancient cities; it considers the killing of one or two men an inadequate expression of royal power; unless at the same time a herd of wretches stands under the executioner's axe, it thinks its cruelty has been forced to accept control.

True happiness lies in bestowing safety on many, in calling them back to life from death's very door, and in earning the civic garland by showing mercy. No decoration is more worthy of an emperor's eminence, or more splendid than that garland awarded for saving the lives of fellow citizens; not enemy weapons torn from them in defeat, not chariots crimson with barbarians' blood, not spoils won in war. This is power worthy of the gods', to save men's lives, whether crowds or the whole citizen-body; but to kill men in great numbers and without distinction is the power of a great fire and of ruin.

BOOK 2

1. There is a single utterance of yours, Nero Caesar, which especially prompted me to write on mercy. I remember hearing it with some admiration when it was made, and subsequently repeating it to others—a noble and magnanimous remark, of great compassion,

which suddenly left your lips spontaneously, without being intended for the ears of others, and made apparent to all the goodness in you that contends with your lofty position. Your prefect Burrus,* an outstanding man born to serve such an emperor as you, was on the point of executing two robbers, and was pressing you to record the names of the men and why you wanted them punished; you had put this off many times and he was insisting that it should at last be done. Both of you were reluctant, and having produced the document, he was handing it over to you, when you exclaimed, 'Ah, if only I had never learned to write!' What a laudable statement, one that all nations should have heard—those dwelling inside the Roman empire and those on its borders whose freedom is scarcely assured, and those who rise up against it in their strength or courage! It should have been delivered to an assembly of all mankind for princes and kings to swear their allegiance to it! What a remarkable utterance it was, worthy of the general innocence of the human race, for which that long-ago age should be restored! Truly it would now be fitting that men should banish envy, the source of every evil of the heart, and agree to aspire to justice and goodness, that piety and integrity should rise anew, together with honour and moderation, and that vice, having misused its lengthy reign, should finally give way to an age of happiness and virtue.

2. That this in large measure will happen, is something, Caesar, we should like to hope and trust in. Men will tell one-another of your heart's kindness, which will spread gradually throughout the entire body of the empire, and all things will take shape in your own likeness. It is from the head that good health comes: through it are all parts of the body active and alert, or sunk in inertia, according as the spirit that animates them lives or withers. There will be citizens, there will be friends of Rome, worthy of this goodness, and righteousness will return to the whole world; everywhere your hands will be spared. Allow me to linger longer on this point, but not simply to gratify your ears (for this is not my way; I would rather give offence by telling the truth than pleasure by flattering). What, then, impels me? Apart from wanting you to be as familiar as possible with your own good deeds and sayings, so that what is now a natural instinct may become a principle, I consider this fact, that many forceful but despicable sayings have entered human life, and are commonly aired as famous, as, for example: 'Let them hate, provided they fear,' and

the Greek verse that resembles it, where a man bids the earth be convulsed with fire when he is dead, and others of this sort. And in some way or other great writers, in dealing with a monstrous and distasteful topic, have found a happier phrase in giving form to violent and impulsive feelings; never yet have I heard an utterance full of spirit from lips that are good and forbearing. What, then, is my point? Although it happens seldom, against your will, and with considerable reluctance, yet there are occasions when you must write something which makes you an enemy of your own power to write, but do it you must, as now you do, with considerable hesitation, with much deferral.

3. And, to avoid by chance being sometimes deceived by the attractive name of mercy and directed into an opposite quality, let us see what mercy is, what its nature is, and what its limitations.

Mercy consists in controlling the mind when one has the power to take revenge, or in the forbearance of a superior towards an inferior in determining punishment. It would be safer to put forward more definitions, in case a single one does not sufficiently cover the subject, and, so to speak, loses its case; therefore mercy can also be described as the inclination of the mind towards mildness in exacting punishment. The next definition will find objections, despite coming very close to the truth: if we describe mercy as the moderation that removes something from the due and merited punishment, the protest will be raised that no virtue bestows on a man less than he deserves. However, everyone understands the fact that mercy consists in stopping short of the penalty that might have been deservedly fixed.

4. Men of limited judgement regard strictness as the opposite of mercy; but no virtue has a virtue as its opposite. What, then, is set in opposition to mercy? It is cruelty, which is nothing other than harshness of mind in claiming punishment. 'But there are some men who do not claim punishment and yet are cruel, such as those who kill strangers they meet, not for financial gain, but for the sake of killing, and, dissatisfied with killing, they vent their cruelty, men like the notorious Busiris and Procrustes,* and the pirates who flog their prisoners and consign them, alive, to the flames.' This is cruelty, I grant; but because it neither has revenge in view (for no injury was received) nor expresses anger at a particular offence (for no crime came before it), it falls outside the scope of our definition; for this limited the mind's lack of restraint to the claiming of punishment. We can describe the attitude that finds torture pleasurable, not as

cruelty, but as brutality; we can call it madness: for madness has various types, and none is more beyond dispute than that which causes the murder and mutilation of men. I shall give the description 'cruel', therefore, to those who have a reason to punish but show no control in exacting it, to men like Phalaris,* who, they say, tortured men who were indeed guilty, but used methods beyond what was human or credible. We can escape the charge of sophistry by defining cruelty as an inclination of the mind to harsher thoughts. Mercy rejects this quality, bidding it stand far away from her; strictness is her natural counterpart.

It is appropriate at this point to ask what pity is; for many praise it as a virtue, describing as good the man who shows pity. But this quality also is a defect of the mind. Both cruelty and pity are closely related to strictness and to mercy, and so we must shun them; for appearing to the world to be strict, we descend into cruelty, and appearing to be merciful, we descend into pity. In the case of the latter our mistake may involve us in less risk, but in both we err equally, as both find us falling short of the truth.

5. Accordingly, just as religion does honour to the gods, while superstition profanes them, so all good men will show mercy and gentleness, but will avoid pity; for it is the defect of a small mind that succumbs to the sight of others' suffering. It is, therefore, most frequently seen in the worst specimens of humanity; old women and wretched females, who are moved by the tears of the most abandoned felons, and would, if they were allowed, break open their prison. Pity looks, not to the cause of these men's condition, but to the condition itself; mercy operates together with reason. I am aware that the Stoic school is regarded unfavourably by the ill-informed as excessively harsh and quite unsuited to giving advice to princes and kings; it is criticized for maintaining that the wise man does not show pity or forgiveness. Such a position is hateful, if formulated in the abstract; for it appears to leave no hope to human error, but rather to consign all offences to punishment. If this is the case, what kind of philosophy is it that tells us to forget the lessons of our own humanity and to close up the surest haven against misfortune, that of helping one-another? But no school is more kind and gentle, none more loving of mankind and more devoted to the common good, so that its guiding principle is to be useful and helpful, and to consider not merely self-interest but that of each and every person on earth. Pity is a mental

sorrow caused by the sight of others' wretchedness, or a sadness induced by the sufferings of others, which it believes happen without their deserving them; but no sorrow falls on the wise man; his mind is tranquil, and nothing can happen to cast a cloud over it. And nothing becomes a man so much as a greatness of mind; but no mind can be great and sorrowful at the same time. Sadness blunts the mind's powers, scattering and restricting them; not even when disaster strikes him personally will this happen to the wise man, but instead he will beat back all Fortune's anger and smash it first; he will always maintain the same calm, unperturbed appearance, an impossible thing to do if he were susceptible to sadness.

6. There is the further point that the wise man exercises foresight and has a plan of action at the ready; but what issues from a troubled source is never clear and uncontaminated. Melancholy is not suited to discerning facts, to thinking up useful solutions, to avoiding dangers, or to weighing justice; he does not, therefore, feel pity, because this can only be felt when the mind is afflicted by sorrow. All the other things that I wish those who feel pity to do, he will do gladly and with a noble spirit; he will bring help to another's tears but he will not add his own; he will offer a hand to the shipwrecked man, hospitality to the exile, a few coins to the needy; he will not follow the practice of most of those who wish to appear compassionate, flinging the coins insultingly and with distaste for those they help, afraid of being touched by them, but rather he will give as one human being to another out of the common store; he will grant to the tears of a mother the life of her son, he will order the prisoner's chains to be struck off, he will release the gladiator from his training, and bury even a criminal's corpse, but all of these things he will do with a mind at peace and a face composed. Accordingly, the wise man will not extend pity but rather assistance and benefit, and, as he is born to help all and to further the common good, he will give each man his share of this. Even to wretches who deserve blame and correction he will show a due measure of his goodness; but those who are in distress and struggling through misfortune will find him far more willing to come to their aid. Whenever he can, he will come between Fortune and her victim; for in what circumstances will he make better use of his resources or his strength than in restoring what has been struck down by chance? Moreover, he will not turn aside his face or his sympathy from a man because he has a withered leg, or is starving and in rags, and is old and props himself on a stick; no, all who are worthy will receive his aid, and, like the gods, he will look graciously on the miserable.

Pity is allied to wretchedness; for it consists partly of wretchedness and is derivative from it. You would know that your eyes are weak, if they also fill with tears at the sight of another's bleary eyes, just as, believe me, it is not mirth, but a disease, always to laugh when others laugh, and to stretch one's own jaws when everyone else yawns.

Pity is a failing of minds that feel unduly distressed by suffering, and if anyone requires a wise man to show it, this is tantamount to requiring him to wail and groan at the funerals of men he does not know.

7. 'But why will he not grant pardon?' Come now, let us now also decide what pardon is, and we shall realize that it should not be granted by the wise man. Pardon consists in the cancellation of punishment that is deserved. Those who hold this as doctrine give a rather lengthy explanation of why it is the wise man's duty not to grant pardon; I, to speak briefly as if stating another's view, explain it as follows: 'Pardon is extended to a man who ought to be punished; but a wise man does nothing which he ought not to do, and leaves undone nothing which he ought to do; accordingly, he does not cancel a punishment which he ought to exact. But the favour you wish to win by pardon he will confer on you in a more honourable way; for the wise man will show forgiveness and consideration, and he will make matters right; he will do the same as he would if he pardoned, but he will not pardon, since the man who pardons is admitting his failure to do something he ought to have done. To one man he will give simply a verbal caution, sparing him any punishment if he sees that he is young and capable of reforming; another who is evidently labouring under the shame of his crime will be told to go free, because he was led astray, because wine caused him to fall; he will send his enemies away unharmed, sometimes even praising them if honourable motives stirred them to make war, in order to maintain loyalty, or to keep a treaty, or their freedom. All these things come about through mercy, not through pardon. Mercy has freedom to decide; not the letter of the law, but what is fair and good determines the sentence it passes; it has power to acquit and to assess the damages at whatever value it pleases. It takes none of these actions as if it were doing less than is just, but as if the greatest justice resided in that action it has decided upon. But to pardon is to waive

the punishment of one you judge worthy of punishment; pardon is
the cancellation of punishment that is due. The superiority of mercy
lies primarily in this, that it declares that those who escape punishment should not have been treated in any way differently; it is more
rounded than pardon, and more honourable. There is dispute, in my
view, about words here, but about the facts there is agreement. The
wise man will cancel many punishments and save many men whose
character may be unsound but yet capable of reform. He will take as
his model good farmers, who cultivate not only the trees that are
straight and tall, but also fit props to the ones that for some reason
have grown crooked, to make them grow straight; other trees they
trim, so that their branches do not prevent them from growing to a
height; to some that are weak, because they have been planted in bad
soil, they give nourishment, and to others that suffer from the shade
cast by their neighbours they open up the sky. The wise man, then,
will see what method of treatment to use on what type of character,
how the crooked may be straightened . . .'*

NATURAL QUESTIONS

BOOK 6: ON EARTHQUAKES

TO LUCILIUS

1. Lucilius, my excellent friend, news has reached me that Pompeii, Campania's renowned city, has been devastated by an earthquake that also shook all the neighbouring districts. The city is on a lovely bay, set back some way from the open sea, and bounded on the one side by the shores of Surrentum and Stabiae, on the other by those of Herculaneum, and it is there that the shores meet. This actually happened in the days of winter, a time that our ancestors were accustomed to claim was free from such danger. This earthquake occurred on the fifth day of February [under the consulship of Regulus and Verginius],* and it caused widespread havoc in Campania, which had never been safe from such a disaster but had always escaped damage, with its fears coming to nothing. Part of the town of Herculaneum has collapsed, with even the buildings that are left now being far from stable, and the colony of Nuceria, though it has escaped disaster, has much to lament. Naples as well lost many private houses but no public buildings, since the great disaster brushed only lightly against it; some villas, indeed, fell to the ground, but the rest over a wide area suffered from the shock without sustaining any damage. These misfortunes were compounded by others: reports tell of a flock of six hundred sheep being killed and of statues being split, and of how some individuals subsequently lost their wits and wandered around unable to control themselves. The fabric of the work I have set myself to write, and the very concurrence of the disaster at this time, require that I unravel the causes of these phenomena.

It is necessary to find comfort for the distressed and to absolve them from their terrible fear. For what can any man consider sufficiently safe if the very world is shaken and its most solid parts are made to sway? If the one thing in the world which is fixed and cannot be moved, so that it supports the weight of everything bearing down on it, begins to waver; if the earth loses its defining characteristic of stability, where will our fears finally come to rest? What hiding-place will humans find, what place of refuge will they seek in their anxiety, if their fear

grows from below and is drawn from the bowels of the earth? All
succumb to panic when buildings creak and give signs of collapsing.
That is when every person dashes headlong outside, abandoning his
household gods and entrusting himself to the open air. What bolt-
hole do we look to, what help, if the very world is the agent of ruin,
if what protects and supports us, upon which our cities lie, which
some have described as the foundation of the universe, leaves its
position and starts to totter? What comfort—I do not say what
help—can you have when fear has cut off all escape? What is, I say,
sufficiently fortified, what has the strength to protect both others as
well as oneself? I will keep the enemy at bay by means of a wall, and
fortresses of sheer height will forestall even great armies by their
difficulty of approach; a harbour offers us defence from a storm; roofs
ward off the violent downpourings from clouds, the rain that falls
without end; if you flee from a blaze it does not give chase; to combat
threats of thunder and of the sky there are the remedies of houses
below ground and caves dug deep into the earth. The well-known
fire from heaven does not penetrate the earth, but is beaten back by
the slight obstruction of the ground. When plague occurs we are at
liberty to change the place where we dwell. Escape is possible
from every disaster. Bolts of lightning have never consumed whole
peoples with their fire; a season of pestilence may have drained a city
of its inhabitants, but has never done away with it altogether. But the
disaster of an earthquake stretches far and wide, is beyond preven-
tion, voracious, and brings harm to all and sundry. For not only
does it swallow up individual houses or households or cities; it
engulfs entire peoples and regions, sometimes covering them in
ruins, sometimes burying them in a deep chasm, and does not even
leave any sign that what no longer exists at one time did. Soil spreads
over the most splendid cities, without any trace of their former
appearance.

Not a few dread this form of death in particular, in which they
plunge into an abyss along with their own homes, and are swept
away, alive, from the number of the living, as though it were not the
case that every death comes to the same end. Among the other indi-
cations of her fairness Nature has this as a cardinal point: when we
arrive at death, we are all on an equal footing. Accordingly, it makes no
difference whether a single stone strikes me down, or an entire mountain crushes me; whether I am entombed by the weight of a single

house and breathe my last under its little pile of dust, or my head is buried by the entire world; it does not matter whether I give up the ghost in the open air of daylight or in some bottomless pit of the yawning earth, whether I fall into that abyss alone or together with a great mass of nations tumbling down beside me. How great a throng of people accompanies my death makes no difference to me. Death has the same force wherever it strikes.

Let us, therefore, show a brave spirit in the face of this disaster, which cannot be avoided or foreseen, and let us now shut our ears to those who have disowned Campania and sought new places to live after this misfortune, saying that never again will they set foot in that district. For who gives them the assurance that they will have better foundations to stand on in this soil or that? All places are subject to the same lot, and if they have not yet suffered such disturbance, it is possible they may. Take this spot on which you stand so confidently: perhaps this night, or this day before the night comes, will split it apart. What makes you think that those places that have already been wasted by Fortune's strength, or those that are propped up by their own ruins, have better conditions? For we are in error if we believe that any part of the world enjoys a dispensation or immunity from this peril. All areas are subject to the same law; nothing was created by Nature to be immobile; different things fall at different times, and just as in great cities now one house is shored up, now another, so in this world of ours now this part fractures, now that.

At one time Tyre was notorious for its falling buildings; Asia at one and the same time lost twelve cities; last year Achaea and Macedonia fell victim to the same disastrous force, whatever it is, that has now attacked Campania. Fate goes the rounds and returns to any place it has long passed by. Some districts it troubles seldom, some regularly; nothing does it allow to be exempt and free from harm. Not only we humans, who are born a thing short-lived and mortal, but cities also, districts and coasts of the earth, and the very sea are the slaves of fate. Despite this we make ourselves assurances that Fortune's blessings will last for ever, and we believe that happiness, whose constancy is the most fickle of all human affairs and swiftest to fly, will have weight and permanence in the case of some person. And as men assure themselves that all things will last for ever, it does not occur to them that the very ground on which we stand is not secure. For the fault in Campania or Achaea is not to be found only there but wherever there is ground; the earth does not stay together well, and for several reasons it separates, not disintegrating as a whole but collapsing in its parts.

2. What am I doing? I had promised comfort against infrequent dangers, and here I am proclaiming dangers to be feared all around. I say that no lasting peace is possible for something that is capable of destroying and of being destroyed. But I place this very truth in the category of consolation, indeed very powerful consolation, since it is fear beyond all remedy that fools have: reason dispels terror from the minds of sensible men; the uneducated derive great confidence from a lack of hope. Accordingly, consider that these words were spoken to the human race, which were addressed to men in a state of confusion when caught suddenly between fire and the enemy:

> For the vanquished one safety remains: hope not for any safety.*

If you wish to fear nothing, consider that all things are to be feared. Observe how we are crushed by trivial reasons. Without a certain proportion neither food, or drink, or wakefulness, or sleep is a benefit to our health. You will soon understand that we are trifling, weak little bodies, lacking stability and liable to be destroyed by no great effort. Without doubt the only danger we have to face is the quaking of lands, their sudden disintegration and dragging down whatever lies on their surface!

He has a high opinion of himself, the man who dreads lightning-bolts and earthquakes and the chasms in the earth they cause. Is he willing to be aware of his own weakness and to fear a cold in his head? This, of course, is the condition we have been born into, this the fortunate physical state we have been allotted, this the noble stature to which we have grown! And this is why we are unable to die unless parts of the world move, unless the sky thunders, unless the earth caves in! We are finished off by the pain of a fingernail, and not even of the whole nail but merely a crack on one side of it! Should I also fear earthquakes, when my breathing is blocked by a thick catarrh? Am I to feel dread at the sea being displaced from its foundations and the tide rushing in with greater force than usual and drawing more water in its wake, in case I should be drowned, when some people have been choked to death by a drink slipping down the throat the wrong way? What folly to be terrified of the sea, when you know you can die from a drop of water!

There is no greater consolation for death than one's own mortality; indeed for all those perils that frighten us in the outside world there is no greater consolation than the fact that countless perils lurk in our own breasts. For what greater madness is there than collapsing at the sound of thunderclaps and creeping below the earth through fear of lightning-bolts? What greater folly is there than fearing the swaying of the earth or the sudden collapse of mountains or the incursions of the sea as it is cast beyond the shore, when death is present on all sides and rushes upon us from every quarter, and nothing is too insignificant in size to have enough strength to bring destruction on the human race? So true is it that we should not be reduced to panic by such perils, as though they harboured more evil than an ordinary death, that on the contrary, when it is necessary to quit life and eventually breathe our last, it should make us happy to die in a more impressive manner. It is necessary to die somewhere, sometime; the earth we know may well stand firm and keep itself within its own boundaries, not buffeted by any violence, but it will one day be above me. What is the difference whether I put the earth on top of me or the earth puts itself on top of me? The earth is parted and burst by the vast power of whatever disaster it may be, carrying me off into a bottomless abyss. So what? Is death easier to bear on a level surface? What have I to complain of if Nature does not want me to lie in a commonplace death, if she places part of herself on top of me? My friend Vagellius* puts it extremely well in his famous poem: 'If fall I must,' he says, 'from heaven would I choose to fall.' I might say in the same way: 'If I must fall, let the world shatter when I fall, not because it is right to hope for a disaster to befall humanity but because it is a considerable consolation for dying to see that the earth, too, is subject to death.'

3. It will be of benefit to keep in mind this point also, that none of these things is the work of the gods, and that neither sky nor land is struck by divine anger; such happenings have causes of their own; they do not feel rage on command but are victims of certain defects, just as our own bodies suffer disorder, sustaining damage at the very moment they appear to inflict it. Our ignorance of the truth makes all these phenomena terrifying in our eyes, and all the more so since their very infrequency adds to our fear; we are less struck by events that we are accustomed to; it is the unusual that gives rise to greater fear. But why do we find anything unusual? It is because we comprehend

Nature, not with our reason, but with our eyes, giving thought, not to what she can do, but only to what she has done. We are punished, therefore, for this indifference in being frightened by things as new when in fact they are not new but simply unusual. What is the consequence of this? Does it not inspire a religious dread in men's minds, and even among a whole people, if the sun appears in eclipse, or the moon (that hides its face more often) is hidden from us in part or in its entirety? And this is far more true of such phenomena as torches driven across the firmament, a large part of the heavens burning, comets, a plurality of suns, stars appearing in the daytime, and the unexpected passage of fires that draw in their wake a long trail of light.

Every one of these things that make us wonder also makes us afraid. And since ignorance is the cause of our experiencing fear, is it not of considerable value to be rid of this ignorance, and so, of your fear? How much better would it be to examine the causes, indeed to focus with the entire mind on this inquiry. For it is impossible to find anything more worthy than a subject which not only attracts but absorbs the mind.

4. Accordingly, let us ask what it is that sets the earth moving from its depths, what drives such a huge mass of weight; what has so much more strength than the earth that by its force it causes so great a load to shake; why the earth sometimes quakes, sometimes is broken up and sinks down, now is separated into parts and gapes wide, in some places maintaining for a long time the gap created by its collapse, in others moving swiftly to bridge the gap; why at times it channels inside itself rivers of remarkable size, and at times forces new ones to its surface; why it sometimes reveals veins of hot water, and sometimes makes the water cold; why it sometimes sends forth fire through an opening previously unknown in a mountain or a rock, and sometimes subdues fires that have been known, indeed famous, for ages. The earth sets a thousand wonders in motion and alters the appearance of places, carrying away mountains, raising up plains, causing valleys to swell up and new islands to rise in the ocean. It is a worthy enterprise to investigate the causes behind these occurrences.

What, you ask, will justify this effort? The reward will be to know Nature, and no prize is greater than this. The subject has numerous features which will prove useful, but the perusal of this material contains nothing more beautiful in itself than that by means of its own splendour it engages the minds of men and is cultivated, not for the sake of profit, but for the wonder it excites. Accordingly, let us investigate the reasons why these phenomena occur. This examination gives me such pleasure that, although in my younger days I published a volume on earthquakes, I would still like to test myself and discover if age has added anything to me in the matter of knowledge, or at least in the matter of attention to detail.

5. Some have supposed that the cause of earthquakes lies in water, others in fire, others in the earth itself, others in the air, others in several of these, and yet others in all of these; certain authorities said that it was clear to them that such elements provided a definite cause of earthquakes, but it was not clear to them what the cause was.

I will now pursue these theories one by one. Before anything else I must state that the old theories were crude and insufficiently precise. Men were still wrong with regard to the truth; all things were new to those making their first attempts; subsequently those same theories were polished. It is nonetheless true that any discoveries made should be acknowledged as received from those men. It was the attainment of a great spirit to unveil the hidden places of Nature's realm and, not content with her outward appearance, to look within and to probe the secrets of the gods. He who hoped that the truth could be discovered contributed most to its discovery. And so it is with indulgence that we should listen to the men of early times. Nothing reaches completion at its beginning; this applies not only to this subject, which is the most important and complex of all (and in which, even when what is achieved is considerable, every age will discover something to do), but to every other business, in which initial efforts have always fallen far short of the completed knowledge.

6. Not one man alone has said that the cause of earthquakes lies in water, and not in one way alone. Thales of Miletus* holds that the whole earth is supported by liquid lying beneath, on which it floats, whether you call it the ocean, or the great sea, or the hitherto elementary water of a different nature, that is, a liquid element. It is this water, he maintains, that supports the earth's disc, just as the water it presses down on supports a large, heavy ship.

It is needless for me to supply the reasons for his belief that the heaviest part of the universe cannot be upheld by air, which is so insubstantial and transient; for the question under consideration at this moment is not the earth's location but earthquakes. By way of proof that waters exist as the cause of earthquakes, and that it is these waters that cause this earth to shake, he advances the following proposition: in every earthquake of some size new springs normally burst forth (just as happens also in the case of ships, which take in water if they tilt and lean to one side, and, if they are submerged due to the excessive weight of what they are carrying, the water either flows over them or at least rises more than usual on the right or left).

It does not require a lengthy deduction to show the falsity of this view. For, if water did support the earth and cause it to shake at times, earthquakes would be continuous, and we should marvel, not at the earth being shaken, but at it staying at rest; again, it would be shaken in its entirety, not just in part, for it is never just half of a ship that is buffeted. But the fact is that earthquakes affect only part of the earth, not all of it. How, then, is it possible for something which is carried as a whole not to be shaken as a whole, if what carries it causes it to be shaken? 'But why do waters burst forth?' In the first place, there are many times when an earthquake has occurred without any new waters starting to flow. Secondly, if this were the reason why water suddenly burst forth, it would pour round the sides of the earth, just as we see happening in the case of rivers and the sea, where the increase in water appears mainly over the sides of ships whenever they sink. Finally, there would never be such an insignificant eruption of water as you claim, like the seeping of bilge-water through a crack, but rather an enormous deluge from liquid that has no limit and supports all of the earth.

7. Certain writers have attributed earthquakes to water but have differed in their explanations. Throughout the whole earth, one of them states, run many kinds of water. In some places there are rivers that never cease to flow, whose great size makes them navigable even without the assistance of rainfall; for instance, there is the Nile, that carries huge quantities of water all summer long; elsewhere, there are the Danube and the Rhine, which flow midway between the pacified and the hostile, the former curbing the attacks of Sarmatians* and forming the boundary between Europe and Asia, the latter keeping at bay the Germans, a people who thirst for war. Reflect now as well on the lakes of great expanse and inland waters surrounded by people unknown to one another, and marshes a boat cannot struggle through, impassable even to those who live on their edges. Again, there are the numerous springs, the numerous sources of rivers discharging sudden streams from places unseen, the numerous rushing

torrents that come together at one time, their strength as short-lived as it is sudden.

Every type and form of water exists also within the earth. There, too, some are carried down with a mighty rush and fall in headlong cascade; others, moving more slowly, recede in shallows and flow smoothly and quietly. There is no denying that waters collect in huge reservoirs and lie motionless in many underground places. We need no lengthy proof that numerous waters are to be found in the place where all waters exist; for the earth would not be capable of producing so many rivers, unless it discharged them from some reservoir, and one of considerable size. If this is true, it must be the case that from time to time a river under the earth exceeds its normal size and, deserting its banks, violently attacks whatever stands in its way; there will thus be a movement of the earth at some part where the river has launched its assault, and, until it subsides, the river will administer this lashing. It can happen that the flowing stream eats away some region and in this way drags down a specific mass whose collapse leads to the shaking of what lies on top.

Now it is the case that a man allows too much to his eyes and does not know how to extend his mind beyond them, if he does not believe that there exist in the hidden regions of the earth bays of an enormous sea. I see nothing to prevent or hinder the sea from gaining access to the earth through secret openings, and from having some kind of shoreline even in the hidden depths. There is also the point that there the sea takes up as much or possibly even more space than here, since the upper regions had to be shared with so many living creatures; the concealed regions, however, being deserted and without owners, afford readier access to water. What stops this subterranean water from rolling like waves and from being propelled by winds that are created by every opening in the earth and by every part of the atmosphere? A storm of larger than normal proportions is capable of moving with some violence any part of the lands it crashes against. For in our upper world as well many places set far back from the sea have been lashed by its sudden approach, and the tide which we heard in the distance has invaded villas overlooking the sea. In the lower world also the subterranean sea can rise up and cast things back, and both of these movements are accompanied by a disturbance of our world above.

8. I do not think you will spend much time hesitating about whether you believe in the existence of subterranean rivers and a hidden sea

beneath us. For where do the rivers we know make their way from, where do they come to us from, if the source of their waters is not shut up inside the earth? I ask you: when you see the Tigris arrested and dried up in mid-journey, not diverted in its entirety but by degrees, with no loss obvious to the eye, at first contracted then wasted away, where do you imagine it goes if not to concealed regions of the earth, particularly as you see it rising up again no smaller than its size when it flowed before? Consider also that we see Alpheus, made famous by poets, sink in Achaea and, crossing the sea, pour forth again in Sicily the beautiful spring of Arethusa.*

Again, are you unaware that among the theories that explain the summer inundation of the Nile there is the view that it bursts forth from the earth and owes its rise, not to waters from above, but to waters produced from the depths of the earth? Indeed, I have listened to two centurions whom Nero Caesar had dispatched to investigate the source of the Nile* (his devotion to the other virtues is matched by a particular devotion to the truth). Their account was that, after being furnished with help by the king of Ethiopia and recommended to the neighbouring kings, they had completed a lengthy journey and penetrated far inland. 'Next,' they said, 'we came to enormous swamps that the natives did not know the way out of and no one could hope to know, so entangled in the water was the vegetation, so impassable on foot or by boat the water, since only a small boat capable of taking just one man can navigate the muddy, overgrown marsh. There,' he said, 'we saw two rocks from which a vast quantity of river-water was falling.'

But whether that is the Nile's source, or merely an addition to it, whether that is its place of origin or it simply returns to the earth's surface from an earlier course it followed underground, is it not your own belief that, whatever the reason, the water rises to the surface from a great subterranean lake? For it must be true that the earth has waters scattered in a great many places and so gathered in one place that it can disgorge them with such intensity.

9. In the judgement of certain men, and indeed men of considerable repute, fire is the cause of earthquakes. Anaxagoras* in particular holds that virtually the same cause causes both the earth and the atmosphere to shake. The atmosphere, which is dense and compacted into clouds, is burst by moving air in the lower region within the earth, and experiences the same force that is accustomed to break

open clouds in our own part of the world. From this clash of clouds and from the rush of air that is forced out fire flashes forth, and, seeking an exit, it makes an assault on all that blocks its path, tearing asunder all opposition, until either it gains a way out to the sky through narrow paths or effects its escape by force and destruction.

Others take the view that fire is indeed the cause of earthquakes, but assign a different cause: buried fire blazes up in many different places and destroys all that is near it. Whenever these areas that have been consumed fall away, they argue that there then follows a movement of those parts which, stripped of the support which lies beneath, begin to slip until they collapse, as nothing rushes in to receive their weight. Then chasms, then huge gulfs open up, or, when they have hesitated a long time, they come to rest upon those objects that remain standing beneath them. This we see happening here with our own eyes whenever fire afflicts a section of a city; when beams have been burnt through or the pillars that lent support to the upper storeys have been destroyed, then the roofs, after swaying for a long period, fall in, wavering for some time in their collapse until they settle upon something solid beneath them.

10. Anaximenes* says that the cause of the earth's movement is the earth itself, which does not feel the shock of something that strikes it from outside but something inside itself and of itself; for, he maintains, certain parts of the earth fall in, if either moisture has dissolved them or fire has eaten them away or a blast of air has caused them to split. But even without the influence of these elements, he argues, no reasons are lacking for some part of the earth to separate or be torn away from the mass; for in the first place all things become unstable over a long period of years, and nothing is safe from the passage of time, which wears away even these solid objects of great strength. Accordingly, just as old buildings collapse in spite of not being struck, when some of their sections have more weight than strength, so in this whole body of the earth it comes about that its parts become weakened by age, and once weakened they fall, causing the parts above them to quake; in the first place they do this at the time of breaking away (for nothing large is cut away without causing to move whatever it clung to); secondly, when they fall they meet something solid and bounce back like a ball, that leaps up when it falls, and rebounds repeatedly whenever it is sent from the ground into a new flight; indeed, if these parts have fallen among stagnant waters, this

very fall shakes the neighbouring regions with a wave which has been cast up by the sudden huge weight thrust down from above.

11. Certain authorities do assign the cause of earthquakes to fire but offer different explanations. When heat reaches intensity in several places, of necessity it causes a vast cloud of vapour to billow up that has no way of escape and by its own force exerts pressure on the air. If the vapour creates extreme pressure, it breaks through everything in its way, but if it is comparatively weak, it brings about no more than a movement of the earth. We see water boil when fire is put below it. What happens in the case of this small volume of enclosed water we may believe happens to a far greater extent when violent, massive fire stirs up vast quantities of water; at such times the fire causes whatever it strikes to shake through the vaporization of the billowing water.

12. Most of the greatest thinkers subscribe to the view that earthquakes are caused by air that moves. Archelaus,* an authority on ancient matters, says as follows: 'Winds are carried down into the hollow regions of the earth. Then, when all the spaces are now full and the air has thickened to its greatest extent, the moving air which comes in on top of the air already there presses and pushes down on it, at first driving it together with frequent blows, then forcing it out; at that point, as it seeks room, the air opens up all the narrow passages and attempts to break out of its prison. In this way it ensues that the earth is moved, as the moving air struggles and looks for an escape-route. Accordingly, when an earthquake is on the point of occurring, it is preceded by peaceful and quiet atmospheric conditions, obviously because the force of air which is accustomed to rouse the winds is held back in the earth's interior.' Even now, at the time of this earthquake in Campania, although it was the changeable winter season, the atmospheric conditions throughout the preceding days were still. 'What is your conclusion? Has the earth never been shaken when the wind was blowing?' Very rarely: for rarely have two winds blown at the same time, though this can happen and is usual. If we accept this, and it is agreed that two winds operate at the same time, why can it not happen that the one wind stirs up the upper atmosphere and the other the lower?

13. You may put in this category of belief Aristotle and his pupil Theophrastus (a man not of divine eloquence, as the Greeks thought, but of a charming eloquence that was lucid and effortless). I will set out the explanation both men favoured: 'There is constantly from

the earth some degree of evaporation, which is sometimes dry, sometimes mixed with moisture. This is produced from the depths of the
earth, and once it has risen as high as it can go, when it has no higher
place to go, it is carried back and rolled in on itself. Then the strife
caused by air moving back and forth tosses aside all obstacles and,
whether the air is blocked or forces its way out through narrow passages,
it creates a movement and disturbance of the earth.'

Strato,* who particularly cultivated this area of philosophy and
was an investigator of the natural world, belongs to the same school
of thought. The position he arrived at is as follows: 'Cold and hot
always move away in opposite directions, they cannot coexist. Therefore
cold flows into the place vacated by the force of heat, and in turn heat
exists in the place from which cold has been banished. That what I
say is true and that both move contrary to one-another would appear
to you from the following: in the season of winter, when there is cold
on the surface of the earth, wells are warm, just as much as caves and
all subterranean recesses, because heat makes its way there, giving
place to the cold that takes possession of the higher regions; when
this heat reaches the lower parts and collects there as much as it can,
its strength increases in proportion to its density. Here it comes upon
other air that of necessity gives way to it, crammed together as that
cold air is and compressed into a corner. The same result occurs in
an opposite way: when a greater force of cold is carried down into the
caverns, all the heat concealed there, yielding to the cold, makes for
the narrow passages and is driven along with great energy, because
the nature of the two does not permit harmony or delay in one place.
Accordingly, the air as it takes flight, desiring to escape in every way,
thrusts back and tosses about all that is near it. And for that reason
a bellowing sound is usually heard before an earthquake occurs, as the
winds are creating a disturbance in the hidden depths.' (Otherwise it
could not happen that, as our own Virgil says:

> Beneath our feet the ground bellows and the lofty ridges move,*

if this were not the work of winds.)

'Then this conflict proceeds to go through the same phases: an
accumulation of heat takes place, and, once more, its eruption, at which
time the cold elements are held in check and give way, though they
will shortly become more powerful. While the force rushes to and fro
and the air moves this way and that, the earth is shaken.'

14. There are those who hold that air, and no other cause, is responsible for earthquakes, but for a different reason than the one that found favour with Aristotle. Listen to the argument these men advance: our body is irrigated by blood and also by air, which travels by its own routes. But we have certain rather narrow receptacles for breath through which air merely passes, no more, and certain others of wider dimension, in which the air gathers and from there is channelled to the different parts of the body. In similar fashion the whole body of the whole earth affords the passage through it of water, which takes the place of blood, and of winds, which one might simply call breath. These two elements rush together in some places, while in others they are stationary. But in the case of our body, as long as we enjoy good health, the movement of the veins also maintains its rhythm without disturbance, whereas, whenever an ailment occurs, the veins pulse more rapidly and breathing in and out indicates strain and fatigue. The same is true also of the earth: as long as it maintains its natural condition, it remains unshaken; when something goes wrong, then its motion is that of a sick body, since the air that was flowing through it in a regular current is struck more violently, causing its veins to shake. But this is different from what was said a little earlier by those whose view is that the earth is a living creature; otherwise, the earth would feel an agitation all over, similar to that experienced by a living creature; for in us a fever afflicts some parts of the body more moderately, others more violently, but it spreads through all the parts with equal uniformity.

You must, therefore, consider if any of the air from the surrounding atmosphere makes its way into the earth. As long as it has a means of escape, it slips through without inflicting any harm. If it hits anything and is met by something that impedes its progress, then at first it becomes weighed down by the atmosphere that pours in upon it from behind, but then with difficulty it makes its escape through some crack, bursting out more violently according to the narrowness of the opening. This cannot take place without conflict, and conflict inevitably involves movement. But if this air finds not even a crack through which to flow, it masses together there and rages, being driven around this way and that, casting some objects aside and cutting through others, since it is very extenuated and at the same time very robust, and bursts through barriers, however great, splitting and scattering by its force whatever it enters. That is when the earth is buffeted: for either it opens up to give space to the air, or, once it has given space, it loses its foundation and sinks into the very cavern from which it dispatched the air.

15. Certain men hold the following view: the earth is perforated in many places, having not only those places of access which it first gained at the time of its origin, enabling it, as it were, to breathe, but many others imposed upon it by accident: in some areas water washed away regions from the earth's surface, while others were cut through by torrents, and others still laid open after being burst asunder by vast tides. Through these apertures air enters: if it is enclosed by the sea and driven deeper down, and the water prevents it from coming back out, then it is rolled around, once its way out and way back are simultaneously shut off, and, because it is unable to extend straight ahead, as is natural to it, it stretches upwards, and beats apart the earth that weighs down on it.

16. Now at this point I must state a theory which recommends itself to a large number of authorities, and will perhaps cause most of us to defect from our own view. It is evident that the earth is not without air: I refer not only to the air by which it holds itself together and joins the parts of itself, which is to be found also in rocks and dead bodies, but also to that vital and active air by which all things are nourished. If the earth did not have this, how would it pour air into so many trees and so many plants that derive life from no other source? How would the earth foster so many different roots that are sunk into it in various ways, some penetrating only the earth's surfaces, others sunk deeper, unless it possessed an abundance of the breath that generates so many different growths, and nurtures them with its own food and drink? So far I have referred to minor considerations: this whole heaven, enclosed by fiery ether, the highest part of the universe, all these stars, that one cannot begin to number, all this assembly of heavenly bodies, and, to pass over other things, this sun driving its course so near to us, larger by far than the whole globe of the earth, all derive their sustenance from terrestrial matter, sharing it among themselves, and are evidently supported by no other means than by the earth's exhalations. This is what nourishes them and provides their pasture. Now, the earth would be incapable of nourishing so many things of such magnitude, greater even than itself, if it were not filled with breath which it pours forth day and night from all parts of itself; for an earth from which so much is sought and consumed must possess a huge abundance of things. And indeed it is produced for the time when it needs to be sent forth (for the earth would not have a constant supply of air to nourish so many heavenly bodies, unless these bodies in turn kept running back and paid their several dues, one for another), but nonetheless it must be the case that the earth abounds in air, is filled with it, and produces it from a hidden store. There can, therefore, be no doubt that within the earth is concealed a great quantity of air and a wide-ranging atmosphere occupies the unseen spaces beneath the earth. If this is true, it follows inevitably that the body of the earth, filled as it is with an extremely moveable substance, is often subject to movement. For surely no one can doubt that there is anything as restless, as variable, or as delighting in unruliness as air?

17. Accordingly, it follows that air exercises its own nature, and that something which wants to be constantly in motion will sometimes cause motion in other things. This takes place whenever it is banned from following its course. For as long as air is not obstructed, it flows peacefully along; when it is met with resistance and held back, it rages and tears its barriers asunder, just like the well-known 'Araxes chafing at his bridge':* as long as a river has a channel that is smooth and unrestricted, it unfolds its waters in orderly sequence; when its path is checked by boulders brought in by man or falling by chance, then it looks for energy from the obstruction, discovering the more strength, the more barriers are put in its way. For all that water which comes up from behind and gathers volume on itself, proving unable to sustain its own weight, acquires its force by means of destruction and escapes by rushing forward together with the very objects that were lying in its path. The same thing comes about with air: the stronger and more mobile it is, the more swiftly it bursts forth and the more violently it sweeps away every hindrance. This causes an earthquake, obviously due to a movement of that part of the earth below which the conflict occurred.

The following point also proves the veracity of what is said: many times when an earthquake takes place, if only a particular section of the earth is broken open, a wind blows from there for a period of many days, as is reported to have happened in the case of the earthquake suffered by Chalcis. You will find this in the writings of Asclepiodotus, a student of Posidonius,* where he treats of this very subject of natural phenomena. You will find in the works of other authors too that the earth has gaped open in one place and from there wind has blown for a considerable time, clearly having created for itself the route along which it moved.

18. The main cause of the earth moving is, therefore, air, which is swift by nature and changing from one place to another. As long as it is not subjected to force and stays hidden in an unoccupied space, it lies harmless and causes no disturbance to its surroundings. When a cause coming from outside vexes it, driving it together and forcing it into a confined space, it simply yields ground, if still allowed to, and wanders to and fro. When the opportunity to escape is cut off and it meets obstacles on every side, then,

> With mighty moaning of the mountain
> About the barriers,*

it rages, and tears apart the barriers it has pummelled for so long, hurling them aside, displaying greater violence the stronger the impediment with which it has struggled. Then, when it has ranged around the whole space that confines it and still cannot escape, it bounds back from where it met the strongest resistance, and is either spread through unseen openings formed here and there by the resultant movement itself of the earth, or bursts through some newly made wound. This is the way of it: so great a force cannot be restrained, and no compact body holds back this wind. For, breaking open any kind of fetter and carrying away with it every weight, it pours through the smallest cracks and creates a space for itself. Through the uncontrollable power of its nature it gains its liberty, and particularly when stirred up it asserts its rights for itself. But air that moves is a thing that cannot be conquered: nothing will exist that,

> By authority restrains or by chains and prison curbs
> The struggling winds and roaring tempests.*

Without doubt the poets wanted this space where the winds lurk in confinement below the earth to be regarded as a prison, but they failed to grasp that what has been shut in is no longer wind, and that it is impossible to shut in what is wind. For whatever is in a confined space is at rest and is stationary atmosphere; all wind is in a state of flight. And now a further argument is added to these, making it evident that moving air is what causes an earthquake: our own bodies also are not given to trembling, unless at a time when some cause disturbs the air inside them, making it contract through fear, or grow weak through old age or feeble through sluggish veins, or become paralysed through cold, or be thrown off its normal course by an attack of illness. For, as long as the air keeps flowing without doing harm and maintains its accustomed course, the body experiences no trembling; when something happens which hinders its function, then it ceases to have sufficient strength to support what it had borne in its state of vigour, and, as it fails, it causes a shaking in whatever it had maintained when it was healthy.

19. Because we have a duty, let us listen to Metrodorus of Chios* stating his preference in advancing his own opinion. For I do not allow myself to omit even those views of which I disapprove, since it is better that there should be a full range of all theories and that the ones I disapprove of should suffer my condemnation rather than my neglect. What, then, does he say? 'When a man sings into a large jar, his voice runs through the whole vessel with a kind of quavering and resonates. There is only a slight projection of the voice but nonetheless it travels all around, not only making contact with the surrounding vessel but also creating a disturbance in it. Likewise, the huge caverns that lie below the earth contain air of their own which is struck and disturbed by other air, whenever it falls from above, just as those vacant spaces I spoke of a little earlier vibrate when they receive a shout.'

20. Let us now come to those who have stated as a cause of earthquakes all the factors I have described or several of them. Democritus thinks several are responsible. He says that an earthquake is brought about sometimes by air, sometimes by water, sometimes by both. This is how he extends his theory: 'A particular part of the earth is hollow; into this a great concentration of water flows. Some of this water is thin and so more fluid than the rest. When it is thrown back by the heavy mass coming on top of it, it dashes against the earth and sets it in motion; for water cannot fluctuate without creating movement in what it pushes against.' And now we must speak in the same way about water also as we did about air: 'When it gathers together in a single place and stops holding itself in check, it inclines in one direction and opens up a route at first by its own weight, then by its force. For it has been enclosed for a long time and so can only go out by descending a slope, and cannot fall straight down in a moderate way or without striking hard against the things through which or into which it falls. But if, once it has already started to sweep along, it is made to halt at some point and that force of current rolls back on itself, it is driven back on the earth that contains it and violently assaults any part of the earth that lacks stability. Moreover, at times the earth becomes saturated with moisture gathered deep inside it, so that it settles lower and its very foundations are weakened. Then it is crushed where the weight of converging waters exerts the heaviest pressure upon it. Indeed, air sometimes drives water, and if it exerts a strong force, it obviously moves that part of the earth against which it has carried the gathered water. Sometimes the air is forced into subterranean pathways, and in looking for a way out, it sets everything in motion. Again, the earth can be penetrated by winds, and moving air is too thin to be kept out and too violent to be opposed when it is stirred up and swift in its motion.'

Epicurus says that all these factors can be causes, and he ventures to propose a number of other causes. He is critical of those who maintain that one single factor is the cause, as it is difficult to give a certain assurance about theories that depend upon conjecture. 'Accordingly,' as he says, 'an earthquake can be caused by water, if it washes away and erodes certain parts of the earth which, once weakened, can no longer support what they sustained when unimpaired. Earthquakes can be caused by the pressure of moving air: for perhaps the air inside the earth is disturbed by other air entering, perhaps the earth receives a shock when some part of it suddenly collapses, and this causes the earth to assume movement. Perhaps some part of the earth is supported by a kind of column and by some sort of piling, and when they become flawed or give way, the weight set above them trembles. Perhaps a warm force of moving air turns to fire, and like lightning sweeps down, wreaking havoc on all obstacles. Perhaps marshy and stagnant waters come under attack from some blast, and therefore either a blow shakes the earth or the disturbance of the air increases by its actual motion, and rousing itself, journeys all the way from the depths to the surface of the earth.' It remains the view of Epicurus, however, that there is no greater cause of earthquakes than air.

21. It is my conviction as well that it is this moving air that can accomplish such great things. Nothing in nature is more powerful than air, nothing possesses more energy, and without it not even the most robust elements have power: air stirs up fire; waters are static, should you take away the wind, and take on energy precisely when driven by a blast of air. Air is also capable of scattering large tracts of

the earth, of lifting up new mountains from down below and of setting hitherto unseen islands in mid-ocean. Who doubts that air carried into the daylight Thera and Therasia, and that island which in our own lifetime was born before the sailors' eyes in the Aegean Sea? According to Posidonius, there are two ways in which the earth is moved. Each of these has its own term: one is a 'thrust below', when the earth is shaken and moves up and down, the other a 'tilt', when, like a ship, it leans to one side or the other. My own view is that there is also a third way, which is described in our own vocabulary: our ancestors had good reason for speaking of the earth's 'tremor', which is unlike either of the other two; for on such occasions things are neither thrust nor tilted but vibrated, an event resulting in minimal damage, just as a tilt is far more destructive than a thrust: for unless a movement restoring the tilt swiftly rushes in from the other side, the inevitable consequence is a collapse.

22. As these movements bear no resemblance to one another, their causes also differ. Let us first, then, talk of a shaking movement. If ever large loads are dragged through streets by a row of several vehicles and the heavier strain causes their wheels to slip into ruts in the road, you will be aware of buildings shaking. Asclepiodotus reports: when a rock was torn from the side of a mountain and fell, buildings in the vicinity fell down because of the ensuing shock. The same thing can occur under the earth, so that something may be loosened from overhanging cliffs and fall with a loud crash and noise into a cavern lying below, coming down the more violently, the greater the weight or the height; and in this way there is movement in the whole roof of the subterranean valley. We can believe that rocks are not only torn off by their own weight, but also that when rivers travel over them the constant moisture makes the joints in the stone weak, and every day carries away something of the mass that the stone is attached to, scraping off the skin, as it were, that holds the stone in position. Then continuous attrition throughout the ages weakens those parts that it rubs into each day, to the point where they cease to function as a support for their load. That is when rocks of enormous size fall down, then that crag, falling headlong, will not allow any obstacle it strikes to stand still,

With a roar it comes on, and all is seen of a sudden to collapse,*

as our Virgil says.

23. This will be the cause of that motion that causes the earth to quake from below; I pass now to the second type. The earth is of a porous nature and contains many empty spaces. Through these apertures air passes, and when in large quantities it flows in and does not come out, it makes the earth tilt. Others as well, as I described a little earlier, have found this explanation attractive; whether you will be impressed by a crowd of authorities, it has also found favour with Callisthenes,* a man whom we should hardly despise. For he possessed remarkable intelligence and would not tolerate the rage of his king. This is the everlasting crime of Alexander, which no excellence, no success in war, will redeem; for whenever anyone says, 'He killed many thousands of Persians,' the response will be, 'And he killed Callisthenes'; whenever it is said, 'He killed Darius,* whose kingdom was the greatest of his day,' the response will be, 'And he killed Callisthenes'; whenever it is said, 'He conquered everything as far as the ocean, and even made an assault on the ocean itself with ships it had not seen before, and extended his empire from a corner of Thrace all the way to the furthest boundaries of the east,' the response will be, 'But he killed Callisthenes.' Granted that he surpassed all the exploits in antiquity of generals and kings, not one of his exploits will be as great as that crime. In the books in which he describes how Helice and Buris sank below the waves, what disaster plunged them into the sea, or the sea into them, this Callisthenes says what I have already said in an earlier part of this work: 'Air enters the earth through unseen openings, as it does everywhere and so beneath the sea as well. Then, when that route by which it had descended is blocked, and the waters standing in its rear have cut off its way back, it is carried this way and that, and running into itself it makes the earth totter. That is why regions close to the sea are most frequently troubled, and therefore this power of the sea to move the earth has been assigned to Neptune. Anyone who has learned the first principles of literature knows that in Homer he is called the "Shaker of the Earth".'

24. I myself also agree that air is the cause of this disaster. With regard to this air I will argue how it enters the earth, whether it is through fine apertures our eyes cannot detect or through larger openings that are more extended, and whether it comes just from the depths or through the earth's surface as well.

We cannot believe this last notion. For even in our own bodies the air is kept out by the skin, and it has no way of gaining entrance except by the parts through which it is inhaled, and even when we have breathed it in, it cannot settle except in the part of the body that is relatively open: for it is not in the sinews or flesh that it lingers but in the guts and the wide cavity of the inner region. We may infer the same about the earth from the fact also that it is not on the earth's surface or around the surface that an earthquake occurs but underground, in its depths. A proof of this is that seas of enormous depth are buffeted, obviously because of the movement of the ground over which the seas are spread. And so it is probable that the earth is moved from far below, and that air is formed there in mighty caverns.

'No!' he says. 'Just as when we shiver with cold, the result is trembling, so the earth too is shaken by the arrival of air from outside.' This cannot in any way happen. For the earth ought to experience cold so that the same thing happens to it as it does to us when we are compelled to shudder because of an external force. I would concede that something similar to the condition we experience does happen to the earth, but not for a similar reason. It must be afflicted by an inner source of harm deep inside. Perhaps the most convincing proof of my argument can be this: when the enormous destruction of an earthquake opens up the ground, sometimes entire cities are drawn in and buried by that gaping hole. Thucydides says that around the time of the Peloponnesian War the island of Atalanta was submerged, either entirely or to a very great extent. We have Posidonius' authority for the same thing happening at Sidon. But in this regard we have no need of witnesses: we remember in our own day that internal movement has torn apart lands, resulting in the separation of regions and destruction of plains. I will now explain how, in my view, this comes about.

25. When with great force moving air completely fills an empty space below the earth, and starts to struggle and to think of how it can get out, it repeatedly dashes against the very sides it is hidden within, above which cities are sometimes situated. These sides are sometimes so shaken that the buildings positioned on top of them fall down, sometimes to such an extent that the walls which support the entire roof of the cave tumble down into that empty subterranean space, and entire cities fall into the vast depths. Should you believe it, they say that Ossa was at one time joined to Olympus and then became separated from it due to an earthquake, and all of a single huge mountain was split into two parts. Then the Peneus flowed

away and proceeded to drain the marshes that used to infest Thessaly, carrying off into its own stream the waters that had formed stagnant pools, having no way of escape. The river Ladon, which flows midway between Elis and Megalopolis, was poured forth by an earthquake.

What do I prove by these instances? That air collects in spacious caverns (by what other name should I call these empty spaces beneath the earth?); were this not the case, large expanses of the earth would be shaken, and simultaneously many regions would experience disturbance: as things are, small districts only are afflicted, and never does an earthquake extend for two hundred miles. This recent one which has filled the world with stories did not go beyond Campania. Why should I explain that, when Chalcis rocked, Thebes stood firm; when Aegium suffered shocks, Patrae, so near to it, only heard about the earthquake? That mighty shock which buried two cities, Helice and Buris, stopped on the nearer side of Aegium. Accordingly, it appears that the area over which an earthquake spreads is only as great as that of the empty space that extends beneath the earth.

26. To prove this point, I could have used, or misused, the authority of great men who record that Egypt has at no time suffered from an earthquake; they offer as an explanation of this the fact that the country has grown entirely from mud. For, if Homer is to be believed, the distance of Pharos from the mainland was that which a ship under full sail could measure in a day's voyage. But Pharos has been moved into contact with the mainland: for the swollen Nile, as it flows down, carries with it a large volume of mud which it deposits from time to time on the existing land, and constantly extends Egypt by adding to its size each year. As a result the land consists of a rich, muddy soil, and it does not contain within it any openings, but grows into a solid as the mud dries. Its formation was that of compressed sediment when the components were glued together, and no empty space could come between these, as liquid and soft elements were constantly falling upon the solid base.

But both Egypt and Delos have earthquakes, though Virgil ordered the latter to stand still:

He granted that the land be tilled and, free from earthquake, should scorn the winds.*

The credulous race of philosophers, on the authority of Pindar,* has also denied Delos earthquakes. Thucydides says that it was indeed free from such disturbances in the past but had an earthquake in the time of the Peloponnesian War. Callisthenes speaks of such an event at another time as well. 'Among the many portents', he says, 'that gave warning of the destruction of the two cities, Helice and Buris, particularly remarkable were a vast pillar of fire and the earthquake on Delos.' His reason for wishing Delos to be thought of as stable is that it is set upon the sea and has hollow crags and porous rocks to allow any trapped air a way back; this is why islands have firmer soil and cities are less at risk the closer they come to the sea. Pompeii and Herculaneum have come to appreciate that this is not true. Add to this now the fact that every seashore is liable to experience earthquakes: Paphos, for example, has collapsed not once alone, and so, too, Nicopolis has rocked and become familiar with this ruinous phenomenon; Cyprus is surrounded by deep sea, and yet knows earthquakes; even Tyre itself suffers as much from earthquakes as from erosion by the sea.

These are the reasons usually advanced to explain the earth shaking.

27. But there are reports of certain things having occurred which are peculiar to this Campanian earthquake, and these require an explanation. They say that a flock of six hundred sheep died in the district of Pompeii. There is no reason for supposing that fear caused this to happen to those sheep: we have stated that plague is accustomed to occur in the wake of great earthquakes, and there is little surprise in this. For many deadly substances lurk in the earth's depths: the very atmosphere there, which is stagnant either through a fault in the earth or from inertia and the everlasting darkness, or because it is tainted by the poison of the internal fires, brings harm to those who inhale it. When it is sent forth from its long stay, it contaminates and defiles this pure, clear atmosphere, bringing new types of disease to those who breathe in the unaccustomed air. There is the further consideration that unwholesome and lethal waters lurk in these hidden places, as they are never moved by use, never stirred up by a free, fresh breeze. They are dense, therefore, and wear a mantle of heavy, unending fog, and so harbour within them only what is fatal and hostile to our bodies. Also, the atmosphere which mixes with them and lies among those swamps, on emerging, scatters its poison over a wide area and brings death to those inhaling it. Again, flocks, that are usually the first victims of the plague's onset, feel its effects more readily the more greed they show: under the open sky they consume large amounts of water, which has the greatest risk of pollution in time of plague. It does not surprise me that sheep have been infected, being of a comparatively weak constitution and holding their heads closer to the ground, since they took in the exhalations of the tainted air near the ground itself. This air would have harmed humans as well, if it had come out in greater quantity; but it was extinguished by the abundance of pure air before it reached a height where it could be inhaled by people.

28. You should understand that the earth contains many deadly things from the fact that so many poisons grow spontaneously, not scattered by hand, as the soil evidently harbours seeds contributing to illness as well as to health. Is it not true that in several parts of Italy a poisonous vapour is exhaled through certain openings, which is harmful for men and beasts alike to breathe? Birds as well, if they encounter the vapour before its virulence is tempered by better weather, fall down in mid-flight, their bodies livid and their throats swollen as if they had been violently choked.

As long as this air keeps itself inside the earth, flowing out from only a contracted opening, it only has the power to kill creatures that look down into it and enter it of their own accord; once it has been concealed for ages in the grim subterranean darkness, it grows into a poison, becoming more toxic by the very delay and more deadly the more it remains inert; when it succeeds in getting out, it launches the undying evil and infernal pollution of gloomy cold, and casts a dark stain upon the atmosphere of our region. For better elements yield the victory to worse. At such a time even that pure air we enjoy is transformed into foul air: this breeds sudden and continuous deaths and monstrous forms of disease, arising from unknown causes. Again, the disaster is of short or long duration according to the poison's strength, and there is no cessation of the plague until that infected air is purified by the clearing of the sky and the buffeting of the winds.

29. Now the fact that several people have run around as though mad or panic-stricken is caused by fear, which shatters minds even when it afflicts individuals and comes in moderation; what of its effect when it fills a crowd with terror? When cities collapse, when populations are crushed, when the earth is shaken, is it any wonder that minds have wandered bereft between sorrow and fear? It is no easy thing to keep one's wits in the midst of great disasters. Accordingly, the tendency is for those of most unstable personality to experience such fear that they lose control of themselves. No one in fact succumbs to terror without some loss of sanity, and all who are afraid resemble madmen. However, fear brings some quickly back to their senses, while others it drives more violently astray and turns them into madmen. This is why during wartime people wander about with their minds distracted, and never will you find more examples of prophesying than when fear compounded with religious feeling strikes the mind.

30. It causes me no surprise that a statue was split in two, since I have described how mountains were parted from mountains and the ground itself was torn asunder from its depths:

> Once, men say, these lands were torn apart by some great devastation
> (Such is the power to change of Time that lasts through all ages).
> They say they leapt apart, these lands, though at first they had been one.
> With mighty force came the sea, slicing from Sicily a vast flank of Italy,
> And with its narrow channel flowed twixt fields and cities the sea had
> sundered.*

You see whole districts torn from their foundations and what had been situated nearby lying now on the far side of the sea; you see cities and peoples torn asunder when part of Nature is stirred up and has driven the sea, or fire, or air forward in a particular direction. Their strength is astonishing, deriving as it does from the whole: for although it spends its fury in only one part, yet that fury is spent with the force of the universe. So it was that the sea ripped Spain from its connection with Africa, and Sicily was cut off from Italy by that flood commemorated by the greatest poets. But considerably more force lies in those currents which come from down below the earth: for whatever has to force its way through narrow passages becomes more violent.

As to what great things these tremors of the earth effect and what wondrous sights they produce, enough has been said. Why, then, is anyone astonished that the bronze of a single statue, not even solid but hollow and thin, has been broken up, when perhaps moving air, while seeking a way out, has shut itself up inside it? But who is not aware of this? We have seen buildings whose corners have broken up moving and coming together again. Again, certain things that were not well fitted in their place and were put together rather carelessly and loosely by masons have been made compact by the continuous shaking of an earthquake. But if whole walls and entire houses are cracked, and the sides of great towers, however solid they may be, are split, and the pilings that give support to great structures scattered, what grounds does anyone have for thinking it worth observing that a statue from top to bottom has been severed equally in two?

31. But why is it that an earthquake has persisted over several days? For Campania did not stop experiencing constant tremors, the earthquake decreasing in violence, it is true, but still causing huge damage, since it shook buildings already shaken, and as they were barely standing it needed merely a push and not a strong force to make them collapse. Evidently all the air had not yet escaped but was still moving from one place to another, despite the greater part of it having been discharged. Among the arguments proving that moving air causes such phenomena, you should certainly not hesitate to advance this one as well: when the largest tremor to vent its fury on cities and countries has been created, another of equal scale cannot follow, but mild tremors succeed the greatest shock, since the violence of the original quake has by now enabled the struggling winds to escape their confinement; then there is not the same power in the remnants of the remaining air, and they are not required to battle, since now they have found a route and follow the path by which the original, greatest force of air exited.

This point also I judge worthy of recording, as it was a man of considerable reputation and learning who observed it (as it happened, he was taking a bath when this earthquake occurred): he declares that when in the bath he saw the tiles that paved the floor separate one from the other and join together again, and that, as the floor opened up, water was received into the joints, but when the floor closed back together again, the water bubbled up and leaked out under the pressure. I have heard the same man recounting how he had seen earthen walls shaking more gently and more frequently than the nature of an unyielding substance allows.

32. I will say no more, Lucilius, my excellent friend, about the causes themselves of earthquakes: now I address those matters that pertain to reassuring our minds, for it is more important for us to have courage than learning; but the one does not come about without the other. For only through the liberal arts and the contemplation of nature does the mind acquire strength. What man has not been strengthened and given fresh heart to face all misfortunes by this very disaster in Campania? What grounds do I have for living in fear

of man or beast, of arrow or spear? More serious perils await me: lightning-bolts, earthquakes, and vast parts of nature seek my life. And so with great courage must death be challenged, whether it attacks us with an assault that is savage and knows no bounds, or with a death which is an ordinary, everyday experience. It makes no difference how threatening is its onset or how great the ruin it draws down on us; what it seeks from us is of little account: it is something that old age is likely to take away from us, or an earache, or an excess of corrupt liquid in our bodies, or food that disagrees with the stomach, or a slight injury to the foot.

A trivial thing is the life of man, but in no way is it a trivial achievement to hold that life in contempt. The man who despises it will view with untroubled mind the fury of the sea, though all the winds stir it up, though the tide, because of some upheaval of the world, turns the entire ocean upon the land. Untroubled, he will gaze upon the grim and fearsome countenance of a thundering sky, even if heaven shatters and combines its fires to destroy all things, particularly itself. Untroubled, he will view the ground yawning wide, its framework shattered, even though the regions of the dead are revealed to his eyes. He shall stand over that abyss with no fear in his heart and perhaps will leap into that void where he will have to fall. What do I care how great are the means by which my death is caused? To die itself is no great thing. If, then, we wish to be happy and not to be exercised by fear of men or of gods or of events, if we wish to hold in contempt the needless promises and idle threats of fortune, if we wish to live in tranquillity and to compete with the very gods in happiness, we must hold our life in readiness. Whether it comes under attack from treachery or disease, from the swords of enemies or of one's fellow countrymen, from the collapse of falling tenements, from the immense force of fire that wraps in its embrace cities and fields with equal devastation, let it be taken by whatever misfortune desires its end.

What debt do I owe life other than to encourage it as it departs and to send it on its way with good wishes? 'Go with courage, go with good fortune! Show no hesitation: Nature is reclaiming you. It is not a question of fact but of time; you are doing what must at some time be done. Ask no questions, feel no fear, and do not step back as though you are about to enter something bad. Nature who gave you birth is waiting for you, and a better and safer place. There no earthquakes are to be found, no winds rush to join battle in a great crash of clouds, no conflagrations lay waste cities and regions. There is no fear of shipwrecks swallowing whole fleets, no armies are arrayed with opposing banners, no soldiers in their many thousands show an equal madness to destroy one another, no plague exists, and funeral pyres blazing in common and without distinction for whole nations that fall. Death has no importance: what do we fear? It is a burden: better that it should fall on us once rather than threaten us for ever. Should *I* be afraid to die, when the earth perishes before I do, when the forces that cause shaking are shaken themselves, and can only do harm to us through inflicting it on themselves? Helice and Buris in their entirety were claimed by the sea: am *I* to fear for this one little body of mine? Ships sail over two towns, two indeed known to us, of which record preserved in writing has made us aware: how many other towns have been submerged in other places, how many peoples has either the land or the sea encompassed? Am *I* to refuse an end to my own life, when I know that my existence has an end? Indeed, when I know that all things are finite, am I to fear my final breath?'

Accordingly, Lucilius, as far as you can, muster your courage against the fear of death: it is this fear that makes us abject; this is what disturbs and destroys the very life it spares; this is what enlarges in our minds all such things as earthquakes and lightning-bolts. You will view all these with a steady eye if you reflect that there is no difference between a short and a long time of life. We lose only hours: suppose the sum is a matter of days, of months, of years: we lose only what is going to be lost in any case. What does it matter, I ask you, if I reach them? Time flows on, abandoning those who crave it most; I own neither the future nor the past, and am suspended on a point of swift-footed time: and it is of no small importance that I have shown moderation! It was an elegant response that the wise Laelius* gave to a man who said to him, 'Sixty years of age are mine': 'These sixty years you speak of are *not* yours.' Do we not understand even from the fact that we tally up the years lost to us the terms of a life beyond our grasp and the allotment of a time that is never ours to enjoy? Let us fix this in our minds, let us say this to ourselves time and again: 'We must die.' When? What concern of yours is that? How? What concern of yours is that? Death is a law of nature; death is a contribution

and an obligation required of mortals; death is a cure for all ills: whoever feels fear has been longing for death. Forget all else, Lucilius,
and concentrate your thoughts on this one thing: not to fear the name
of death. Through long reflection make death one of your close
acquaintances, so that, if the situation arises, you are able even to go
out and meet it.

EXPLANATORY NOTES

ON PROVIDENCE

3 *Lucilius*: also the addressee of the *Letters* and of the *Natural Questions*. There is no information on him independent of that which can be retrieved from Seneca's works. He is presented as coming from a town at the gulf of Naples (Naples or Pompeii), a knight, and is said to have held a post of procurator of Sicily. He is interested in philosophy, but leaning towards Epicureanism, and writes prose and poetry.

6 *Cato*: the younger Cato (Marcus Porcius Cato), who during the civil war in 46 BC preferred suicide to being granted pardon by Julius Caesar.

Petreius and Juba: both were opposed to Caesar and sought death in single combat after his victory at Thapsus in 46 BC.

7 *our friend Demetrius*: a Cynic teaching in Rome at the time; Seneca also refers to him in *Letters* 20.9, 66.14, 91.19; *On Benefits* 7.1.3, 7.11, and 8.2.

8 *Mucius by fire . . . Cato by death*: according to legend Gaius Mucius Cordus Scaevola demonstrated to Porsena in 507 BC how determined the Romans were to defend their native land by scorching his right hand. Gaius Fabricius Luscinus (consul in 282 and 278 BC) fought against the Samnites and Pyrrhus. Publius Rutilius Rufus (consul 105 BC) was unjustly convicted of extortion and withdrew to Asia. For Cato see note to p. 6.

Sulla's proscriptions: Lucius Cornelius Sulla (*c*.138–78 BC), as dictator, sought to re-establish the power of the senate. Under his rule 'proscription' lists of political opponents, condemning them to death, were published.

is Lucius Sulla fortunate: allusion to the *cognomen* 'Felix' which Sulla adopted.

Cornelian law: a law on murder, stipulating severe punishment, which Sulla introduced.

Regulus: see note to p. 137.

9 *rebuffs of a cantankerous wife*: on Terentia, Maecenas' less than laudable wife, see also *Letters* 114.6. Gaius Maecenas was a friend of Augustus and patron to Horace, Virgil, and others.

elixir of immortality: Plato's dialogue *Phaedo* juxtaposes the description of Socrates' suicide through drinking hemlock with a discussion of the immortality of the soul.

Pompey, Caesar, and Crassus: the three formed the so-called first Triumvirate in the 50s BC, which dominated Roman politics.

Vatinius: a supporter of Caesar, he defeated Cato in the candidature for the praetorship in 55 BC.

13 *an Appius and a Metellus*: two distinguished blind politicians. Appius Claudius Caecus (censor in 312 BC) was the leading politician of his time, responsible

for the Via Appia, an important water-main into Rome (the Aqua Appia), and the refusal of a peace with King Pyrrhus of Epirus. Lucius Caecilius Metellus defeated the Carthaginians, probably in the year of his consulship (251 BC) in a battle during the First Punic War.

14 *that brave man Demetrius*: see note to p. 7.

15 *Steep is the way . . . lest I headlong fall*: from Ovid, *Metamorphoses* 2.63 ff. The sun-god Phoebus tries to convince his son Phaethon that he should not ride the chariot of the sun.

And though . . . ravening Lion: Ovid, *Metamorphoses* 2.79 ff; translations of both Ovid quotations by A. D. Melville, Oxford World's Classics, 1996.

ON ANGER, BOOK 3

18 *Novatus*: see the first note to *On the Happy Life*.

20 *as I said in my earlier books*: in 1.9.2, 1.17.1, 2.13.1.

23 *Democritus*: a Presocratic philosopher, whose physical and ethical doctrines were crucial influences on Epicurean doctrine.

25 *an extremely hot-tempered orator*: Marcus Caelius Rufus (*c.*84–48 BC). Charged with public order offences in 56 BC, he was defended by Cicero and Marcus Crassus, but also delivered a speech in his own defence. Cicero's extant speech *For Caelius* includes occasional references to it.

26 *Pythagoras*: the legendary philosopher and mathematician of the sixth century BC. The movement established by him enjoyed a revival in the first century BC. Several of Seneca's philosophical teachers appear to have had an interest in his teachings.

27 *Pisistratus*: (*c.*600–528/7 BC) seized control of Athens in around 560, was removed from power soon afterwards, but returned ten years later to rule Athens up to his death.

29 *Speusippus*: (*c.*407–339 BC) philosopher, nephew of Plato and his successor as head of the Academy.

30 *King Cambyses*: Persian king (529–522 BC), son of Cyrus. His reign and decline is described in Herodotus, Book 3.

31 *Harpagus*: as described in Herodotus 1.108 ff. Harpagus saved the life of the infant Cyrus when the Persian king Astyages had ordered him to be killed. The king punished Harpagus by killing his son and serving him his flesh.

32 *Darius . . . Magian*: Darius' conspiracy against the Magian who had ruled Persia after the death of Cambyses is described in Herodotus 3.67 ff.

33 *Lysimachus*: see note to p. 210.

Marcus Marius: Marcus Marius Gratidianus, son of a sister of Sulla's political opponent Gaius Marius. He prosecuted Quintus Lutatius Catulus, who had been disloyal to Gaius Marius, as tribune in 87 BC and drove him to suicide. After Sulla's victory he was executed as described here, on the instigation of Catulus' son.

34 *Catiline*: Lucius Sergius Catalina, notorious for his attempt to seize power in Rome in 63 BC, thwarted largely due to Cicero, who was consul in that year.

Sextus Papinius: flogged and tortured in AD 40, on the order of the emperor Caligula (Gaius Caesar).

Betilienus Bassus: Cassius Dio (59.25.6) refers to the killing of a Betillinus Cassius and seems to mean the same case.

35 *Cambyses*: see the note to p. 30. Cambyses' expedition against the Ethiopians is described in Herodotus 3.17 ff.

36 *Cyrus' anger . . . river Gyndes*: the incident is described in Herodotus 1.189.

37 *Antigonus*: probably the Macedonian king Antigonus I (*c.*382–301 BC), one of Alexander the Great's generals (not his grandfather, as Seneca mistakenly claims in sec. 23).

Silenus: a proverbially ugly, aged satyr, often shown as accompanying Dionysus.

Philip: Philip II, king of Macedonia 359–336 BC.

38 *Thersites*: an ugly, abusive soldier in the Grecian army at Troy (*Iliad* 2.212 ff.).

Asinius Pollio: Gaius Asinius Pollio (76 BC–AD 4), politician and orator, follower of Caesar, then supporter of Antony, with strong literary interests. He retired from politics in the early 30s BC.

43 *the deified Julius*: i.e. Julius Caesar, who was proclaimed a god after his death.

44 *he gave me the twelve fasces*: the rods which the Roman state officials carried who accompanied holders of high offices.

48 *Ennius*: Quintus Ennius (239–169 BC), poet chiefly known for his *Annals*, a historical epic on Roman history from the beginning to historical times, and the foundational work on Roman identity before Virgil's *Aeneid*. Several writers of the first century AD express disapproval of Ennius, who was seen as unsophisticated and coarse by that time.

Hortensius: Quintus Hortensius Hortalus (114–49 BC), a celebrated orator and advocate, eventually eclipsed by Cicero.

Diogenes the Stoic philosopher: probably Diogenes of Babylon (*c.*240–152 BC), head of the Stoa.

Lentulus: probably Lucius Cornelius Lentulus Crus, who was praetor in 58 BC, followed Pompey in the civil war, and died a day after him in Egypt.

49 *Vedius Pollio*: Publius Vedius Pollio was the son of a freedman and an aide to Augustus, who is said to have despised his love of luxury (Tacitus, *Annals* 1.10.5).

CONSOLATION TO MARCIA

53 *Marcia*: a close friend of Augustus' wife Livia, and daughter of A. Cremutius Cordus (see next note), her prolonged mourning for the death of her son Metilius was the occasion for Seneca's essay.

53 *Aulus Cremutius Cordus*: historian who wrote under Augustus and Tiberius and treated the period of the Principate down to at least 18 BC. He refused to celebrate Augustus and instead glorified leading 'Republicans' like Cicero and Brutus. Sejanus had him prosecuted (see Tacitus, *Annals* 4.34 f.). He committed suicide in AD 25.

Sejanus: L. Aelius Sejanus, prefect of the Praetorian Guard under Tiberius, who rose to extraordinary influence and was eventually removed by the emperor.

55 *Marcellus*: Marcus Claudius Marcellus (42–23 BC), famously referred to in Virgil, *Aeneid* 6.860–6.

56 *Drusus*: Nero Claudius Drusus (38 BC–AD 9). His first child was Germanicus Julius Caesar.

57 *Julia Augusta*: i.e. Livia, who was renamed thus on her adoption into the Julian family (*gens*) under the terms of Augustus' will.

Areus: Arius Didymus, a Stoic philosopher and adviser to Augustus.

61 *an outstanding verse*: probably by Publilius Syrus of Antioch, a former slave, who lived in the first century BC. He is quoted elsewhere by Seneca, and it has also been suspected that Seneca adapted some of his epigrams in his tragedies. It became a commonplace in the early empire that his epigrams expressed moral ideas better than serious dramatists.

65 *The Fortunate*: see note to p. 8.

66 *Paulus*: Lucius Aemilius Paullus (consul 182 BC; died 160 BC). He ended the Second Macedonian War in 168 by his victory against the Macedonian king Perses in the battle of Pydna; it was in this battle that his two sons died. The other two sons were (after adoption) Quintus Fabius Maximus Aemilianus and Publius Cornelius Scipio Aemilianus.

67 *Lucius Bibulus . . . and Gaius Caesar*: Seneca must be thinking of Marcus Calpurnius Bibulus, Gaius Julius Caesar's colleague in the consulship in 59 BC. The inactivity of Bibulus is encapsulated in the joke (related by Suetonius, *Life of Julius Caesar* 20.2) that theirs was the consulship not of Bibulus and Caesar, but of Julius and Caesar.

Tiberius Caesar . . . adopted: Drusus (poisoned by Sejanus in AD 23) and Germanicus.

from the Rostra: a speaker's platform in Rome, decorated with the prows (*rostra*) of captured warships.

68 *Lucretia and Brutus*: the rape of Lucretia and the outrage it caused marked the beginning of the end of the reign of Tarquinius Superbus, the last Roman king before the establishment of the Republic.

Cloelia: a Roman girl sent as hostage to the Etruscan king Porsenna, who escaped by swimming the Tiber (see Livy 2.13).

Gracchi: Tiberius Sempronius Gracchus and Gaius Sempronius Gracchus, social reformers of the late second century BC, who became the proverbial instigators of civil unrest.

Livius Drusus: Marcus Livius Drusus was killed in 91 BC, when he was tribune. See note to p. 144.

70 *From Hesperia's side Sicily did sever*: Virgil, *Aeneid* 3.418.

Charybdis: a dangerous whirlpool later identified with the Strait of Messina.

Arethusa's fountain: the Arcadian river-god Alpheus is said to have pursued the nymph Arethusa across the sea to the island of Ortygia near Syracuse. Her spring there was said to have a subterranean connection with the river Alpheus, in the Peloponnese.

that natural prison: ancient quarries near Syracuse were used in this way.

Dionysius: Dionysius II, who succeeded his father Dionysius I as tyrant of Syracuse in 367/6 BC.

75 *Gnaeus Pompey*: Gnaeus Pompeius Magnus, Julius Caesar's great rival for power. After his defeat by Caesar at the battle of Pharsalus he fled to Egypt, where he was stabbed to death, apparently by a slave.

the daggers of Catiline: referring to the attempt on Cicero's life during his consulship in 63 BC, when he was opposing Catiline's plot to seize power (see note to p. 34).

the king's bequest: left by King Ptolemy of Egypt, who committed suicide soon after Cato arrived to carry out the annexation of the island in 58 BC.

76 *the world which . . . renews itself*: allusion to the Stoic doctrine of conflagration, according to which the universe is destroyed and arises anew in a cyclical process.

77 *And . . . his allotted span*: Virgil, *Aeneid* 10.472.

78 *Rutilius*: Publius Rutilius Rufus (*c.*160–after 92 BC), a Stoic, legal expert, military commander, and politician. He was convicted of extortion by a court controlled by knights and sent into exile, where he wrote historical works.

82 *the changing Syrtes*: see note to p. 96.

ON THE HAPPY LIFE

85 *Gallio my brother*: Seneca's older brother Annaeus Novatus, who later changed his name to Junius Gallio after adoption by the senator Junius Gallio. He was proconsul of the province of Achaia in AD 51/2 and suffect consul in 53/5. He committed suicide in 66, a year after Seneca. *On Anger* is also dedicated to him, apparently before his adoption.

86 *vote-counting*: on the arrangements and procedures in Roman elections see Lily Ross Taylor, *Roman Voting Assemblies from the Hannibalic War to the Dictatorship of Caesar* (Ann Arbor, Mich., 1966).

a better and more reliable light: Seneca means a criterion. Hellenistic philosophy was especially concerned with criteria in ethical and epistemological contexts.

87 *shine brightly on the outside but have no value within*: a metaphor from architecture; decorative surfaces (marble, plaster) were often only veneer.

87 *Nature is the guide I choose*: See Introduction, p. xiii.

88 *a state of peace*: Stoic moral doctrine seeks to induce a state of unperturbedness.

every impulse to cruelty is born from weakness: cf. Cicero, *Tusculan Disputations* 4.25.

The highest good is a mind: cf. Seneca, *Letters* 106.2: 'you ask: is the good corporeal? The good exercises an effect; for it is beneficial. What exercises an effect, is a body. The good exercises an impulse on the mind and in some way forms and comprises that which is essential to the body.'

The power of the mind: the autonomy of the good manifests itself in independence from external influences and in the supreme role accorded to virtue.

a trivial collection of things: on the notion of indifferents see the Introduction, p. xi.

89 *For as far as pleasure is concerned*: Seneca responds to an unstated objection from an Epicurean point of view.

90 *then let it look back to the past*: referring to the Epicurean calculus of pleasure, which draws not just on experiences currently registered but also on the recollection and anticipation of pleasant experiences.

91 *places that fear the aedile*: the aediles were responsible, among other things, for the 'care for the city', which included some policing functions.

The highest good is untouched by death, it knows no ending: the implication is that pleasure as conceived by the Epicureans means pleasant sensations; the ability to experience them can obviously be curtailed by death. The Epicureans would feel misrepresented.

Nature . . . whose counsel it takes: Seneca polemically engages with the Epicurean Lucretius' use of personified Nature in *On the Nature of the Universe* 3.931–62.

given us only for a day: the allusion to Lucretius continues; cf. 3.971: 'no man possesses life in freehold—all as tenants.'

confident in spirit and for either end prepared: Virgil, *Aeneid* 2.61.

92 *For God as well*: see the Introduction, p. xiii, on the Stoic conception of the divine being that governs the universe.

93 *not of his belly*: a standard way of referring to the Epicurean conception of pleasure.

plucks the ear: the gesture represents an appeal to memory (cf. Pliny, *Natural History* 11.251).

restraint: on the notion of restraint or temperance see Cicero, *On Ends* 1.47.

94 *Nomentanus and Apicius*: the former was a well-known debauchee (Horace, *Satires* 1.1.102); the latter had a reputation as a gourmet (a cooking manual has come down to us under his name).

96 *but in your hand is a tambourine*: an allusion to the priests of the eastern goddess Cybele, called *Galli*, who were usually eunuchs and danced during processions while striking tambourines.

caught in the waters off the Syrtes: a notoriously dangerous area of shoals and sandbanks off the coast of North Africa; the Trojans suffer shipwreck there in Virgil, *Aeneid* 1.

97 *with hunting noose . . . ring of hounds*: quotations (from memory) from Virgil, *Georgics* 1.139–40.

98 *born under a monarchy*: the kingdom of the divine rational being is meant.

99 *virtue is all that one needs to live happily*: on the sufficiency of virtue for happiness see the Introduction, p. xii.

What . . . is the difference here?: Seneca is drawing a distinction between the foolish, unwise men and those who are making progress towards virtue.

100 *the gout that afflicts me*: similar references to the condition are in Seneca, *Letters* 53.6, 78.9.

Zeno: (335–263 BC), the founder of the Stoic school.

Rutilius or Cato: for Rutilius see note to p. 78; for Cato, note to p. 6.

Demetrius the Cynic: see note to p. 7.

101 *my life is o'er . . . run*: Virgil, *Eclogues* 4.653.

102 *Yet fails in no weak enterprise*: Ovid, *Metamorphoses* 2.328.

103 *Whine away*: we are probably supposed to think of dogs; cf. *Letters* 72.8.

yet lives a life of wealth: Seneca is probably defending himself here.

when Marcus Cato was extolling Curius and Coruncanius: we do not know in what context exactly the younger Cato referred to these figures of the early third century BC.

a few small silver coins: Valerius Maximus mentions (2.9.3) that Gaius Fabricius Lucinius in 275 BC excluded Publius Cornelius Rufinus (consul 277 BC) from the senate, on the grounds that he was setting a bad example by owning ten pounds of silver.

107 *Sublician Bridge*: an ancient wooden bridge, destroyed by a flood a few years after Seneca's death, according to Tacitus, *Histories* 1.86.

a Socrates: the archetypal philosopher.

Thebes: Bacchus/Dionysus descends from the Theban royal family through his mother, Semele. In the classical period a cult of Dionysus existed in the city; the myth of Pentheus, treated in Euripides' tragedy the *Bacchae*, is situated in Thebes.

on a foreign litter: spoils and captives were displayed on a carriage during triumphal processions.

109 *one of whom gives him wings. . .*: allusions to well-known myths: the swan of Leda, the bull of Europa, the act of adultery committed with Alcmene, the cruel treatment of Vulcan/Hephaestus as described in Homer's *Iliad*, the punishment of Prometheus, the abduction of Ganymedes, the removal of Saturnus from power.

110 *the holy rattle*: particularly associated with the priests of the Egyptian goddess Isis.

110 *that prison*: Socrates was held in an Athenian prison, having been convicted of introducing new gods and corrupting the Athenian youth, and was forced to commit suicide there.

subject-matter for his jokes: the reference is to Aristophanes' *Clouds*, where Socrates is lampooned.

111 *criticize Plato . . .*: Plato allegedly sought money from Dionysius of Syracuse and turned away pupils who could not pay. Aristotle is said to have received money from the Macedonians. Democritus allowed land inherited from his father to fall into dereliction. Alcibiades, when young a close associate of Socrates, had a reputation for scandalous behaviour. Phaedrus was a pupil of Socrates.

to the lowest abyss . . .: the text is not preserved in its entirety.

ON THE TRANQUILLITY OF THE MIND

112 *SERENUS*: Annaeus Serenus, a young prefect in Nero's guard, to whom Seneca dedicated two further treatises. This is the only genuine dialogue among Seneca's *Dialogues*; in the others the addressee is not given a speaking part. On the treatise see B. Inwood, 'Seneca and Self-assertion', in *Reading Seneca* (Oxford, 2005), 322–52, esp. 348–51.

I would to a doctor: the commonplace comparison between philosopher and healer; contrast Cicero, *On Ends* 3.24.

113 *the variety of its markings*: extravagant and expensive wooden tables were a status symbol in Rome from the late Republic onwards.

by the purple or the lictors' rods: holders of high offices wore a toga with a purple border and were accompanied by officials who carried rods with an axe sewn into them (*fasces*, see note to p. 44) as symbols of their power.

Zeno, Cleanthes, and Chrysippus: Cleanthes of Assos (331/30–232/1 BC) was successor of Zeno as head of the Stoa; Cleanthes in turn was followed by Chrysippus of Soloi (281/77–208/4 BC).

114 *direct my speech*: a touch of old-fashioned Romanness, reminiscent of Cato's famous saying, 'seize the subject, and the words will follow'.

115 *Democritus*: see note to p. 23.

117 *Achilles is like this*: the reference is to the grief suffered by Achilles over the death of Patroclus (Homer, *Iliad* 24.10 ff.).

118 *Campania*: a famously lush and corrupting region, a favourite setting for luxurious villas.

Thus each man ever flees himself: Lucretius, *On the Nature of the Universe* 3.1068.

Athenodorus: of uncertain identification; perhaps the Stoic Athenodorus of Tarsus, who was friendly with the younger Cato.

121 *prytanis*: originally an Athenian title for a state official, but later adopted by other Greek cities.

sufes: judge or chief magistrate (a Carthaginian term).

Thirty Tyrants were dismembering it: the oligarchs who ruled Athens after its collapse during the Peloponnesian War against Sparta (404 BC).

Areopagus: an ancient Athenian tribunal which also had an informal guardianship of the state.

122 *Harmodius*: together with Aristogiton, Harmodius plotted to kill the tyrant Hippias at the Panathenaic festival of 514 BC. Both were venerated as heroes after the eventual expulsion of Hippias.

Curius Dentatus: Roman general who achieved victories against the Samnites (290 BC) and Pyrrhus (275 BC).

123 *Isocrates laid his hand on Ephorus' shoulder*: Isocrates (436–338 BC) was an Athenian orator, who influenced political opinion and Athenian self-perception mainly through written speeches. Ephorus of Cyme (*c.*405–330 BC) is the major source for Diodorus Siculus, whose work (unlike Ephorus') is extant.

124 *Cato*: reference is to the younger Cato (see note to p. 6).

125 *Bion*: the Cynic writer Bion of Borysthenes (3rd cent. BC); his brand of popular morality appealed to Horace too.

Diogenes: the famous Cynic (*c.*412/403–324/321 BC). Anecdotes about him are collected in Diogenes Laertius 6.70–3.

127 *flames at Alexandria*: referring to the fire in 48 BC.

129 *As Cicero says*: reference is to Cicero's speech *For Milo* 92.

130 *Publilius*: see note to p. 61.

131 *Sejanus*: see note to p. 53.

Croesus: on his defeat by Cyrus, Croesus, the king of Lydia, was to be burned alive, but a sudden shower extinguished the flames. The story is in Herodotus 1.86.

Jugurtha: a Numidian client king who rose against Rome at the end of the second century BC. In his *Jugurthine War*, the historian Sallust represents the lengthy war against him as an indication of the decline of aristocratic rule in Rome.

Ptolemy . . . Mithridates: Ptolemy, king of Mauretania (AD 23–40), was exiled to Rome; Mithridates, a ruler of Pontus, was later restored to his throne and eventually brought down by his son Pharnaces.

133 *Democritus*: see note to p. 23.

134 *our master Zeno*: see note to p. 100.

Gaius: the emperor Caligula.

Phalaris: the proverbially evil tyrant of Acragas (Agrigento, Sicily) in the sixth century BC, who was reputed to roast his enemies alive in a brazen bull.

135 *Heraclitus*: Presocratic philosopher. Traditionally known as 'the weeping philosopher', and contrasted with Democritus, 'the laughing philosopher'.

136 *Rutilius*: see note to p. 78.

137 *Regulus*: the reference is to Marcus Atilius Regulus (consul in 267 and 256 BC). He was captured fighting the Carthaginians in the First Punic War and died in captivity. Later a legend arose that he was sent to Rome by the Carthaginians in order to negotiate a prisoner exchange, advised against it, and voluntarily returned to Carthage, where he was brutally killed.

138 *Scipio*: the context seems to require that Publius Cornelius Scipio Africanus (236–183 BC) is meant, who defeated Hannibal.

Asinius Pollio: see note to p. 38.

the tenth hour: by Roman reckoning this would be two hours before sunset.

139 *the Freedom-Giver*: i.e. Liber, one of the Roman names for Bacchus, god of wine.

Solon and Arkesilaos: Solon (fl. *c.*600 BC), Athenian sage, poet, and lawgiver. Arkesilaos (316/5–242/1 BC), philosopher and head of the Academy in the mid-third century.

sometimes it is a pleasure even to be a madman: a fragment of the comic playwright Menander (no. 421 Kock), cf. Horace, *Odes* 4.12.28.

no great genius has ever existed without a dash of lunacy: this commonplace idea is not to be found in the works of Aristotle which have come down to us, but cf. Pseudo-Aristotle, *Problemata* 30.1.

ON THE SHORTNESS OF LIFE

140 *Paulinus*: Pompeius Paulinus, a knight of Arelate (Arles), who was in charge of grain distribution in Rome from AD 48 to 55.

Life is short, but art long: a translation of Hippocrates' first aphorism (IV 458 Littré).

Aristotle: in his *Tusculan Disputations* (3.69) Cicero attributes an almost identical saying to Theophrastus, Aristotle's pupil and successor as head of his school, the Peripatos. This may be explained either as an error or as a conscious decision on Seneca's part that the distinguished doctor Hippocrates should be set against a philosopher of equal distinction.

141 *in the greatest of poets*: the identity of the poet is a matter of dispute.

143 *a letter sent to the senate*: it was standard practice for the emperor to communicate with the senate by letter when he did not attend its sessions (the historian Tacitus frequently quotes or paraphrases from such communications in his *Annals*). In this case Seneca is our sole source of information.

144 *Murena, Caepio, Lepidus, Egnatius*: men who conspired against Augustus between 29 and 23/22 BC.

by his daughter: the scandalous behaviour of Julia eventually led to her being exiled from Rome in 2 BC.

Iullus . . . with an Antony: Iullus, whose name has been restored here by Waltz's conjecture, was the second son of Marcus Antonius and Fulvia. He was executed for adultery in 2 BC.

Catiline and Clodius and Pompey and Crassus: the suppression of Catiline's conspiracy was the high point of Cicero's consulship in 63 BC. Cicero testified against Publius Clodius Pulcher in a trial about the profanation of the rites of Bona Dea in 61. Clodius in turn was instrumental in bringing about Cicero's exile in 58 for executing Roman citizens without trial during the Catilinarian conspiracy. Pompeius and Crassus were not as helpful as they might have been in having Cicero recalled from exile.

in a letter to Atticus: the letters to Atticus which have come down to us do not include this statement, but the collection is incomplete.

Livius Drusus: M. Livius Drusus introduced social legislation as a tribune in 91 BC. The reference to the brothers Gracchus, social reformers of the second half of the second century, marks the laws out as extreme and divisive. Both patricians and knights opposed his measures in the senate. Information on his end from elsewhere clearly suggests that he was murdered.

147 *fasces*: see note to p. 44.

149 *the greatest of poets*: Virgil, *Georgics* 3.66–7.

Fabianus: on Papirius Fabianus (*c*.35 BC–AD 35), who represented an important intellectual influence on Seneca, see the Introduction, p. viii.

153 *a foolish passion once confined to the Greeks*: Seneca must be thinking of Hellenistic grammarians working in Alexandria, whose exegetical efforts extended to literal-minded questions.

Duilius: Gaius Duilius was consul during the First Carthaginian War and led the Roman fleet to victory off Mylae in Sicily in 260 BC.

Curius Dentatus: see note to p. 122.

154 *Valerius Corvinus was the first conqueror of Messana*: Manius Valerius Maximus Messalla (consul in 263 BC) forced the tyrant Hieron II of Syracuse to accept a peace agreement with Rome and was granted a triumph for the capture of Messana (today Messina).

was the first to exhibit lions without chains in the circus: during a public festival in 93 BC, when Sulla held the office of *praetor urbanus*.

King Bocchus: the father-in-law of Jugurtha (see note to p. 131).

stabbed by the lowest of slaves: see note to p. 75.

155 *pomerium*: the ancient sacred boundary of Rome, representing the limits of divine surveillance.

Carneades: the most celebrated Academic philosopher of the second century BC, Carneades was a sceptic, who did not advance doctrines of his own but criticized the teachings of the dogmatic schools.

158 *Jupiter . . . a lover's embraces*: when Jupiter slept with Alcmene, in the guise of her husband Amphitryon, he made the night last twice (or three times) its normal length. Hercules was born from the union.

158 *the Persian king*: Xerxes; cf. Herodotus 7.45–6. He was defeated by the Greeks under Athenian leadership at Thermopylae and Salamis in 480 BC, and at Plataea in 479.

159 *Marius*: after serving in the war against the Numidian king Jugurtha, Gaius Marius held the consulship several times between 104 and 86 BC (having held it once before in 107).

Quintius: L. Quintius Cincinnatus was dictator in 458 BC and again in 439. Allegedly he was called away from his plough in 458.

160 *those charged with responsibility for the corn-market*: organizing the grain supply for the capital was a logistically challenging and politically sensitive task.

CONSOLATION TO HELVIA

163 *my best of mothers*: Seneca is consoling her on account of his exile; see also the Introduction.

164 *stepmother*: stepmothers featured as stereotypical villains in literature and popular discourse.

168 *Sciathus and Seriphus, Gyara and Cossura*: the first three are small islands in the Aegean; Cossura is situated off Sicily.

this rock: Corsica, Seneca's place of exile.

Scythia: the region to the north and north-east of of the Black Sea.

169 *Miletus*: Miletus was the oldest and the most powerful of the twelve Ionian cities in Asia Minor (western Anatolia).

a greater Greece: i.e. Magna Graecia, the name for the area of southern Italy colonized by Greek settlers from about the eighth century BC.

Asia claims the Etruscans as her own: according to a tradition first in evidence in Herodotus (1.94), the Etruscans are Lydians, who came to northern Italy in the second half of the thirteenth century BC.

the people of Tyre inhabit Africa: Carthage was founded by Phoenicians from Tyre; later Spain became a sphere of influence.

Greeks occupied Gaul: a reference to the people from Phocaea, see below.

Gauls Greece: strictly Greek Asia Minor, where the Gauls were settled after their various invasions in the third century BC.

the Pyrenees did not prevent the Germans from crossing over: this erroneous reference must be to the Celtiberians, who crossed from Gaul into Spain.

Diomedes: the passage contains several references to the story of Aeneas, the Trojan prince who was legendarily the founder of the Roman people, as told by Virgil in the *Aeneid*. Aeneas meets Evander, whose son joins him in battle; Diomedes, who prevailed in a single combat against Aeneas at Troy and later settled in Italy, refuses to join forces with Aeneas' enemies.

170 *the Greeks who now inhabit Marseilles, having left Phocis*: the city was founded *c.*600 BC by Phocaeans (people from Phocaea in Asia Minor, not from Phocis in Greece).

Varro: M. Terentius Varro (*c.*116–27 BC), polymath and scholar.

Marcus Brutus: Marcus Junius Brutus (*c.*85–42 BC), one of the conspirators against Julius Caesar, and a Stoic philosopher.

172 *Marcellus*: Marcus Claudius Marcellus (consul 51 BC) was fiercely opposed to Caesar and retired to Mytilene after Pompey's defeat at Pharsalus. He was recalled by Caesar in 46 BC; Cicero's speech *For Marcellus* presents itself as a revised version of the expression of thanks delivered on the day. Marcellus was murdered in Athens while on his return journey.

173 *Phasis*: a river in Colchis at the Black Sea.

174 *Parthians . . . revenge from them*: for the defeat of the Roman army under Crassus at the battle of Carrhae in 53 BC.

Gaius Caesar: the reference is to the emperor Caligula.

175 *would return to their enemy rather than prove false*: a reference to Marcus Atilius Regulus (see note to p. 137).

our dictator, the man who gave audience to the Samnites' envoys: Manius Curius Dentatus (see note to p. 122).

Apicius: see note to p. 94.

177 *Menenius Agrippa*: consul in 503 BC. In the context of the mediation mentioned here, he told a story about the parts of the human body and how each has its own purpose in the greater function of the whole.

Atilius Regulus: see note to p. 137.

178 *Scipio*: Gnaeus Cornelius Scipio Calvus (consul 222 BC).

179 *Thirty Tyrants*: see note to p. 121.

Aristides: a leading Athenian politician at the beginning of the fifth century BC.

182 *Cornelia*: the mother of the Gracchi (see note to p. 68).

Cotta: C. Aurelius Cotta, exiled in 91 BC for encouraging Italian unrest against Rome. He returned in 82 BC.

184 *Consider my brothers*: see the Introduction, p. vii.

185 *your sister*: it is unclear whether the mother's sister or a sister-in-law is meant.

186 *the woman . . . in place of her husband*: Alcestis, who in Greek mythology agreed to die in place of her husband Admetus (see Euripedes' *Alcestis*).

ON MERCY

See the Introduction (p. xxiii) for the circumstances of publication of this treatise.

192 *If safe their king . . . loyalty behind*: a quotation from Virgil, *Georgics* 4.212–13, where bees and their devotion to their 'kings' are at issue. The example of bees is developed in sec.19.

196 *Lucius Cinna*: Gnaeus Cornelius Cinna Magnus (consul AD 5).

197 *Salvidienus . . . Egnatius*: see note to p. 144.

200 *the elder Dionysius*: Dionysius I (*c.*430–367 BC) was tyrant of Syracuse.

Lucius Sulla: see note to p. 8.

Let them hate, if only they fear: a quotation from the archaic poet Accius.

202 *Father of his Country*: the honorific title bestowed on Augustus by the senate and the people in 2 BC.

204 *sentence him to the sack*: the traditional Roman punishment for a parricide was to be drowned in a sack along with a cock, snake, dog, and monkey.

205 *Vedius Pollio*: see note to p. 49.

210 *Lysimachus*: one of Alexander's generals (*c.*360–281 BC). He survived Alexander and eventually died in battle, so the scenario here must be hypothetical.

213 *your prefect Burrus*: Sextus Afranius Burrus, head of the Praetorian Guard and joint senior adviser (with Seneca) to the young Nero; see also the Introduction, p. ix.

214 *Busiris and Procrustes*: Busiris was a mythical king of Egypt who used to sacrifice to the gods all strangers who set foot on his shores; Procrustes was a giant who made visitors fit a bed, by lengthening or shortening them.

215 *Phalaris*: see note to p. 134.

218 *be straightened . . .*: the rest of the essay (the remainder of Book 2 and probably a third book) is lost.

NATURAL QUESTIONS, BOOK 6: ON EARTHQUAKES

219 *under the consulship of Regulus and Verginius*: Seneca seems to date the earthquake to the year 63 through his reference to these two consuls, while Tacitus dates it to 62 in *Annals* 15.22.2. This has prompted scholars to suspect interpolation of the reference to the consuls here. See R. Syme, *Tacitus* (Oxford, 1958), ii. 742.

222 *For the vanquished . . . safety*: Virgil, *Aeneid* 2.354.

223 *My friend Vagellius*: we do not know a poet of that name. Possibly the name has been garbled in the process of transmission.

225 *Thales of Miletus*: one of the celebrated seven sages of antiquity, he is credited with predicting a solar eclipse which modern scholars have dated to 585 BC. Water is also given primeval importance in Egyptian and Babylonian myths.

226 *Sarmatians*: these people lived in the west and south of what is today Russia.

228 *the beautiful spring of Arethusa*: see note to p. 70.

whom Nero Caesar had dispatched to investigate the source of the Nile: Pliny the elder, *Natural History* 6.181, mentions this mission; it seems to have served commercial rather than scientific purposes.

Anaxagoras: (*c.*500–428 BC), the first philosopher to settle in Athens.

229 *Anaximenes*: Anaximenes of Miletus; the most productive phase of his life is traditionally given as 546 to 525 BC.

230 *Archelaus*: (*fl.* 5th century BC), Greek philosopher, a pupil of Anaxagoras.

231 *Strato*: Strato of Lampsacus (died 269/8 BC). He was a Peripatetic philosopher, head of the school after Aristotle's successor, Theophrastus.

Beneath our feet . . . lofty ridges move: Virgil, *Aeneid* 6.256.

234 *Araxes chafing at his bridge*: Virgil, *Aeneid* 8.728.

Asclepiodotus, a student of Posidonius: Posidonius (*c.*135–51 BC) was a scientist, historian, and leading Stoic philosopher of his time. He was open to influence from Aristotle's school, which had pioneered the empirical study of the natural world. His pupil Asclepiodotus is known to us for his work on military matters.

235 *With mighty moaning . . . barriers*: Virgil, *Aeneid* 1.55–6.

By authority . . . roaring tempests: Virgil, *Aeneid* 1.53–4.

236 *Metrodorus of Chios*: a pupil of Democritus (see note to p. 23), who lived in the fourth century BC. He was interested in physics as well as meteorological and astronomical phenomena.

238 *With a roar . . . collapse*: Virgil, *Aeneid* 8.525.

239 *Callisthenes*: a nephew of Aristotle, who compiled a work on the 'deeds of Alexander' while in the latter's entourage. In early 327 BC he alienated Alexander by his opposition to *proskynesis*, the oriental form of abasement before the monarch, was falsely implicated in a conspiracy, and executed.

Darius: Darius III, king of Persia. He died in 330 BC as the result of a plot, after he had been decisively defeated by Alexander.

241 *He granted . . . scorn the winds*: Virgil, *Aeneid* 3.77.

on the authority of Pindar: the poem referred to is not extant in the works of the Greek poet Pindar (518–438 BC).

244 *Once, men say . . . the sea had sundered*: Virgil, *Aeneid* 3.414–19.

247 *the wise Laelius*: Gaius Laelius (*c.*190–129 BC), a politician and close friend of Publius Cornelius Scipio Aemilianus and thus a member of the so-called 'Scipionic circle'. He was nicknamed 'the wise', and made a central character in Cicero's *On Friendship*.

American Literature

British and Irish Literature

Children's Literature

Classics and Ancient Literature

Colonial Literature

Eastern Literature

European Literature

Gothic Literature

History

Medieval Literature

Oxford English Drama

Poetry

Philosophy

Politics

Religion

The Oxford Shakespeare

A complete list of Oxford World's Classics, including Authors in Context, Oxford English Drama, and the Oxford Shakespeare, is available in the UK from the Marketing Services Department, Oxford University Press, Great Clarendon Street, Oxford OX2 6DP, or visit the website at www.oup.com/uk/worldsclassics.

In the USA, visit www.oup.com/us/owc for a complete title list.

Oxford World's Classics are available from all good bookshops. In case of difficulty, customers in the UK should contact Oxford University Press Bookshop, 116 High Street, Oxford OX1 4BR.